LIFE TAKES PLACE

Life Takes Place argues that, even in our mobile, hypermodern world, human life is impossible without place. Seamon asks the question: why does life take place? He draws on examples of specific places and place experiences to understand place more broadly. Advocating for a holistic way of understanding that he calls "synergistic relationality," Seamon defines places as spatial fields that gather, activate, sustain, identify, and interconnect things, human beings, experiences, meanings, and events.

Throughout his phenomenological explication, Seamon recognizes that places are multivalent in their constitution and sophisticated in their dynamics. Drawing on British philosopher J. G. Bennett's method of progressive approximation, he considers place and place experience in terms of their holistic, dialectical, and processual dimensions. Recognizing that places always change over time, Seamon examines their processual dimension by identifying six generative processes that he labels *interaction, identity, release, realization, intensification*, and *creation*.

Drawing on practical examples from architecture, planning, and urban design, he argues that an understanding of these six place processes might contribute to a more rigorous place making that produces robust places and propels vibrant environmental experiences. This book is a significant contribution to the growing research literature in "place and place making studies."

David Seamon is a Professor of Architecture at Kansas State University in Manhattan, Kansas, USA. Trained in geography and environment-behavior research, he is interested in a phenomenological approach to place, architecture, and environmental design as place making. His books include *A Geography of the Lifeworld* (Routledge Revivals Series, 2015). He is on the editorial boards of *Environmental Philosophy; Phenomenology & Practice; Journal of Environmental Psychology*; and *Journal of Architectural and Planning Research*. He edits *Environmental and Architectural Phenomenology*, which in 2014 celebrated twenty-five years of publication.

LIFE TAKES PLACE

Phenomenology, Lifeworlds, and Place Making

David Seamon

Routledge
Taylor & Francis Group

NEW YORK AND LONDON

First published 2018
by Routledge
711 Third Avenue, New York, NY 10017

and by Routledge
2 Park Square, Milton Park, Abingdon, Oxon OX14 4RN

Routledge is an imprint of the Taylor & Francis Group, an informa business

© 2018 Taylor & Francis

The right of David Seamon to be identified as author of this work has been asserted by him in accordance with sections 77 and 78 of the Copyright, Designs and Patents Act 1988.

Library of Congress Cataloging in Publication Data
Names: Seamon, David, author.Title: Life takes place : phenomenology, lifeworlds and place making / David Seamon.Description: New York, NY : Routledge is an imprint of the Taylor & Francis Group, an Informa Business, 2018. | Includes bibliographical references and index.
Identifiers: LCCN 2017052826 | ISBN 9780815380702 (hbk) | ISBN 9780815380719 (pbk) | ISBN 9781351212519 (ebk)
Subjects: LCSH: Place (Philosophy)
Classification: LCC B105.P53 S43 2018 | DDC 114--dc23
LC record available at https://lccn.loc.gov/2017052826

ISBN: 978-0-8153-8070-2 (hbk)
ISBN: 978-0-8153-8071-9 (pbk)
ISBN: 978-1-351-21251-9 (ebk)

Typeset in Bembo
by Taylor & Francis Books

CONTENTS

FIGURES AND TABLES

Figures

Tables

ACKNOWLEDGMENTS

In writing this book, I wish to thank five scholars who have written superlative phenomenologies of place: Edward Casey, Jeff Malpas, Robert Mugerauer, Edward Relph, and Ingrid Leman Stefanovic. Their efforts have provided much of the groundwork for the argument I present, though I know that each will agree or disagree with my perspective and conclusions in different ways. I thank several colleagues who generously read drafts of chapters: John Cameron, Vicki King, Claudia Mausner, Sue Michael, Jenny Quillien, and Stephen Wood. I much appreciate their perceptive suggestions and criticisms that have made the book stronger and better integrated. I thank Kansas State University colleague Ray Streeter for assisting me with the book's graphics. I am grateful to several friends and colleagues who responded to my request that they provide me with definitions of place, which I examine in Chapter 5. These individuals are Bob Barzan, Julio Bermudez, John Cameron, Anja Claus, Linda Finlay, Tonino Griffero, Jing Han, Lena Hopsch, Susan Ingham, Vicki King, Thomas Larsen, Peter Laurence, Jeff Malpas, Claudia Mausner, Sue Michael, Dan Palmer, Aya Peri-Bader, Grant Price, Jenny Quillien, Edward Relph, Kerstin Sailer, Eva Simms, Ingrid Leman Stefanovic, Petr Urban, Jeremy Wells, Tim White, and Stephen Wood. I thank my departmental colleague Gary Coates, who coaxed me to Kansas State University over thirty years ago and has been a faithful friend and ally without whom my professional life would be so much less engaging and rewarding. I am particularly grateful to educator and phenomenologist Max van Manen for providing me with the original impetus for writing this book, which is considerably stronger because of his thoughtful critique and gracious support, even on points of conceptual and methodological disagreement.

I thank Ben Bennett, representative of the Estate of J. G. Bennett, for giving me permission to draw on passages from Bennett's writings. I thank Paul Krafel for permission to reproduce several drawings from his book, *Shifting*. Portions of Chapters 2, 10, and 16 are reproduced from the article, "Lived Bodies, Place, and Phenomenology," first published in the *Journal of Human Rights and the Environment* (Seamon, 2013b). I thank journal editor Anna Gear and Edward Elgar Publishing for allowing me to make use of those sections. Portions of Chapters 3, 13, and 15 are reproduced from the article, "Understanding Place Holistically: Cities, Synergistic Relationality, and Space Syntax," first published in the *Journal of Space Syntax* (Seamon, 2015c). I thank journal editor Daniel Koch and London's Bartlett School of Architecture for allowing me to make use of those sections.

I am grateful to Australian artist Sue Michael for allowing me to reproduce her wonderful place tryptic, *Booleroo Centre Yard*, on the book's front cover. Boleroo Centre is a small town in the Southern Flinders Ranges region of South Australia. In providing background for the painting, Michael described the ninety-three-year-old woman who tended this backyard garden: "She often worked all morning and afternoon in her garden, all through the seasons. Even on unbearably hot days, she could be found pulling weeds from beneath the shrubs."

The ideas, aims, and hopes that I put forward in this book have been deeply influenced by three remarkable thinkers with whom I have had the good fortune to study directly: first, geographer Anne Buttimer, who introduced me to phenomenology and pointed to its regenerative possibilities for environmental and architectural studies; second, philosopher Henri Bortoft, who taught phenomenology phenomenologically and whetted my interest in Goethean science and phenomenologies of wholeness and belonging; and, third, philosopher J. G. Bennett, who made me realize how much there is in the world to know, particularly the less effable. These three thinkers have contributed mightily to who I am intellectually, emotionally, and ethically. I am indebted to them profoundly.

I dedicate this book to my late mother and father, who bore me into a world I could not understand. Finding ways to know and accept that world led me to phenomenology and helped me to realize that the most inhospitable of places offers hope and possibilities, often in ways unimaginable until one has moved beyond and then looks back in grudging gratitude.

David Seamon
Bluestem Café
Aggieville
Manhattan, Kansas USA
October 1, 2017

1

LIFE TAKES PLACE

An Introduction

As I finished writing this book, Hurricane Harvey struck Houston, Texas, inundating the city with nine trillion gallons of water that would make a liquid cube two miles high and four miles square. Described as "the most extreme rain event in American history," this "thousand-year" storm devastated Texas communities and uprooted Texan lives. "What do we do when there ain't no place to go home to?" asked one teary-eyed survivor, who forsook her house in a kayak that her son had just happened to see floating by his house next door. "We want to go home," the son explained, "but we don't have no home to go to."[1] Extreme weather events like Harvey bring public attention to the overwhelming significance of place, place experience, and place attachment in human life. Most of the time, however, this overwhelming significance is taken for granted as daily living proceeds matter-of-factly and uneventfully. In this book, I draw on phenomenology to examine why and how place, places, and place experiences are integral to human life and what happens existentially and experientially when, like the Harvey survivors, people lose their places.

As a thematic hook to focus my argument, I draw on the colloquial expression, "life takes place," which is a puzzling phrase when one thinks about it. Why does life "take" place? Does "take" mean "requires" as in the phrases "learning takes effort" or "healing takes time"? What could it mean that life requires place? In today's hypermodern times, does the phrase even make sense as human life so often involves autonomous individuals making their way in worlds independently of any environments or places in which those individuals find themselves? Though the unsettling experiences of Harvey survivors suggest otherwise, could it be today that "life takes place" has much less existential and geographical traction than for past peoples and past places?

These questions are the crux of this book and, in the last several decades, have become central to research in a wide range of disciplines and professions. This interest in place began in humanistic geography and architectural phenomenology in the 1970s. In the last two decades, this research has intensified, particularly because of the phenomenologies of place provided by environmental thinkers Edward Casey (1997, 2009), Jeff Malpas (1999), Robert Mugerauer (1994), Edward Relph (1976, 1981), and Ingrid Stefanovic (2000). Drawing on and extending these earlier phenomenological studies, I argue that life in fact *does require place*, and I work to explain why this requirement is so.[2]

What recent phenomenological work on place offers is a provocative new understanding about human life and human experience. These phenomenologists claim that *human being is always human being in place*. As Casey (2009, p. 14) declares, "To be is to be in place." If this contention is true, then life does indeed take place. In fact, one can claim that human life is impossible without place. We are always emplaced in that we always already find ourselves present to some world, whether that world is relatively temporary (attending a meeting in an unfamiliar city) or permanent (tending a family farm one's entire life). Understanding this perpetual, unavoidable emplacement is the main aim of this book.

In the examination of place that I offer, I draw on phenomenology because it is the Western philosophical tradition that provides the most conceptual and practical guidance for examining and understanding human experience, consciousness, and meaning. My aim is a phenomenology of place that draws on situations and experiences relating to specific places and place experiences as a means to understand place more broadly, including a more thorough explication of *how* "life takes place." From a phenomenological perspective, one can define place as *any environmental locus that gathers human experiences, actions, and meanings spatially and temporally*. A more sophisticated phenomenological definition is offered by philosopher Jeff Malpas (1999, p. 36), who describes place as "an open and interconnected region within which other persons, things, spaces, and abstract locations, and even one's self, can appear, be recognized, identified and interacted with."

These two definitions suggest that places work as spatial fields that gather, activate, sustain, identify, and interconnect things, human beings, experiences, meanings, and events. Both definitions assume that places range from intimate to regional scale and include such environmental situations as a favorite park bench, a house associated with unpleasant childhood memories, a neighborhood to which one is deeply attached, or a taken-for-granted geographical locale where one has lived her entire life. Experientially, places are multivalent in their constitution and complex in their dynamics. On one hand, places can be liked, cherished, and loved; on the other hand, they can be disliked, distrusted, and feared. For the persons and groups involved, a place can invoke a wide range of supportive, neutral, or undermining actions, experiences, and memories.

Grounding Place as a Phenomenon and Concept

In attempting a phenomenology of place, one faces the important question of real-world evidence. Ideally, a book offering a broad, conceptual understanding of place should ground that understanding in firsthand experience of specific places and place events. For example, one potential real-world context would be several in-depth, longitudinal, participant-observation studies of two or three actual places, selected in such a way as to offer provocative evidence for comparisons and contrasts. These studies would provide thorough descriptions of these places as physical environments, as situations and events, and as ordinary (or perhaps, in some cases, extra-ordinary) worlds for their users and others associated with those places. These real-world discoveries would provide a testing ground and springboard for broader conceptual claims about place.

In this book, I take a different methodological route for considering how life takes place. The experiential evidence for the phenomenological claims I make is a serendipitous cross-section of primary and secondary sources that include newspaper accounts, imaginative literature, and well-respected field studies and conceptual explications of places and place experience. In Chapter 2, I discuss my phenomenological method more fully, but here I offer some examples of real-world places and place experiences so that readers have an incipient sense of the kinds of situations and events that I attempt to clarify conceptually. In later chapters, I draw one source of place descriptions from articles in two American newspapers of record – *The New York Times* (*NYT*) and *The Wall Street Journal* (*WSJ*). While writing this book, I set myself each day to study these two newspapers and to note articles that made some aspect of place the primary focus. Obviously, almost any newspaper article deals with place, since all reporting requires journalists to ask *where?* I gave primary attention to entries that discussed some focal aspect of places not subject to recurring newspaper coverage because of significant current events.[3] Here, for example, is a summary of eight articles that appeared in the two newspapers on Wednesday, March 1, 2017, a particularly fruitful day for stories about places, which ranged from an up-and-coming Parisian suburb to a disintegrating French town:

- Commercial developers are transforming the Parisian suburb of Aubervilliers, a long-time stronghold of communism, into a toney business district envisioned as an alternative to Paris's expensive city center (*WSJ*, p. B8).
- After a sixty-eight-year ban, North Dakota lawmakers are considering state legislation allowing the return of parking meters. Supporters argue that the meters would free up spaces regularly taken by downtown workers and make parking easier for shoppers and restaurant patrons (*WSJ*, p. A1).
- As a way for cell-phone addicts to be untethered from their devices and to engage with actual places and events, a company called Yondr has developed a lockable neoprene pouch in which one places her phone, which is only

accessible again when she leaves that place or event and taps the pouch on an unlocking pod: "For some of us, it takes being locked out of the digital world to realize the extent to which these pieces of electronics have sucked us away from the real one" (*WSJ*, p. B4).

- The Cloudmount Ski Resort in northeastern Alabama is facing financial ruin because of this winter's unseasonably warm temperatures. Making use of a snow-making machine, the resort's owner is typically assured of forty to fifty days of skiing, but this winter has provided only six. There are very few ski resorts in the American Deep South, and Cloudmount is "a gateway for first-time skiers in the south who want to learn the basics before heading to bigger mountains in the northeast or out west" (*WSJ*, p. A7).

- A chapel in a shopping mall in Paramus, New Jersey, is closing after nearly fifty years of religious services. Officially known as St. Therese's Chapel, this small space above a Marshall's department store is open daily from 7 am to 9:30 pm and provides Mass for almost 1,000 worshippers weekly. The chapel must close because mall management has other plans for the space (*NYT*, p. A23).

- New York City Mayor Bill de Blasio vows to reduce the 60,000 people living in homeless shelters by 2,500 over five years. His aim is to move homeless individuals into more stable residential situations where they can receive community services and be helped to find and succeed with permanent housing. The task is difficult because of insufficient affordable housing and low wages that don't keep pace with the city's high rents (*NYT*, p. A23).

- The Canadian prairie city of Medicine Hat, Alberta, is on the leading edge of a countrywide effort to end homelessness through a "housing first" strategy whereby anyone identified as homeless is provided a home with no pre-conditions, including sobriety. The argument is that only after people have stable housing can they deal with other life challenges, such as mental illness or drug and alcohol addiction: "The stability of home allows people to gradually address their problems" (*NYT*, p. A4).

- The southern French provincial town of Albi (population 49,000) is losing the "vitality and buzz" of its historic core, which is marked by vacant storefronts, empty residences, and deserted streets. Remaining retail functions are mostly tourist shops and chain clothing stores. Albi's deteriorating city center symbolizes many other French towns, where "the interplay of the human-scale architecture, weathered stone and brick, and public life had been one of the crucibles of French history and culture . . . ." Today, many of these towns are endangered, and, in Albi's case, largely undermined by a shopping mall and by large grocery stores built at the town's periphery (*NYT*, p. A1).

Though these eight stories cover a spectrum of environmental and geographical scales, they each have phenomenological significance because they depict some aspect of place as it contributes to the experiences and lives of people associated with that place: the threat to the future of an Alabama ski resort; the loss of a worship space in a New Jersey mall; the efforts of New York City and Medicine Hat, Alberta, to find ways to provide homeless populations with stable homes. In some examples, the place itself is given more attention (Albi's decline); in other examples, experiencers are highlighted (cell-phone users locking up their devices so they can engage with a place or event). I introduce these stories at the start of this book so that readers fathom the wide range of place types and environmental situations relevant to a phenomenology of place. In later chapters, I draw on additional newspaper articles to illustrate, via actual places and place experiences, broader conceptual themes and patterns that mark place phenomenologically.

Outlining the Book

My major focus in this book is the significance of places in human life and how they might be envisioned and made to strengthen human wellbeing. My conceptual perspective and research method are grounded in phenomenology, which, in Chapter 2, I introduce broadly and identify some of its core concepts relevant to understanding place. In Chapter 3, I consider how place might be considered holistically and identify two contrasting ways of understanding wholes and wholeness. On one hand, I speak of *analytic relationality*, a situation in which any whole, including place, is pictured as a set of parts among which are located a series of linkages that, when measured, identify stronger and weaker connections and relationships. On the other hand, I speak of *synergistic relationality*, a situation in which any whole, including place, is pictured as a dynamic, generative field that sustains and is sustained by parts integrally interconnected both physically and experientially.

My main aim in this book is to develop a phenomenology of place grounded in synergistic relationality. To accomplish this possibility, I make use of *progressive approximation*, a multivalent means for examining phenomena holistically developed by British philosopher J. G. Bennett. Progressive approximation draws on the qualitative significance of number to provide a method to examine a phenomenon from different vantage points guided by the interpretive possibilities of one-ness, two-ness, three-ness, and so forth. For example, Bennett demonstrates how one-ness can be used to locate the phenomenon as a whole, just as two-ness helps to identify important contrasts and complementarities. In turn, three-ness helps to locate relationships, actions, and processes integral to the phenomenon. In Chapter 4, I introduce Bennett's progressive approximation and argue that it is implicitly phenomenological in that it offers a creative way to explore the experiential dimensions of any phenomenon from multiple perspectives guided by the interpretive significance of number. In Chapter 5, I consider place in terms of one-ness, arguing that human beings are always already emplaced, though the specific nature of that emplacement involves a wide range of place types and place experiences. In Chapter 6, I consider place in terms of two-ness and discuss several existential binaries that include movement/rest, insideness/outsideness, ordinariness/extra-ordinariness, and homeworld/alienworld.

In Chapters 7–14, I consider place in terms of three-ness. This explication is the most extensive portion of the book because, according to Bennett, three-ness involves relationships, processes, and actions. Bennett associates three-ness with what he called *triads*, which he uses to identify six different processes that I draw on to understand how, over time, places can become stronger, weaker, or remain in stasis. In Chapters 7 and 8, I consider how Bennett's six processes might contribute to a generative understanding of place, place experiences, and place meanings. I identify six different place processes that I label *interaction, identity, release, realization, intensification,* and *creation*. In Chapters 9–14, I examine each of these processes in turn and discuss their value for understanding places as they are and for making those places better through design, planning, policy, and advocacy. In Chapter 15, I examine how these six processes interact dynamically to support robust places, on one hand, or faltering places, on the other. In the book's last chapter, I identify potential concerns and criticisms of the phenomenology of place I present here and offer a critical rejoinder. I end by discussing the future of places in our hypermodern times.

Perhaps the most controversial aspect of this book is my use of Bennett's progressive approximation. If the crux of phenomenological effort is openness to the phenomenon, how can one justify a research method that uses a predefined structure – the qualitative significance of number – to examine and understand the phenomenon? In responding to this concern, I point out, first, that nothing can be seen purely as it is in itself. Always, we understand the thing from our personal, cultural, intellectual, and historical points of view. We cannot get beyond our own knowledge and experience: They direct what we see and how we interpret what we see. For sure, a major aim of phenomenology is "the pristine innocence of first seeing" (Spiegelberg, 1982, p. 680) whereby one "sets aside" taken-for-granted understandings, viewpoints, and predilections. The difficult methodological question, however, is how this "setting aside" is to be accomplished practically. This difficulty of seeing the phenomenon afresh is the major reason I use Bennett's method of progressive approximation: I hope to demonstrate that it offers an innovative means for encountering a phenomenon like place and understanding it in ways one would perhaps not consider or bring forward otherwise.

Though Bennett himself was not a phenomenologist, I argue that there is much about progressive approximation that is phenomenological. I find Bennett's method invigorating phenomenologically because it offers a way to examine phenomena from different but complementary perspectives normally unnoticed or ignored. A picture of the phenomenon arises that is multidimensional but integrated. This possibility of comprehensive wholeness is particularly appropriate for a complex, ever-shifting phenomenon like place and is perhaps best demonstrated by the six place processes whereby one realizes dynamic interconnections not readily envisioned otherwise. These six place processes offer an unusual but valuable way to think about how specific places work dynamically – how they shift over time and how they might be strengthened by creative plans and actions that accurately engage with those places and respect their possibilities.

Notes

1 This information on Hurricane Harvey is drawn from articles in the *New York Times*, Saturday, September 2, 2017, p. A1, pp. A10–A11, p. A18. The survivor accounts quoted are on p. A10.

2 The research on place is voluminous; reviews include Cresswell, 2014; Gieryn, 2000; Gruenewald, 2003; Hay, 2002; Janz, 2005; Lewicka, 2011; Manzo, 2005; Manzo and Devine-Wright, 2014; Patterson and Williams, 2005; Seamon, 2013b; Seamon and Gill, 2016; Trentelman, 2009.

3 For example, during the time I was writing this book, one recurring news story was the ten-month effort of Iraqi coalition forces to retake the northern Iraqi city of Mosul, held by the Islamic State since July 2014. Obviously, this story relates to place but in a dramatic, out-of-the-ordinary way that speaks more to the phenomena of "conflict within and between places" and the "devastation of place via war." Because my research concern is a phenomenology of place as it is ordinarily, in a settled, day-to-day way, I focused on stories describing places in their everydayness, whether that every-dayness related to the place's remaining the same or shifting in some supportive or undermining way.

2

PRELIMINARIES FOR A PHENOMENOLOGY OF PLACE

Principles, Concepts, and Method

Arising in continental Europe in the early twentieth century, phenomenology is a way of understanding that emphasizes the description and interpretation of human experience, awareness, and meaning, particularly their unnoticed, taken-for-granted dimensions. The German philosopher Edmund Husserl (1859–1938) was the founder of phenomenology, which he envisioned as "the descriptive, non-reductive science of whatever appears, in the manner of its appearing, in the *subjective* and *intersubjective* life of consciousness" (Moran, 2005, p. 2). Over time, other European philosophers, including Martin Heidegger (1889–1976) and Maurice Merleau-Ponty (1908–1961), shifted their phenomenological explications beyond "consciousness" toward related philosophical topics such as the nature of human being, the various experiential modes by which human meaning arises, and the central role of bodily presence and action in human life.[1]

In this chapter, I describe phenomenology as a way of knowing, and I discuss some of its major principles and concepts. My hope is that this introductory background prepares readers for the phenomenology of place that I offer in following chapters. In providing a preliminary description, I define phenomenology as *the directed effort to see the things and experiences of the world more clearly and completely*. These things and experiences as people experience them are *phenomena*. Any object, event, situation or experience that a person can see, hear, touch, smell, taste, feel, intuit, know, understand, or live through is a legitimate topic for phenomenological investigation. There can be a phenomenology of friendship, of jealousy, of home, of travel, of seeing, of learning, of blindness, of change, of community, of power, of economy, of architecture, of landscape, of plants, and so forth. All these things are phenomena because human beings can experience, encounter, or live through them in some way.

The aim of phenomenological study, however, is not idiosyncratic descriptions of phenomena, though such descriptions are often a useful starting point for phenomenological research. Rather, the aim is to use these descriptions as an evidentiary field from which to locate underlying commonalities that mark essential, non-contingent features and qualities of the phenomenon. The phenomenologist *pays attention* to specific instances of the phenomenon with the hope that these instances, in time, will point toward more general qualities and characteristics that accurately describe the foundational structure or *constitution* of the phenomenon. The pivotal phenomenon that I consider in this book is *place,* which incorporates place experiences, place actions, place meanings, and place events.

Describing Phenomenology

Most simply, phenomenology focuses on human experience. Philosopher Robert Sokolowski (2000, p. 2) defines phenomenology as "the study of human experience and of the ways things present themselves to us in and through such experience." Philosopher David Cerbone (2006, p. 3) writes that "Phenomenology invites us to stay with 'the experience itself,' to concentrate on its character and structure rather than whatever it is that might underlie or be causally responsible for it." To describe phenomenology more fully, I discuss five principles grounding most phenomenological research and introduce what each principle means for the phenomenology of place I offer here.

1. Understanding Grounded in Experience

As I have already emphasized, phenomenologists give attention to concrete human experience and the lived reality of everyday life. Phenomenologist Max van Manen explains that the aim is to discern "the primordialities of meaning as we encounter and live with things and others in our lived experiences and everyday existence" (van Manen, 2014, p. 28). At first glance, the use of the word "lived" in phrases like "lived experience" or "lived meaning" may seem tautological – what, other than "lived," can experience be? For phenomenologists, however, "lived" is an essential descriptor because it "announces the intent to explore *directly* the originary or prereflective dimensions of human existence: life as we live it" (van Manen, 2014, p. 28). Van Manen (2014, p. 39) writes:

> Lived experience is active and passive living through experience. Lived experience names the ordinary and the extraordinary, the quotidian and the exotic, the routine and the surprising, the dull and the ecstatic moments and aspects of experience as we live through them in our human existence.

In this sense, any phenomenological articulation of human beings and their worlds must be grounded in an awareness, a language, and a conception that arise from, remain with, and return to lived experience and meaning. The foundation for conceptual and applied claims is human actions, situations, events, and understandings as they happen matter-of-factly in the unfolding world of human life, which is "the ultimate setting for ourselves and for all the things we experience" (Sokolowski, 2000, p. 44). On one hand, this unfolding world is inestimably more than what any one person can experience or know. On the other hand, for each person, this unfolding world is always only what he or she uniquely experiences and understands it to be. As philosopher John Compton (1997, p. 208) explains,

> The world is inexhaustible and transcends us; we are inevitably out in the middle of it; it is experienced independently of us. At the same time, the world is what, in the most inclusive sense, we experience (or perceive) it to be. There is no world "behind" or "beneath" the world of primordial lived experience.

As Compton indicates, there is always an existential gap between how we experience and know the world and what that world actually is. There is always a conceptual gap between how we experience and know the world and how adequately we translate that everyday experience and knowledge into interpretive and theoretical formulations. The aim of phenomenological research is to pay heed to the comprehensive nature of human experience and to facilitate reflexive understandings that portray human experience as accurately and multivalently as possible. In the phenomenology of place that I present here, I draw on J. G. Bennett's method of progressive approximation to provide an understanding of place that is multidimensional and alert to aspects of experience and meaning that might otherwise remain hidden.

2. Phenomena Approached Openly

If phenomenology's topical focus is human experience and meaning, its methodological focus is empathetic contact with the phenomenon. The aim is an openness whereby the phenomenon is offered a supportive space in which it can most accurately and comprehensively present itself in a way in which it is what it is. One way that Husserl described phenomenology was "back to the things themselves," by which he meant setting aside personal, cultural, ideological, and conceptual prejudices so that one might offer the phenomenon a supportive venue in which it appears in a way that is most real and complete (Moran, 2000, p. 9). One of the most incisive descriptions of phenomenological method is Heidegger's enigmatic directive "to let that which shows itself be seen from itself in the very way in which it shows itself from itself" (Heidegger, 1962, p. 58). How, in other words, might we encounter the phenomenon so that it freely has the space to be what it is rather than what we might suppose, imagine, claim, or dictate it to be?

The central means by which phenomenologists work to facilitate an openness to the phenomenon is the *phenomenological reduction*, which refers to ways to evoke a progressively deepening awareness of the phenomenon so that it is seen in a stronger and clearer light. Van Manen (2014, p. 215) contends that this reduction incorporates contrasting but complementary modes of encountering the phenomenon – on the one hand, suspending any obstacles that block the phenomenon (called "bracketing" or the "*epoché*"); on the other hand, moving closer to the phenomenon via careful, persistent, deepening contact (called the "reduction" proper). Van Manen (2014, p. 220) writes: "The *epoché* describes the ways that we need to open ourselves to the world as we experience it and free ourselves from presuppositions. . . . The aim of the reduction is to re-achieve a direct and primitive contact with the world as we experience it or as it shows itself – rather than as we conceptualize it."

In the phenomenology of place I offer here, I attempt to maintain an openness to the phenomenon in two ways. As a source of accurate lived descriptions of real-world places and place experiences, I draw on a range of materials, including novels, newspaper articles, place research, and design and planning efforts emphasizing place making. To conceptualize place phenomenologically, I draw on earlier phenomenological work, particularly the perceptive studies of geographer Edward Relph (1976, 2009) and philosophers Edward Casey (1997, 2009) and Jeff Malpas (1999, 2006). I also draw on Bennett's method of progressive approximation to examine place from multiple perspectives, including place-as-process. I describe Bennett's multifaceted method more fully in the last part of this chapter.

3. People Immersed in World

Phenomenologists claim that human experience, awareness, and action are always *intentional* – i.e., necessarily oriented toward and finding their significance in a world of emergent meaning. Human beings are not just aware but aware *of something*, whether an object, living thing, idea, feeling, environmental situation, or the like (Sokolowski, 2000, pp. 8–11). Merleau-Ponty (1962, p. *xvii*) explains that the distinguishing feature of intentionality is that "the unity of the world, before being posited by knowledge in a specific act of identification, is 'lived' as ready-made or already there." In this sense, intentionality relates to "the ways we are 'attached' to the world" and means that, experientially, we can never separate or "'step out' from the world and view it from some detached vista. We are *au monde*, meaning simultaneously 'in' and 'of' the world" (van Manen, 2014, p. 62).

The concept of intentionality leads to a central phenomenological claim: *that human beings are always already inescapably immersed, enmeshed, and entwined in their worlds that, most of the time, "just happen" without the intervention of anything or anyone* (Seamon, 2014a, p. 5). How, phenomenologically, do we describe the lived ways in which selves and world are reciprocally related and mutually interdependent?

How, phenomenologically, do we locate and understand the complex, multivalent ways in which we, as human beings, are intertwined, intermeshed, entrenched, and submerged in the worlds in which we find ourselves? Because of this lived intimacy between person and world, one cannot assign specific phenomena to either person or world alone. Everything experienced is "given" but also "interpreted," is "of the world" but also "of the person" (Compton, 1997, p. 208).

Different phenomenologists have clarified this "lived immersion" variously. Husserl emphasized such phenomenological concepts as intentionality, lifeworld, and natural attitude; Heidegger spoke of being-in-the-world and dwelling; and Merleau-Ponty emphasized lived corporeality and the body as an intelligent but pre-predicative subject. In phenomenological research of the last several years, place, place experience, and lived emplacement have become one significant conceptual means for describing and clarifying this human-immersion-in-the-world. In this book, I delineate the wide range of ways in which place contributes to and reflects this lived intimacy between people and the worlds in which they find themselves.

4. Examining Lifeworlds

The everyday structure through which human-immersion-in-the-world unfolds is the *lifeworld* – a person or group's day-to-day world of taken-for-grantedness normally unnoticed and, therefore, concealed as a phenomenon (Dorfman, 2009; Moran, 2000, pp. 181–186; Seamon, 1979). One aim of phenomenology is to disclose and describe the various lived structures and dynamics of the lifeworld, which always includes spatial, environmental, and place dimensions. There is a lived wholeness to lifeworld in that, on the one hand, it refers to the normally unnoticed, automatic unfolding of everyday life as it happens for the individuals and groups involved. On the other hand, the lifeworld incorporates the broader world in which that unfolding happens. In this sense, there is a lifeworld for each experiencing person and group but there is also a lifeworld of the place or situation that embraces those individual and group lifeworlds. This collective lifeworld is grounded and sustained, totally or in part, by the individual and group lifeworlds, just as they are grounded and sustained, totally or in part, by the collective lifeworld in which they find themselves.

Unless it changes in some significant way, we are almost always, in our typical human lives, unaware of our lifeworld, which we assume is *the* way that life is and must be. This typically unquestioned acceptance of the lifeworld is what Husserl called the *natural attitude*, because of which we habitually assume that the world as we know and experience it is the *only* world (Moran, 2000, pp. 144–146). We "accept the world and its forms of givenness as simply *there*, 'on hand' for us" (Moran, 2005, p. 7). Husserl characterized the natural attitude as "naïve" because "we are normally unaware that what we are living in is precisely given to us as the result of a specific 'attitude.' Indeed, even to *recognize* and identify the natural attitude as such is in a sense to have moved beyond it" (Moran, 2005, p. 55).

In this book, I argue that an integral constituent of the lifeworld is place, which is a powerful concept phenomenologically because, by its very nature, it offers a way to articulate more precisely the experienced wholeness of lifeworlds. From a phenomenological perspective, place is not the material environment distinct from the people associated with it but, rather, the indivisible, normally unnoticed phenomenon of person-or-people-experiencing-place. Place is typically complex in its lived constitution; one of my major aims in the phenomenology of place that I present is to provide an interconnected conceptual structure for picturing this lived complexity in an ordered way, including the generative processes whereby places and place experiences shift over time.

5. Identifying Essences and Underlying Patterns Holistically

The primary aim of phenomenological research is a more accurate and thorough understanding of human life, experience, and meaning. The phenomenologist works to penetrate beneath the concrete experience or thing to identify shared patterns and general commonalities that integrate specific instances of the phenomenon into broader structures and patterns not typically recognized (Dahlberg, 2006; Moran, 2000, pp. 134–136; van Manen, 2014, pp. 89–91). Sometimes in phenomenological work, these non-contingent structures and patterns are referred to as *essences* – in other words, "fixed, universal, selfsame and univocal qualities that inform the thing *as such*, at once the ground of its being and its being intelligible" (Burch, 1991, p. 33). Essences are not some set of abstract, cerebrally derived universals that arbitrarily pin down and categorize lived experience. Rather, they are "what endures in time as a remarkable continuity of sense, that is, as a history or motif, in virtue of which the presence of the thing as such is granted in our experience" (Burch, 1991, p. 35). In assuming the experiential presence and existential significance of essences, the phenomenologist presupposes

> a priority of essence in determining the being of beings in themselves, and a notion of "truth" as the conformity of the existent thing to its essence, upon which is grounded "truth" as the correspondence of our essential knowledge with the thing . . . [I]n contrast both to dogmatic metaphysics that presumes a purely theoretical essential insight outside the bounds of all possible experience and to contemporary skepticisms (e.g., deconstruction) that dismantle all essential inquiry, phenomenology must consider essences as they are first constituted in lived experience as a whole, prior to all reflective dichotomies, general ideas, and static forms posited by philosophy.
>
> *(Burch, 1991, p. 33, pp. 34–35)*

Such underlying qualities, configurations, and interconnected structures are the crux of phenomenological understanding. One locates how these interrelated parts and qualities belong together and aims to understand how they are together as they are. One aims to see the phenomenon *in its wholeness* – what philosopher Robert Mugerauer (1988, p. 216) describes as "the gathering together of what already belongs together even while apart." Phenomenological examination is particularly appropriate for place, which provides a spatial and temporal gathering of human life – things, people, situations, and events all together in environmental presence. Working through the lived dimensions of place as an integrated environmental whole and wholeness is a major aim of this book.

The Lived Body and Environmental Embodiment

Having offered an overview of phenomenology, I next discuss several substantive phenomenological themes that are important for the phenomenology of place I present here. These themes most directly relate to the phenomenological interest in the *lived body* – a body that simultaneously experiences, acts in, and is aware of the world that, typically, responds with immediate pattern, meaning, and contextual presence. The phenomenologist most relevant is Maurice Merleau-Ponty, who claims that the lived body is the grounding for human perception, which he understands as the immediate, taken-for-granted givenness of the world always already present before we can catch its presencing. He also recognizes, however, that the lived body incorporates an active, motor dimension that he calls *body–subject* – tacit, unself-conscious corporeal awareness expressed via action and typically in sync with and enmeshed in the physical environment in which the action unfolds. Merleau-Ponty (1962, p. 100) writes:

> [M]y body appears to me as an attitude directed towards a certain existing or possible task. And indeed its spatiality is not, like that of external objects . . . a *spatiality of position,* but a *spatiality of situation* . . . . The word "here" applied to my body does not refer to a determinate position in relation to other positions or to external co-ordinates, but the laying down of the first co-ordinates, the anchoring of the active body in an object, the situation of the body in face of its tasks. Bodily space can be distinguished from external space and envelop its parts instead of spreading them out, because it is the darkness needed in the theatre to show the performance . . . .[2]

In this sense, body–subject is a synergy of pre-reflective but integrated gestures and behaviors. One has mastered a specific corporeal action or set of actions when body–subject has incorporated those actions into its sphere of unself-conscious taken-for-grantedness (Merleau-Ponty, 1962, pp. 138–139). This pre-reflective style of corporeal sensibility evoked through a flow of in-sync actions points toward an intentional bodily unfolding in the world as that world typically sustains the bodily unfolding. Through a repertoire of unself-conscious but corporeally intentional gestures and movements seamlessly interconnected, the body–subject automatically offers up the behaviors, actions, and activities presupposed by and sustaining the person's typical lifeworld (Seamon, 2018b).

In studying place phenomenologically, one can examine the lived body's relationship to the physical environment and spaces in which experiencers find themselves. Relevant here is *environmental embodiment* – the various lived ways, sensorily and mobility-wise, that the body in its pre-reflective perceptual presence encounters and works with the world at hand, especially its environmental and place dimensions (Finlay, 2006, 2011, Chap. 6; Low, 2003b; Seamon, 2014b; Toombs, 1995, 2000). Particularly significant for a phenomenology of place is the environmental versatility of body–subject as expressed in more complex corporeal ensembles extending over time and space and contributing to a wider lived geography (Allen, 2004; Casey, 2009; Toombs, 1995). In my work, I have highlighted two such bodily ensembles: first, *body routines* – sets of integrated gestures, behaviors, and actions that sustain a particular task or aim, for example, darning a sock, preparing a turkey for roasting, or shoveling a sidewalk; and, second, *time–space routines* – sets of more or less habitual bodily actions extending through a considerable portion of time; for example, a going-to-bed routine, a Sunday going-to-church-and-lunch routine, or a daily morning-and-evening dog-walking routine (Seamon, 1979, 2013b; van Eck and Pijpers, 2017).

In relating environmental embodiment to place, the phenomenologist recognizes that the lived body is typically an integral constituent of place and place experience because "lived bodies belong to places and help to constitute them" just as, simultaneously, "places belong to lived bodies and depend on them" (Casey, 2009, p. 327). Through bodily encounters and actions, the person or group contributes to the constitution of a place as, at the same time, those encounters and actions contribute to the person or group's sense of lived involvement and identification with that place. In short, lived bodies and places "interanimate each other" (Casey, 2009, p. 327).

This *interanimation* of lived bodies and places is significant because it suggests that the habitual, unself-conscious familiarity of body–subject is one way by which individuals and groups actualize a taken-for-granted involvement with place. In this regard is the possibility that, in a supportive physical environment, individuals' bodily routines can come together in time and space, thereby contributing to a larger-scale environmental ensemble that I call, after urbanist Jane Jacobs (1961), a *place ballet* – an interaction of individual bodily routines rooted in a specific environment that often becomes an important place of interpersonal and communal exchange, meaning, and attachment (Seamon, 1979). Place examples would include a popular neighborhood café, a lively urban park, a vibrant stretch of city street, or a thriving urban neighborhood. Place ballet points to the possibility that everyday habitual routines regularly happening in material space can transform that space into a lived place with a unique character and ambience (Seamon and Nordin, 1980; van Eck and Pijpers, 2017). This is a theme that emerges throughout the following phenomenology of place.

Place and Phenomenological Method

In doing phenomenological research, one faces the difficult conceptual and methodological question of interpretive accuracy and trustworthiness (Finlay, 2011; Madison, 1988; Seamon, 2017c; Seamon and Gill, 2016; van Manen, 2014; Wachterhauser, 1996). How does the phenomenologist establish a convincing interpretive link between real-world experience and conceptual generalization? In this book, I assume that one methodological means to reduce interpretive error is the use of contrasting but related texts that might offer a multifaceted illumination of the phenomenon being studied – in this case, place, place experiences, place meanings, and place events. By "text," I mean any organized description of place and place experience, whether that description refers to firsthand real-world events or to secondhand literary and scholarly accounts. Here, I draw on the following groups of texts among which I seek to locate thematic and conceptual interconnections via which one might better understand the phenomenon of place:

1. Phenomenologies of place already written. Though the phenomenological literature on place is sizeable, I mostly rely on three major works: Edward Relph's *Place and Placelessness* (Relph, 1976); Edward Casey's *Getting Back into Place* (Casey, 2009); and Jeff Malpas' *Place and Experience* (Malpas, 1999). Though he never explored the phenomenon of place directly, I also rely on Merleau-Ponty's *Phenomenology of Perception* (Merleau-Ponty, 1962) because it contributes to understanding the role of the lived body in place and place experience (Seamon, 2018c).

2. Studies by sociologists, geographers, psychologists, architects, planners, urban designers, and others who provide valuable insights into real-world place experience, place meaning, and place making. Most of these studies are not explicitly phenomenological, but I draw on them in following chapters because they offer empirical or conceptual evidence for my phenomenological claims relating to place.

3. Accounts from imaginative literature that relate to place experiences and place meanings. In this book, I draw on British-African writer Doris Lessing's *The Diaries of Jane Somers* (Lessing, 1984) because this novel offers a heartrending picture of the importance of place for an indigent, ninety-year-old woman named Maudie Fowler. I also draw on three novels by British writer Penelope Lively (1998, 2007, 2011), who frequently considers in her work how characters come to belong to place and how unexpected events in those places lead to characters' lives unfolding differently than they would otherwise.

4.   Recent newspaper articles that deal with place events and place experiences as illustrated by the eight place stories summarized in Chapter 1. During the time of writing this book (October 2016 through September 2017) I set myself each day to study two American newspapers of record – *The New York Times* and *The Wall Street Journal*; I also perused one regional newspaper, *The Kansas City Star* (*KCS*), published in Kansas City, Missouri. My aim was to clip, file, and index any relevant articles and use them as one set of real-world evidence for substantiating more general conceptual themes relating to place. I draw on these newspaper entries to provide one set of empirical evidence for the six "place processes" that I discuss in Chapters 9–14.

5.   The method of progressive approximation developed by British philosopher J. G. Bennett. Progressive approximation offers a conceptual means for exploring any phenomenon from different vantage points; in this book, I use Bennett's approach to consider the holistic, binary, and processual dimensions of places and place experiences. Because it provides the major conceptual structure for the phenomenology of place I develop, I discuss progressive approximation more fully in Chapter 4 and then use it as my major interpretive method in Chapters 5–14.

I use this wide range of texts because I assume that they might offer mutual illumination, amplification, and validation of place as a phenomenon. I call this method *triangulation*, whereby one source of evidence provides insights into other sources of evidence, and one's understanding of the phenomenon is therefore deepened and strengthened. In the literature on qualitative research, triangulation is more typically defined as a research method whereby the researcher draws on multiple methodologies, data sources, evaluators, and conceptual approaches as a means to identify different lived perspectives and to corroborate evidence from different data sources (Creswell, 2007, p. 208; Yardley, 2008, pp. 239–240). Here, my use of triangulation is somewhat different in that the five texts I use for interpretive corroboration are of different descriptive "levels" – in other words, some of these texts are more philosophical and conceptual, while other texts are more experiential and grounded in real-world or narrative evidence. My assumption is that the more conceptual texts shed light on the real-world examples, just as they in turn provide empirical support for my broader conceptual claims. In short, I aim for an appropriate consolidation of experience and thinking and real-world events and conceptual generalization.

The rest of this book examines the phenomenon of place, including place experiences, place meanings, and places as they are lived settings for human life. I begin this phenomenology by arguing, in Chapter 3, that a comprehensive understanding of place incorporates a *synergistic relationality*, whereby place is interpreted as an integrated, intensive whole rather than a set of separated, extensive parts.

Notes

1 Introductions to phenomenology include: Burch, 1989, 1990, 1991; Cerbone, 2006; Finlay, 2011; Moran, 2000, 2001; Morley, 2010; Sokolowski, 2000; Spiegelberg, 1982; van Manen, 2014.
2 Discussions of Merleau-Ponty's understanding of the lived body include: Behnke, 1997; Casey, 1997, pp. 202–242; Cerbone, 2006, pp. 96–103; Cerbone, 2008; Evans, 2008; Finlay, 2006; Gallagher, 1986; Heinämaa, 2012; Jacobson, 2010, pp. 223–224; Leder, 1990; Moran, 2000, pp. 412–430; Morris, 2004, 2008; Pallasmaa, 2005, 2009; Seamon, 1979, 2013b, 2015a, 2018c.

3

UNDERSTANDING PLACE HOLISTICALLY

Analytic vs. Synergistic Relationality

Since the 1970s, when humanistic geographers Yi-Fu Tuan (1974a, 1974b, 1977, 1980), Edward Relph (1976, 1981), and Anne Buttimer (1972, 1976) first realized the need to explore the topic in terms of its everyday lived dimensions, research on place has proliferated. Much of this research is specialized, and one notes such subthemes as "place attachment," "place identity," "place belonging," "sense of place," and so forth.[1] In a review of place research, philosopher Bruce Janz (2005, p. 89) points out that place has become a topic of study in "an unexpectedly wide range of disciplines" because "researchers assume that it gives access to otherwise unavailable features of human experience" (Janz, 2005, p. 89). Another reason for this accelerating interest is the value of place as a concept that "resists theoretical reductionism" and points to the theoretical and practical possibility that "the world cannot be understood in solely causal terms" (Janz, 2005, p. 89).

In examining more fully why place has become a significant research focus, Janz identifies five reasons that relate to the power of the concept to gather together aspects of human experience and meaning conventionally seen in conflict or difficult to integrate theoretically and practically. Janz's five reasons can be summarized as follows:

1. Place speaks to resistance and opposition.
    For example, place can be associated with communitarian or non-instrumentalist theories that allow "moral or traditional considerations of human good to have weight instead of solely relying on instrumentalist reason" (Janz, 2005, p. 91). In a similar way, place can resist cynical, relativist, poststructuralist thinking and counter "frustration with critical strategies that have been good at uncovering the presumed entitlements of modernist

accounts of the world but then have had little to offer in its place" (Janz, 2005, p. 91). Finally, place can confront the homogenizing impacts of globalization by facilitating the recognition that local history, geographical locale, and environmental identity play an important role in human well-being. Place calls into question a key presupposition of globalization: "that we are transcending place and particularity all together" (Janz, 2005, p. 92).

2.   Place breaks down conventional distinctions.

Place becomes a "location of dialogue and critique" in that it can broach differences between the "subjective" understandings of those researched (what anthropologists term the "emic," or the insider's view) versus the "objective" understandings of researchers (the "etic," or the outside observer's view). In a related way, some place research moves beyond observation and explanation to advocate for place and people associated with those places – for example, researchers focusing on individuals and groups who have lost their place or are forcibly displaced. These researchers may become activists for uprooted or placeless individuals and groups (e.g., Larsen and Johnson, 2017; Mbembe, 2001).

3.   Place offers a way to hold sight of both the specific and the general.

If place breaks down distinctions, it also draws on specificity to draw generalizations and broader conceptual principles. Place offers one empirical starting point for theories that "grow from the ground up" (Janz, 2005, p. 93). Studies of real-world places, place experiences, and place meanings, facilitate conceptual understanding (e.g., Manzo, 2003; Manzo and Devine-Wright, 2014). In this sense, place has become "a way of resisting a reductionist postmodernism" that rejects any foundational or essential structures (Janz, 2005, p. 93).

4.   Place offers one way to re-enchant the world.

If place is an integral part of human being, it may offer one means to reinvigorate human life and to criticize planning and development that serve "to close down the imagination and define human life primarily in terms of what can be marketed back to those who dwell there," with the result that environments become banal and placeless (Janz, 2005, p. 94). Janz notes that many researchers who study place "acutely feel its loss and want to give form to that feeling" (Janz, 2005, p. 93).

5.   Place facilitates new modes of disciplinary awareness.

The wide range of disciplines and professions interested in place indicates that the concept may allow researchers "to reflect on themselves in a new way" (Janz, 2005, p. 93). The concept offers an intriguing, untested conceptual and empirical perspective that directs disciplinary research in novel and unusual directions not envisioned otherwise (Relph, 2009; Casey, 2009; Malpas, 1999). Janz suggests that "grappling with as complex an idea as place tends to press [disciplines' standard] methodologies to their limit and tends to bring disciplines back to the source of their material (their duties) as well as the place the discipline holds in relation to other disciplines (their debts)" (Janz, 2005, p. 93).

Conceptual Approaches to the Study of Place

Besides suggesting why place research has gained in academic importance, Janz (2005, pp. 90–91) identifies four major ways in which place has been understood conceptually: first, an *empirical psychological* perspective that assumes "a linear, causal view of place"; second, a *symbolic and structural* perspective that finds the meaning of place "in the 'external' world of symbolic production"; third, a *social-constructivist and Marxist* perspective that assumes place to be "the result of social forces"; and, fourth, a *phenomenological and hermeneutical* perspective that understands place as it involves human experience, agency, and meaning (Janz, 2005, p. 90). For each of these perspectives, Janz briefly highlights its primary value. He explains that the benefit of phenomenological and hermeneutical research is that

> it does not tend either toward idealizing place or materializing it. Place neither simply exists as an abstract idea, nor as stuff "out there" apart from experience. Approaching place phenomenologically and hermeneutically means to recognize that the experience of place brings out something significant about both the world and the [people] experiencing it.
>
> *(Janz, 2005, p. 90)*

In this book, my approach to place is phenomenological, partly because, as Janz suggests, this perspective offers a way to move beyond understandings of place that are either *objectivist* (i.e., interpreting place as an objective environment *outside* experiencers) or *subjectivist* (i.e., interpreting place as a subjective representation, whether cognitive or affective, *inside* experiencers). Rather, I attempt to understand place conceptually and pragmatically as a lived engagement and process whereby human beings both shape and are shaped by the world of places in which they find themselves. Toward this aim, phenomenology is useful because one of its concerns is identifying taken-for-granted foundational structures through which human life is given coherence and continuity (Finlay, 2011; Moran, 2000; van Manen, 2014; Seamon, 2013b).[2]

To provide a conceptual starting point for the phenomenology of place I develop, I identify two contrasting understandings of place – what I call *analytic relationality* and *synergistic relationality*.[3] In analytic relationality, place is understood conceptually as a collection of parts among which are arbitrarily identified a series of linkages then measured and correlated to demonstrate stronger and weaker connections and relationships. This mode of understanding informs much current place research, mostly in a tacit, unquestioned way (Patterson and Williams, 2005). In contrast, an understanding of place grounded in synergistic relationality assumes a phenomenological perspective and works to interpret place conceptually as an integrated, generative field that shapes and is shaped by parts integrally interconnected in a physical and experiential whole. The parts are only parts as they sustain and are sustained by the constitution of the whole. As Malpas (2006, p. 29) explains, place is "constituted through a gathering of elements that are themselves mutually defined only through the way in which they are gathered together within the place they also constitute."

Though Malpas's phrasing is cryptic, his description is a penetrating rendition of a synergistic understanding of place because it pays heed to the indivisible wholeness of place and its parts. Articulating this inseparable interconnectedness is hugely difficult because place as a whole must be understood to know its parts, yet those parts must be understood to know the whole of place (Bortoft, 1996, pp. 9–16). In this chapter, I argue that the perspective of synergistic relationality contributes to an understanding of place that is more accurate, comprehensive, and usable than an understanding grounded in analytic relationality.[4]

Place as Analytic Relationality

In an analytic mode of understanding, relationality is interpreted as a set of correspondences and linkages among parts, the specific properties of which are connected to the specific properties of other parts. The reality of any relationship is portrayed only in terms of the individual identities of self-contained constituents that "merely interact with one another" (Wiggins et al., 2012, p. 209). Any whole is understood conceptually as a complex of interrelated elements often pictured graphically by some set of boxes or sectors connected by a matrix of flow lines and feedback loops. Ontologically, the relationship among the parts is not a whole unto itself but, rather, only a whole as it is a collection of the interlinked parts and their processional interconnections.

One prominent example of analytic relationality is the "General Systems Theory" of biologist Ludwig von Bertalanffy, who envisions a mathematical science of organized wholes, whether the whole be physical, organic, environmental, psychological, social, economic, or historical (Bertalanffy, 1965; Hammond, 2003). He writes:

> The properties and modes of action of higher levels are not explicable by the summation of the properties and modes of action of their components *taken in isolation*. If, however, we know the *ensemble* of the components and the *relations existing between them*, then the higher levels are derivable from the components.
>
> (Bertalanffy, 1965, p. 153)

In Bertalanffy's theory, any whole is called a "system," a term that most broadly refers to an integrated configuration of parts interconnected via some matrix of relationships. Though systems theory is holistic in the sense that any system is interpreted as a cohesive set of elements and linkages, this understanding of wholeness is reductive because there is provided no conceptual or practical way to understand and describe *the whole as whole*. Though systems theory recognizes that the interaction of parts is not static and constant but shifting and dynamic, this approach to wholeness remains piecemeal, since the whole is pictured as an external, materially definable organization of parts and relatable connections. To speak of the whole in terms of ambience, character, presence, or serendipitous unfolding is inappropriate ontologically and epistemologically because the whole has been reified and "separated from the parts that it then dominates" (Bortoft, 2012, p. 15). Philosopher Henri Bortoft (whose work I discuss more fully in the next chapter) argues that the most serious problem with analytic relationality is that it sees things in isolation from one another. This isolationist selectivity loses sight of context and overlooks "the way in which things already *belong* together" (Bortoft, 1996, p. 290). Because the analytic mind is not well practiced in seeing this intrinsic relationality,

> [i]t tries to put *together* what already *belongs* together. Thus the intrinsic relatedness is not seen, and instead, external connections are introduced with a view to overcoming separation. But the form of such connections is that they, too, belong to the level of separation.
>
> *(Bortoft, 1996, p. 290)*

Psychologists Bradford Wiggins, Joseph Ostenson, and Dennis Wendt (Wiggins et al., 2012) point out that the analytic understanding of relationality dominates much academic research today because identifiable parts and connections work as definable variables conveniently measured and correlated quantitatively to offer simple, clear-cut explanations for understanding phenomena originally much more complex: "The hope . . . is that by isolating the variables that matter most within a particular phenomenon from the broader contextual 'noise,' [researchers] can draw out understandings and solutions that were heretofore obscured by complexity" (Wiggins et al., 2012, pp. 210–211).

In relation to analytic research on place, one example is studies of place attachment – the emotional bonds that individuals and groups feel for real-world places (Manzo and Devine-Wright, 2014). In a review of research on place attachment, social psychologist Maria Lewicka (2011) concludes that the central focus has been "the role of individual differences in place attachment," including socio-demographic predictors (e.g., age, social status, home ownership, and length of residence); social predictors (e.g., community ties and sense of security in place); and physical predictors (e.g., building density, presence of green areas, municipal services, access to nature). For understanding place synergistically, Lewicka's most important conclusion is that current place-attachment research has "largely ignored processes [and] the mechanisms through which place attachment develops" (Lewicka, 2011, p. 222). There has been little interest in the interacting network of give-and-take processes and relationships whereby the phenomenon of place comes to be constituted environmentally and temporally. Rather, place is transposed into a static matrix of dependent and independent variables relatable via some degree of measurable correlation and association. For example, one major research finding is that degree of place attachment is typically associated with length of residence in place (Lewicka, 2011, p. 216).

One specific example of an analytic approach to place attachment is psychologist Leila Scannell and Robert Gifford's "tripartite model," which incorporates the three interrelated place components of *physical elements, personal and group meanings,* and *emotional, cognitive, and behavioral aspects* (Scannell and Gifford, 2010). The first component refers to the specific environmental elements and qualities of place to which people are attracted, and the second component relates to the individual and collective understandings from which the place attachment arises. The third component refers to how feeling, thinking, and action are manifested in place attachment. In operationalizing this model empirically, Scannell and Gifford suggest the development of a "place-attachment measurement instrument" (Scannell and Gifford, 2010, p. 6). Their quantitative model illustrates an analytic approach in that it bypasses the lived nature of place and place experience as they sustain and are sustained by felt attachment to the place. Instead, place attachment is understood as a phenomenon separable from place and place experience and then reduced to a passive resultant "produced by" active, causal factors defined via piecemeal human and environmental elements identified *a priori.* The wholeness of place, place experience, and place attachment are largely lost sight of, and place attachment is converted into a measurable, pre-defined interplay of independent and dependent variables.

In a review of place research, environment-behavior researchers Michael Patterson and Daniel Williams (2005, pp. 368–69) associate analytic research like Scannell and Gifford's place attachment model with a *psychometric paradigm* assuming precisely defined concepts represented quantitatively. This approach emphasizes "a need to infuse quantitative operationalization into empirical research on place to make possible the precise, rigorous, and systematic analyses demanded in science" (Patterson and Williams, 2005, p. 368). Patterson and Williams conclude, however, that "structural, holistic understanding cannot be accomplished through the types of concise operational definitions employed in psychometric epistemology" (Patterson and Williams, 2005, pp. 369–370). In discussing the lived nature of human-immersion-in-place, Wiggins et al. (2012, p. 211) make a similar point: "[T]he separation of humans and 'the environment' makes no sense from a [synergistic-relational] perspective because part of what it means to be human is to always and already be human-in-place . . . For [synergistic] relationality, places are what they are, in large part, in relationship to the life that dwells there, including human life."

In a related way, sociologist Thomas Gieryn (2000, p. 466) emphasizes the complex, experiential richness of places. He explains that "place has a plentitude, a completeness, such that the phenomenon is analytically and substantively destroyed" if its parts are arbitrarily broken apart and one or more parts left out or ignored. Neither can the parts of place be ranked higher or lower or be claimed as independent or dependent variables. Rather, the parts of place must remain "bundled" (Gieryn, 2000, p. 466). As Gieryn (2000, p. 466) explains, any place is "an unwindable spiral of material form and interpretive understandings and experiences."

Place as Synergistic Relationality

But if place is Gieryn's "plenitude" and "unwindable spiral," how can it be understood phenomenologically as a synergistic relationality? To broach this question is to examine more carefully what a synergistic interpretation of place entails. In contrast to the analytic perspective, a synergistic perspective on relationality defines the identity and actions of any part by its contextual situation in the larger whole (Bortoft, 1996). The function and impact of any part are not autonomous and self-contained but, rather, "mutually constituted with the broader context within which it is in relationship" (Wiggins et al., 2012, p. 159). In that each part enters into the constitution of every other part, the whole is self-organizing, and one cannot say that the parts are separate from or external to each other as is the case, for example, in Scannell and Gifford's tripartite model of place attachment. Rather, the whole depends on the parts but, equally, the parts depend on the whole. As Malpas (2012b, p. 239) explains, "The relation is itself dependent on what it relates, but what is related is also dependent on the relation."

Quantum physicist David Bohm calls this situation an *implicate order*, by which he means that "everything is enfolded into everything" (Bohm, 1980, p. 177). He contrasts this way of understanding with a situation he terms the *explicate order* – an assembly of interconnected parts understood as external to each other. Bohm's distinction between implicate and explicate orders parallels the distinction between analytic and synergistic relationalities. He writes:

> What distinguishes the explicate order is that what is derived is a set of recurrent and relatively stable elements that are *outside* of each other. This set of elements . . . then provides the explanation of that domain of experience in which the mechanistic order [i.e., analytical relationality] yields an adequate treatment. In the prevailing mechanistic approach, however, these elements, assumed to be separately and independently existent, are taken as constituting the basic reality. The task of science is then to start from such parts and to derive all wholes through abstraction, explaining them as the results of interactions of the parts. On the contrary, when one works in terms of the implicate order, one begins with . . . undivided wholeness . . . in which all parts . . . merge and unite in one unity.
>
> *(Bohm, 1980, pp. 178–179, p. 11)*

In understanding place as synergistic relationality, one can say that each person and group are, first of all, a nexus of human and environmental relationships, including the lived experiences, situations, and meanings that the person or group encounters in relation to the place in which they find themselves. Malpas (2009, p. 22) writes that "Place has an essentially relational structure, and our connection to place is such that we are always already embedded within that structure." Or as psychologist Brent Slife (2004, p. 159) emphasizes more broadly,

> all things . . . have a shared being and a mutual constitution in this sense. They start out and forever remain in relationship. Their very qualities, properties, and identities . . . must depend on how they are related to each other.

Slife (2004, p. 159) goes on to contrast ontological differences between analytic and synergistic relationality. For the former, relationality is only *secondarily* relational because it ignores "the shared being of all things." In reducing relationality to hermetic parts, the researcher arbitrarily abstracts those parts from their lived, real-world context: "In their fundamental realness – in their practical and concrete realities – all things are ontologically related to their context and can qualitatively change as their contexts change . . . . All things, in this sense, are concretely dependent upon, rather than independent of, their contexts" (Slife, 2004, p.159).

In relation to place research, Patterson and Williams (2005, p. 369) argue that a synergistic approach to place must "reject the very notion that place is a concept suited to a precise definition or that conceptual clarity can be achieved via quantitative operationalization or narrowly defined constructs." Rather, the indivisible lived context of place "must be understood structurally (as inter-relationships among elements) and holistically . . ." (Patterson and Williams, 2005, p. 369). Making an argument similar to Slife's, Patterson and Williams emphasize that the major ontological and epistemological weakness of the psychometric perspective is the tendency

> to adopt a "molecular" approach that views phenomena as capable of being reduced to a set of interacting elements or variables, rather than a molar approach that conceives of phenomena more holistically as transactional dimensions whose whole is more than the sum of its parts.
>
> *(Patterson and Williams, 2005, p. 370)*

In her review of the research on place attachment, Lewicka (2011, p. 224) makes a related argument when she points out that, though there are many studies "of correlates and predictors of place attachment, we know very little about the *processes* through which people become attached to places." In suggesting ways in which the lived relationality of people-in-place might be explored, she mentions such research themes as place affordances, environmental embodiment, place habitualities, architectural and environmental pattern languages, and place making as the envisioning of environmental wholeness (Lewicka, 2011, pp. 224–226).

The difficult conceptual and practical matter, however, is how places are to be understood via synergistic relationality. If this approach to wholeness offers a more comprehensive, processual rendition of place, how is this knowledge to be looked for and discerned? How, ontologically and epistemologically, is place to be understood synergistically? These are the central questions I address in the remaining chapters of this book. In the next chapter, I discuss a synergistic approach to wholeness described by British philosopher Henri Bortoft. I then introduce the method of progressive approximation developed by J. G. Bennett via a research approach he calls *systematics*. Bennett's work offers an innovative way to examine any phenomenon from contrasting-but-complementary perspectives and is especially appropriate for studying place as synergistic relationality.[5]

Notes

1 For reviews of place research, see Chapter 1, note 2.
2 For phenomenological discussions of place, see Cameron, 2005; Casey, 1997, 2001a, 2001b, 2009; Donohoe, 2014, 2017a, 2017b; Janz, 2005, 2017; Malpas, 1999, 2001, 2006, 2012a, 2012b, 2015; Moores, 2012; Mugerauer, 1994, 2008; Relph, 1976, 1981, 1985, 1993; Seamon, 2013b, 2013c, 2014b, 2014c, 2015b, 2017a, 2017b, 2018a, 2018b, 2018d; Stefanovic, 1998, 2000.
3 In presenting the two modes of analytic and synergistic relationality, I follow the argument of Wiggins, Ostenson, and Wendt (2012) and Slife (2004). Drawing on Slife, Wiggins et al. use the terms "weak relationality" and "strong relationality," for which I have substituted "analytic relationality" and "synergistic relationality," since "weak" and "strong" suggest a difference in quality and effect. In fact, both conceptions of relationality have their strengths and weaknesses; it therefore seems inappropriate to cast "analytic relationality" as less potent, though in many ways it is, as I shall attempt to demonstrate as the chapter proceeds. Psychiatrist Ian McGilchrist (2009) argues that the contrasting psychological and neurological groundings for analytic and synergistic relationalities can be understood via the human right-brain/left-brain division, which appears to facilitate two dramatically contrasting ways of understanding and being in the world. McGilchrist (2009, p. 137, p. 142, pp. 152–153) associates the left brain with the analytic functions of logic, verbal language, and "abstracted, decontextualized, dis-embodied thinking" (p. 137); he associates the right brain with the synergistic function of intuitive, affective, holistic understandings, including those fostered by the arts and phenomenological awareness.
4 Portions of the following discussion are drawn from Seamon, 2015c.
5 Though not discussed here, a third conceptual approach to the "togetherness" of place is *assemblage theory*, originally associated with poststructural philosophers Gilles Deleuze and Félix Guattari (1987). As assemblages, places are understood as interconnected matrices of human, non-human, and material elements that temporarily coalesce in shifting relationships and spatial and environmental complexes. For example, geo-graphers Paul Robbins and Brian Marks (2010, p. 181) define place assemblages as dynamic environmental structures incorporating "semi-stable socio-natural configura-tions and geographies that emerge over space and time." From the perspective of synergistic relationality, a primary weakness of assemblage theory is its reducing the

"*belonging* together" of place to an arbitrary togetherness largely established by the cerebral determination of the researcher. Places are understood as open-ended, variegated collections of people, things, and environmental elements all momentarily interconnected in a haphazard web of causal and contingent relationships. In this sense, places are not things-in-themselves but momentary spatial and temporal "togetherings" that sooner or later become something else environmentally and place-wise. In addition, the elements, processes, and dynamics of any place assemblage are arbitrarily defined by the researcher, and thus, the comprehensive relationality of the place is reduced to piecemeal parts and linkages in a way similar to the reductionist approach of analytical relationality. For assemblage interpretations of place, see Dovey, 2010 and McFarlane, 2011. A helpful critical commentary on assemblage theory is Storper and Scott, 2016, pp. 1125–1128.

4

EXPLICATING WHOLENESS

Belonging, Progressive Approximation, and Systematics

In Chapter 3, I argued for an understanding of place as it might be interpreted via synergistic relationality. I envisioned place as an interconnected field of intertwined relationships gathering and gathered by a lived intimacy between people and world and held together spatially and temporally. The difficult question is how, via description and interpretation, place, broadly, and actual places, specifically, can be seen and understood as they are unfolding human, environmental, and spatial fields of experience, action, and life?

To answer this question, I draw on two thinkers who have sought ways to remain in contact with the wholeness of the whole – British philosopher and science educator Henri Bortoft (1938–2012); and British philosopher and mathematician J.G. Bennett (1897–1974). Bortoft offers a phenomenology of wholeness by recognizing how the parts of a whole are as they are because of the way they *belong* together. Early in his professional career, Bortoft worked with Bennett, who developed a research approach he called *progressive approximation*. This method of seeing and understanding is grounded in the qualitative significance of number, whereby each whole number – 1, 2, 3, 4, and so forth – offers a unique pathway for understanding different aspects of any phenomenon. In this chapter, I introduce Bortoft and Bennett's understandings of wholeness and explain how Bennett's method of progressive approximation is particularly relevant for a phenomenology of place, which as a phenomenon is remarkably complex environmentally and existentially.[1]

Bortoft's Understanding of Wholeness

To relate synergistic relationality to a phenomenology of wholeness, I begin with Bortoft's insightful hermeneutic-phenomenological work (Bortoft, 1971, 1985,

1996, 2012; Seamon, 2013a; Stefanovic, 1991, 2000). Though he never uses the language of analytic and synergistic relationality to discuss wholeness, Bortoft makes a parallel argument in contending that the whole cannot be explained through a sequential, analytical approach that breaks the whole into a set of parts and then reassembles them piecemeal by cerebral effort (as is the case of analytic relationality). Instead, he claims that the whole can only be understood by entering further into its parts through a mode of careful, intuitive encounter uniting perception, feeling, and thinking. In other words, there is a way to see how the whole is present throughout its parts, so that, in any one of the parts, the whole can be found, sometimes more clearly, sometimes less. As one finds ways to better understand the parts, so the whole to which they belong becomes better understood. In turn, this progressive clarity of the whole sheds additional light on the parts, which become yet more understandable and say more about the whole. The aim is a process of reciprocal insight – a virtuous circle resonating between parts and whole.[2]

The great difficulty, however, is finding a way to move into and encounter the parts as they are in themselves so that the whole is foreshadowed and seen, more and more fully. How do we encounter the parts most advantageously so that we can better see and understand the whole? How can one avoid describing the parts in an inaccurate way or arbitrarily constructing a counterfeit whole unfaithful to the parts? In this sense, any act of understanding or doing is revealing the right parts in their right relationship as they mark out the larger whole. As Bortoft (1971, p. 54) explains:

> If a part is to be an arena in which the whole can be present, it cannot be any old thing. Parts are not bits and pieces, because a part is only a part if it is such that it can bear the whole. There is a useful ambivalence here: "to bear," in the sense of "to pass through" and "to carry"; and "to bear" in the sense of "to suffer," where this is taken in the sense of "to undergo." By itself the part is nothing, not even a part, but the whole cannot be whole without the part. The part becomes significant itself through becoming a bearer of the whole.

If the parts of the whole come into being as they "bear" the whole, so the whole relates to the parts in that it is not a thing marked by their simple summation. Rather, the whole comes to presence within its parts, which are the place for the presencing of the whole. In other words, the parts show the way to the whole, which can be encountered nowhere else except through the parts. Bortoft (1971, p. 56) writes:

> We cannot know the whole in the way in which we know things because we cannot recognize the whole as a thing. If the whole were available to be recognized in the same way as we recognize the things that surround us, then

the whole would be counted among these things as one of them. So we could point and say "here is this" and "there is that" and "that's the whole over there." If we could do this, we would know the whole in the same way that we know its parts, for the whole itself would simply be numbered among its parts, so that the whole would be outside of its parts in just the same way that each part is outside all the other parts. . . . But the whole comes into presence *within* its parts, so we cannot encounter the whole in the same way as we encounter the parts. Thus, we cannot know the whole in the way that we know things and recognize ourselves knowing things. So we should not think of the whole as if it were a thing . . . , for in so doing we effectively deny the whole inasmuch as we are making as if to externalize that [i.e., the whole] which can express presence only within the things which are external with respect to our awareness of them.

Belonging Together

Bortoft argues that, by teaching ourselves to become more sensitive to the dynamic reciprocity between parts and whole, we learn to recognize how parts "belong" to the whole. To make the parts/whole relationship grounded phenomenologically, Bortoft (1996, pp. 59–60) draws on phenomenological philosopher Martin Heidegger's discussion of "belonging *together*" vs. "*belonging* together" (Heidegger, 1969, p. 29). On one hand, the relationship between parts and whole can be understood in terms of "belonging *together*" – a situation where the thing belongs in some larger structure because it has a position in the order of a "together" that is arbitrary, fortuitous, or practically necessary (e.g., names in a telephone directory, books in a library, or parts of an engine). As a result, any parts will more or less suffice (Bortoft, 1996, p. 59). As explained in the earlier discussion of analytic relationality, this mode of togetherness is typically assumed in conventional empirical research whereby the researcher arbitrarily decides on the parts of the whole and then defines and measures their consistency and connections accordingly.

On the other hand, one can envision the relationship between parts and whole as "*belonging* together," a situation in which the "together" is established by the "belonging" (Bortoft, 1996, p. 60). In this case, the parts are together first of all *because they belong* and, thus, each part is essential and integral, contributing to and sustained by the belonging. Grasping the difference between "belonging *together*" and "*belonging* together" is difficult. One accessible example is a song: In terms of "belonging *together*," the song is a set of notes that can be represented via musical notation. In terms of "*belonging* together," however, the song is a unique, integrated sound experience that conveys a character, mood, and meaning grounded in the "belongingness" evoked by the song in its wholeness. The song's notes, rhythm, harmony, and so forth make up its constitution technically and soundwise, but the song *as an experience and "thing in itself"* is entirely different from its musical components. The song "*is* the organization – it is not another note" (Bortoft, 1996, p. 353, n. 13). It is this manner of integral organization that grounds "*belonging* together" and marks the manner of wholeness that synergistic relationality aims to understand and identify.[3]

There is still the confounding question of how a mode of "*belonging* together" is to be recognized and understood. One promising possibility is J. G. Bennett's method of progressive approximation, which I draw on in the remaining chapters as one way to understand place as "*belonging* together" and thus as synergistic relationality. In the rest of this chapter, I introduce Bennett's work, beginning with progressive approximation.

Bennett's Progressive Approximation

Throughout his professional career, J.G. Bennett sought a conceptual means to integrate scientific theory and research with studies of the world's religions and spiritual traditions. He was particularly drawn to the qualitative and symbolic significance of numbers – a theme recognizable in many religious traditions, both East and West (Bennett, 1956, pp. 17–48; Bennett, 1974, pp. 335–339). As a philosopher and mathematician, Bennett became interested in reconciling the materialist, quantitative approach to number in modern Western science with the intuitive, qualitative approach of the world's spiritual traditions. His influential masterwork, *The Dramatic Universe*, was published in four volumes between 1956 and 1966 and attempted to "formulate the rules that enable the possible to be distinguished from the impossible" (Bennett, 1956, p. 229). By the phrase "dramatic universe," Bennett (1956, p. 20) sought do bring attention "to the character that all existence acquires through the presence everywhere of relativity and uncertainty, combined with consciousness and with the possibility of freedom." He assumed that "behind the bewildering diversity and complexity of phenomena, there is an organized structure that holds them all together" (Bennett, 1966a, p. 6).

In his search for this "organized structure," Bennett developed the method of *progressive approximation*, whereby one returns "again and again to examine the same material of experience to search for new depths of meaning and to transform these meanings into understanding" (Bennett, 1956, p. 117). The goal of progressive approximation is "the construction of concepts starting from vague outlines with subsequent filling in of details" (Bennett, 1956, p. 518). As researchers proceed, they examine the same phenomenon but encounter it in contrasting but complementary ways via different vantage points, a manner of seeing that, figuratively, can be compared to experiencing a sculpture, which from different viewing angles offers different aesthetic experiences and understandings. The method consists "in deepening of meanings as opposed to accumulating of facts" (Bennett, 1956, p. 518). As we proceed, we attempt gradually to build up a world-picture, at first in outline only, afterwards filling in details where we find it possible. [We start] with a total concept that is necessarily vague and faulty, rather than with a concept that, though perhaps precise and convincing, is necessarily abstract and incomplete. We shall begin with the total givenness of all experience and, without forgetting the limitations of our powers of perception and thought, try to see that totality as one.

(Bennett, 1956, p. 30)

To clarify the method of progressive approximation, Bennett described two contrasting ways of approaching phenomena, particularly those involving *organized complexity* – i.e., phenomena, like place, that incorporate many different elements, actions, situations, and qualities enjoined spatially, environmentally, and temporally (Bennett, 1966a, pp. 5–7). He pointed out that, on one hand, the researcher can examine the phenomenon *in parts* to draw conceptual and practical possibilities and outcomes. On the other hand, he or she can consider the *whole as whole* and seek to locate some underlying connectedness or integrated structure. One notes that these two contrasting ways of looking and seeing are consonant with differences between analytic and synergistic relationality. As Bennett (1966a, p. 118) explained:

There are two ways of dealing with complex, or multivalent situations. One is to simplify, taking the situation apart and applying a technique of examination and analysis that will allow us to formulate working hypotheses and suggest lines of action. This is the recognized procedure of natural science, and it has proved immensely successful in extending our practical knowledge, and markedly unsuccessful in showing us how all the pieces are to be put together again to form a living whole. The second way is to start from the totality, accepting complexity as an irreducible element in the situation, and then to search for an organized structure that will enable us to examine it as a whole. We shall endeavor to follow the second procedure, recognizing that we cannot hope to know the structure in any absolute sense . . . . Absolute knowledge of *what* [human beings are] would imply absolute knowledge of *why* [they are]. Whereas we can only guess at some partial notion.

Bennett's Systematics

As with Bortoft's approach to wholeness, however, the difficult question for progressive approximation is how it is to be accomplished practically so that one sees the phenomenon more and more thoroughly in an integrated, comprehensive way remaining faithful to what the phenomenon actually is. How, procedurally, does the researcher shift from broad aspects of the phenomenon to more specific aspects and from its general features to more detailed features, interrelationships, and processual aspects? Bennett's answer to these questions is a method of looking and seeing that he called *systematics*. Systematics draws on the interpretive significance of whole numbers to facilitate a deepening familiarity with and understanding of the phenomenon. For example, Bennett associated one-ness with the unity and wholeness of the phenomenon; two-ness, with difference and complementarity; three-ness, with relationship and process; four-ness, with ordered activity, and so forth. The central assumption of systematics is that "there is something inherent in number itself that is fundamental to the way the world is and the way we can understand it. If we are able to penetrate more deeply into the nature of number, then we must become able to see reality more clearly" (Blake, 2003, p. 8).[4]

For Bennett, using whole numbers as an interpretive guide for discovery was one means to facilitate a widening sphere of awareness for looking at, seeing, and knowing the phenomenon – in short, his progressive approximation. As researchers proceed, they examine the same phenomenon but encounter it differently as each number offers a different but more sophisticated vantage point. The result is that the researcher understands the phenomenon from a range of different perspectives, each of which sheds light on new but interrelated aspects. What, in other words, do we learn about the phenomenon when we consider it in terms of one-ness (wholeness), two-ness (complementarity), three-ness (relationship), four-ness (organized activity), and so forth?

In developing systematics as a formalized method of study, Bennett used the word *system* to designate the underlying pattern that a specific number represents. By using the Greek word for the number followed by the suffix –*ad*, he gave each system a name. Thus the *monad* relates to one-ness; the *dyad*, two-ness; the *triad*, three-ness; the *tetrad*, four-ness, the *pentad*, five-ness, and so forth. Bennett argued that each of these systems offers different but equally accurate perspectives on the phenomenon. Each system refers to a "mode of experience that has a characteristic quality that cannot be reduced to simpler terms" (Bennett, 1961, p. 3). The triad, for example, points to something about human experience that cannot be seen via the dyad; in turn, the dyad reveals aspects of human life unavailable via the monad. By exploring a phenomenon via the interpretive guidance of numbers, the researcher gains a more comprehensive and integrated understanding of the phenomenon and is better able to appreciate and to work with it. Systematics assumes that wholeness is relative and revealed in different but complementary ways via the monad, dyad, triad, and so forth. Each system offers a contrasting but equally reliable way of exploring the phenomenon and may help one to locate qualities and features not noticed or expected otherwise.

I emphasize that, in Bennett's systematics, "system" is defined differently from the standard systems-theory definition of "an integrated set of parts and their relationships." Rather, systems in systematics are understood as underlying structures organized via the qualitative significance of whole numbers. Bennett formally defined *system* as "a set of independent but mutually relevant terms," in which *term* refers to "those elements of the system that express a specific

TABLE 4.1 The first six systems of Bennett's systematics framework.

System	Term	Systemic attribute
1 – monad	totality	wholeness
2 – dyad	natures	difference
3 – triad	impulses	relatedness
4 – tetrad	sources	organized activity
5 – pentad	limits	potential
6 – hexad	laws	event as coalescence

character, such as universality, complementarity, dynamism, activity, potential, and so forth" (Bennett, 1993, p. 13). The number of terms in a system identifies its *order*; thus the monad is of the first order and has only one term that is called *totality*. The second-, third-, fourth-, fifth- and sixth-order systems are *dyads, triads, tetrads, pentads*, and *hexads*. Their respective terms are *natures, impulses, sources, limits*, and *laws*. Table 4.1 lists these six systems and their systemic terms and attributes.

As in systems theory, a system in systematics involves a set of elements incorporating an organized whole. According to the systematics definition, however, those elements are an integral part of human experience but *beneath* the directly given phenomenon and grounded in the interpretive possibilities of one-ness, two-ness, three-ness, and so forth (Bennett, 1966a, pp. 7–12). For example, the monad is a system that uses the qualities of one-ness to locate the specific content and identity of the phenomenon, just as the systems of dyad and triad work in a similar way by using the qualities of two-ness and three-ness to locate binaries and relationships that mark the phenomenon. From the perspective of systematics, any phenomenon can be examined through several different systems that range from the one-ness of the monad to the twelve-ness of the dodecad (Bennett, 1966, Chap. 37).[5]

It is important to understand that the numerical sequence of the systems is not derived simply by the addition of another term. The complementarity marked by the dyad does not arise solely by the addition of two wholes but by the formation of a binary. The relatedness marked by the triad does not arise solely by the reconciliation of opposites but by a processual action facilitated in the coalescence of the triad's three terms. Each system in the numerical sequence points toward a progressive complexity of the phenomenon, beginning with its wholeness and then moving toward difference, relationship, activity, potential, and so forth. In sum, the systems "serve only as a means for recognizing certain properties of our experience and for studying them both separately and in their mutual relevance" (Bennett, 1956, p. 35).

In relation to phenomenological understanding, one can say that each system relates to a particular dimension of human experience in relation to the phenomenon studied – in other words, the lived qualities of wholeness, of difference, of relatedness and the like (Table 4.1, third column). As Bennett explains, "By 'system' we shall designate a mode of experience that has a characteristic quality that cannot be reduced to simpler terms. Thus duality has the quality of difference, that cannot be reduced to unity" (Bennett, 1966a, p. 3). A system is said to incorporate "some inner connectedness or mutual relevance of its . . . terms" (Bennett, 1961, p. 3). As one uses each system to examine the phenomenon, one's vantage point shifts, and he or she gains a different but equally representative understanding of the phenomenon. Systematics assumes that these various understandings coalesce into a more thorough, multi-dimensioned account of the phenomenon.

From a phenomenological perspective, one can argue that Bennett's achievement is a multivalent phenomenology of wholeness in which each whole number – 1, 2, 3, 4, and so forth up to 12 – points toward a different mode of togetherness and belonging in relation to the thing studied. Though Bennett never associated systematics with phenomenology, one can argue that the method offers one workable way to locate and gauge phenomena by drawing on the interpretive possibilities of number. Throughout his discussion of systematics, Bennett emphasized the central importance of direct, firsthand experience, for example:

- "The real problem of the philosopher is not to look beyond experience but to understand it" (Bennett, 1956, p. 34);
- "A process of clarification of experience" (Bennett, 1956, p. 230);
- "This approach emphasizes the importance of the qualitative elements in all experience as derivative from the qualitative significance of number" (Bennett, 1963, p. 107);
- "There is no getting outside experience" (Bennett, 1993, p. 11);
- "The question before us is how we can use our experience so that it will increase our understanding" (Bennett, 1993, p. 11).

Some scholars might argue that "systematics" is an unfortunate designation for the method of study that Bennett developed, since the term suggests analytic relationality and Bertalanffy's systems theory as discussed in Chapter 3.[6] In addition, one finds that, in conventional scientific and academic circles, "systematics" more commonly refers to a biological subfield that classifies living things with the aim of understanding their evolutionary history (Schuh and Brower, 2009). When Bennett and his associates coined the term in the 1960s, I do not know if they were aware of these issues of nomenclature and terminology. I agree that Bennett's way of study might be more appropriately named, but "systematics" is the designation that his research group used, and it is the term I draw on in this book. Bennett began systematics research in the late 1940s and played a central role in its continuation until his death in 1974. In 1946, he established the Institute for the Comparative Study of History, Philosophy and the Sciences, a London research group that conducted systematic investigations. In 1963, he founded *Systematics*, an academic journal, published until 1974, that presented a wide range of articles drawing on systematic principles and methods explicitly or implicitly. In presenting the systems of monad, dyad, and triad as they might contribute to an understanding of place, I draw on Bennett's discussion in the four volumes of his *Dramatic Universe* (Bennett, 1956, 1961, 1966a, 1966b) as well as the posthumously published *Elementary Systematics*, a series of introductory lectures on systematics that he gave in London in 1963 and that I edited for publication in the early 1990s (Bennett, 1993).[7]

In following chapters, I explore place systematically in terms of the monad, dyad, and triad. In the rest of this chapter, however, I review the monad and dyad in greater detail. In Chapters 5 and 6, I then consider how each, respectively, might be used to better understand place. In many ways, Bennett's triad is the most complex system because it sheds light on relationships and changes over time – *generative processes*, in other words. Because of its complexity, I present the triad by itself in Chapter 7 and then discuss its value for understanding place in Chapters 8–14.

The Monad

As a one-term system, the monad relates to universality, totality, and diversity in unity (Bennett, 1966b, p. 15).[8] It is "the totality of recurrent elements without distinction" (Bennett, 1966b, p. 20) and helps the researcher to locate the unique qualities that allow any phenomenon to be what it is rather than something else. In its focus on the wholeness of the phenomenon, the monad offers a means to delineate its content, which is multifaceted, wide-ranging, and undifferentiated. At the same time, each phenomenon is unique, and the monad helps one to become aware of the central features grounding that uniqueness: "Every monad is a universe in itself and has a diverse content drawn together by a central quality that makes the monad a recognizable entity" (Bennett, 1993, p. 20).

In looking for the monadic qualities of any phenomenon, the researcher aims to set aside any pre-set picture of what the phenomenon is. Almost always, it incorporates certain core elements or features, but one's first task is to be open to the phenomenon and allow its constitutional elements to reveal themselves as they are. As Bennett (1966a, p. 14) explains,

> The monad is an undifferentiated diversity. We meet this state of affairs whenever we turn our attention to a new situation, large or small. The monadic character of [any phenomenon] is present in all its parts. Every such part appears in its immediacy in an undifferentiated totality of which we know nothing except that it is what it is. But, side by side with this bare knowledge, we are led on by the conviction that it is a structure [and] hope to understand it by examining its content more closely. This combination of

confused immediacy and the expectation of finding an organized structure gives the monad a progressive character. It is what it is, but it holds promise of being more than it appears to be.

As Bennett indicates, the aim is to encounter the phenomenon without distinctions. The researcher works to gather a description of the phenomenon without supposing that any parts mean more or less in terms of what the phenomenon is. We locate the content of the phenomenon by setting it before us and allowing "a description to come forth" (Bennett, 1993, p. 22). Practically, this effort may involve making a list of words and phrases that characterize the phenomenon. At least at first, however, we do not order these qualities, assume their relative significance, or make links among them. The guiding principle is "whether a particular element is relevant or not. To know what is relevant, one must have some sense of what belongs to the structure . . ." (Bennett, 1993, p. 22). The word "belongs" is crucial and echoes Bortoft's emphasis of discovering the *belonging together* of the phenomenon.

What are some examples of phenomena considered as monads? As a simple illustration, Bennett discusses the monad of "school," which is marked by such descriptors as "students," "teachers," "parents," "teaching," "learning," "school building," "classrooms," "community," "textbooks," "reading," "writing," "mathematics," "blackboards," "computers," "curriculum," "exercises," "examinations," and so forth. These descriptors cover a wide range of elements and are various in nature; some involve material objects ("school building," "computers"), some involve people ("students," "teachers"), some involve activities and situations ("learning," "teaching"), and some involve aims and methods ("curriculum," "examinations"). This diversity of the school monad is "not only a difference among things of the same kind but also a difference among things of a different kind. . . . The totality of all these things is the content of the monad" (Bennett, 1993, p. 23).

This monad describes the phenomenon of school broadly, and one realizes that the monads of specific schools would incorporate some common elements but also incorporate variations. For example, the monad for a Montessori school would be identified differently from that of a Waldorf School, which in turn would be different from that of a Catholic school or a school that emphasizes vocational studies. Similarly, the monad for "high school" would be different from the monad for "middle school" or "elementary school." This example of "school" indicates that monads are not defined by sharp, impenetrable boundaries, whether material or conceptual, but are unified by their total character (Bennett, 1966a, p. 15).

Any phenomenon can be considered as a monad, provided it is "sufficiently complete in terms of human experience so that we can have contact with it" (Bennett, 1993, p. 19). In this book, I emphasize the phenomenon of place broadly, and thus the monad of place I delineate in the next chapter focuses mostly on lived qualities that identify place as an integral constituent of human experience and life. At the same time, however, there is a huge range of place types (e.g., room, building, neighborhood, district, town, city, and region) as well as specific places (e.g., France, New England, California, Moscow, Tokyo, Soho, Greenwich Village, Hampstead Heath, Notre Dame Cathedral, Hagia Sophia, and so forth). In this book, I argue that the broad explication of place that I delineate has value for thinking about particular place types and particular places, whatever their functional constitution, geographical scale, or social and cultural structure and aspects.

The Dyad

If the monad relates to the phenomenon as a unity marked by diversity, the dyad shifts one's attention to the phenomenon as described by binaries and contrasts. Bennett defines the dyad as a "two-term system, such that each term is distinct from and yet requires, and even pre-supposes the other" (Bennett, 1993, p. 26).[9] Bennett names the dyad's two terms *natures* and identifies the dyad's attribute as *complementarity* (rather than polarity) because any contrasting elements or qualities are always inextricably together, and one cannot be present without the other: "The two natures of anything are not two parts of it. Instead, these natures are *pervasive* in the sense that they intimately permeate every portion of the thing, even the parts to which they seem opposite" (Bennett, 1993, p. 28).

To clarify this pervasiveness, Bennett (1966a, p. 19) draws on the simple adage, "every stick has two ends," to indicate the mutuality and reciprocity of the dyad's two natures. To break a whole stick into two separate parts is to destroy the stick-as-stick and thereby to undo its wholeness, since the stick is no longer one but two. The habitual ease with which the two natures of the dyad can be thought of as conflicting opposites rather than complements is a perplexing aspect of the dyad, and Bennett emphasizes that "We have to find ways of describing the two terms . . . in such a way as to bring out the connection between contradiction and complementarity" (Bennett, 1966a, p. 19). For example, in thinking about "school" as a dyad, one realizes that, on one hand, a school must maintain learning standards and proctor children who master those standards. On the other hand, that school has responsibilities to the larger world – to parents, to the community of which the school is a part, and to shifts in pedagogy, learning technologies, governmental requirements, and advances in knowledge. These external responsibilities may be much different from and even in conflict with the school's pedagogical duties, but both sets of obligations must be adequately dealt with if the school is to be successful *as a school*.

One dyad that Bennett (1966a, pp. 21–22) discusses is "tree," which, as it is in itself, is different from what it is in relation to the world in which it finds itself. In terms of what it is, any tree can be described by its species, its genus, size, condition, age, coloration, seasonal patterns, and so forth. In terms of what it does, the tree is a part of the world of things and living beings. As a thing, it may be a source of fruit, nuts, or wood, and thus play a role in human worlds; as a living being, it is part of the biological processes of photosynthesis and may be part of a larger forest ecology. Another way to interpret the tree as dyad is via the verticality of its branches and roots. On the one hand, the tree is drawn down into the earth but reaches upward into the sky. One thinks of the tree of life and the powerful sacred symbolism whereby the tree is anchored in this material world but strives heavenly toward some etheric ineffability.

This tree example indicates that any phenomenon involves more than one dyad, and the question becomes selection: Which dyads are most useful for understanding the phenomenon? In answering this question, Bennett offers no exact guidelines, other than the claim that the most helpful dyads incorporate both strength and adequacy – strength, in the sense that the identified dyads contribute to a deepened understanding of the phenomenon; adequacy, in the sense that the dyads apply fully to the range of experience marked by the phenomenon. Bennett emphasizes, however, that, as with the tree and school examples, the phenomenon as dyad can often be usefully envisioned, on one hand, as *what it is*, and, on the other hand, as *what it does*. As he explains,

> Every structure has a twofold nature: one nature makes it what it is and the other what it does. What it is, that is the content, is its own affair; but what it does concerns everything around it . . . . It is infinite in its external connectedness, and it is also infinite to its internal diversity. The two infinities are not the same. They even contradict each other. The inner significance comes from separation from the rest of the world and the outer from contact with it.
>
> *(Bennett, 1966a, p. 19)*

In illustrating these inner and outer natures more precisely, Bennett explicates the two natures of "home" (Bennett, 1966b, p. 19; Bennett, 1993, pp. 27–29), a topic central to this book, since "home" is one manner of place. On one hand, a home turns inward to provide a place of comfort, security, and mutual support for the dwellers who live there. On the other hand, the home turns outward because it necessarily requires connections and exchanges with the world outside – for example, procuring food and other essentials, offering a place of welcome and hospitality for guests, drawing on places and activities beyond the home to complement its more usual experiences and life patterns. Whether these two natures of the home are described as "inner and outer" or "private and public," they are both integral aspects of any home, and each connects to and colors the other. A sofa, for example, may be one's favorite place of relaxation but may also be a primary domestic locale for entertaining guests. A closed entry door secures a sense of shelter and comfort, just as an open entry door allows visitors to be welcomed in.

The key point about the dyad's two natures is that they interpenetrate and cannot be separated because both are integral to phenomena. In this sense, reconciliation is not possible via the dyad. Rather, we must "accept the complementarity of dyads and cease to look for its removal by the suppression or elimination of one of the terms" (Bennett, 1966b, p. 23). In asking how the dyad's unavoidable differences are to be dealt with, we must look to the triad, whereby we shift "from the need to resolve a contradiction to the conditions that make the resolution possible" (Bennett, 1966b, p. 23). Because of its complexity, I devote Chapter 7 to the triad and Chapters 8–14 to the triads of place. First, however, I discuss place in terms of the monad and dyad. This is the focus of the next two chapters.

Notes

1 On Bortoft's relationship with Bennett, see Bortoft, 2012, p. 178 and pp. 205–206; Seamon, 2013a.
2 Bortoft draws the idea of a virtuous circle from the philosophical tradition of herme-neutics, the study of interpretation and understanding. The reciprocal interpretive rela-tionship between parts and whole is known as the "hermeneutic circle," which hermeneuticist Richard Palmer (1969, p. 118) describes as follows: "The whole receives its definition from the parts, and, reciprocally, the parts can only be understood in reference to a whole." Bortoft (1971, p. 49) discusses the hermeneutic circle in relation to reading and understanding a text: "In order to read meaningfully, it is necessary to understand in advance what will be said, and yet this understanding can come only from the reading . . . . More specifically, we must grasp the words to express the sen-tence, but the way of saying the words comes from the sentence. Put this way, it appears paradoxically that we should ever be able to speak, read, or write meaningfully. Put generally, the paradox of the hermeneutic circle is that to understand the whole we must understand the parts, but to understand the parts we must understand the whole."
3 In the introduction to her translation of *Identity and Difference*, philosopher Joan Stambaugh (1969, p. 11) explains what Heidegger means by identity: that "to every being as such there belongs identity, the unity within itself." She goes on to say that "What is new about [Heidegger's] understanding of identity as a relation is that the relation first determines the manner of being of what is related and the how of this relation" (Stambaugh, 1969, p. 12). It is this identity-grounded-in-relation, described in Chapter 3 as synergistic relationality, which marks "*belonging* together."
4 Bennett defines systematics as "the study of structures [i.e., phenomena] as simplified totalities" and explains that "Analytics breaks structures down into their simplest elements and looks for the connections between these elements. Systematics takes the connections as primary and the elements as secondary. This is a very difficult mental exercise for people trained in analytical thinking" (Bennett, 1966a, pp. 9–10). The most thorough discussions of systematics include Bennett, 1956, pp. 17–48; Bennett, 1961, pp. 3–10; Bennett, 1963; Bennett, 1966a, pp. 3–75; Bennett, 1993. Systematics is the conceptual and methodological foundation of Bennett's four-volume masterwork, *The Dramatic Universe* (Bennett, 1956, 1961, 1966a, 1966b).
5 Bennett identifies systems beyond twelve-ness and the dodecad as *societies*, which he defines as "multi-term systems with an indefinite number of members" (Bennett, 1961, p. 38).
6 For a comparison of general systems theory and systematics, see Bennett, 1963, 1970.

7 In justifying their qualitative significance, Bennett (1956, p. 28) writes that "Numbers have a meaning in their own right. The number two is not merely the symbol of duality; 'twoness' depends upon and defines the separation of opposites. The number three is indissolubly connected with the very idea of relatedness. Three as a class concept is an abstraction from experience – three as a relationship is an integral part of experience itself. This leads us to seek for a property which can be called the *concrete significance of number.*"

8 Introductions to the monad include Bennett, 1966a, pp. 14–18; Bennett, 1993, pp. 18–26 and pp. 99–101.

9 Introductions to the dyad include Bennett, 1966a, pp. 18–23; Bennett, 1993, pp. 27–35 and p. 101.

5

THE MONAD OF PLACE

In this chapter, I consider place as a monad, which, first of all, accommodates the phenomenon as a whole without identifying distinctions. A systematics approach requires that one begins by locating the phenomenon as a unity. Whereas place as a monad points to the central role of emplacement as a non-contingent aspect of human experience and human life, place as dyad and triad makes a start at refining the lived dimensions of lived emplacement and understanding places as they change over time.

The monad of place is significant both theoretically and practically. Theoretically, the monad is crucial to all disciplines and professions dealing with environmental, architectural, and place concerns because the monad of place helps one to realize that human beings and worlds are always integrally together. As a multifaceted phenomenon incorporating and shaping the environmental fabric of taken-for-granted daily life, place is an essential, inescapable constituent of human-being-in-the-world. Practically, this lived togetherness of people and place is important because it demonstrates that environmental and place qualities are integral to human being. The monad points to the need to envision effective policy, planning, design, and advocacy as they support, via robust place making, this lived togetherness grounded in place. Ideally, the practical aim is a *"belonging together"* in place rather than a "belonging *together*."

Aspects of the Monad of Place

How is the monad of place to be located and described? As I illustrated through the example of "school" in Chapter 4, one method is to generate a list of descriptive words and phrases. The aim is to identify recurring characteristics of the phenomenon and, eventually, to establish which of these characteristics are more or less central. To generate such a list, I contacted thirty-five individuals interested in or associated with place research. My email request was that they ponder "place" and

> make a list of words and short phrases that come into your mind as you ponder. Whatever comes up is fine. There are no right or wrong descriptors. I don't want specific places (e.g., favorite places). Rather I'm trying to locate what one might term the "core" or "heart" of place, and this listing exercise is one means toward that ends. Your list can be a few descriptors or many.
>
> *(December 29, 2016)*

Twenty-seven individuals answered my request, though some of these responses offered declarative statements about place rather than a list of words and phrases, as I requested. So that readers have a sense of these responses, I reproduce eight lists in Table 5.1.[1] In perusing these lists, one notes that each is unique, though some broader themes begin to be emerge – e.g., states of being and feeling ("embodied," "belonging," "attachment"), spatial and relational qualities ("groundedness," "between," "bounded openness/opening"), and lived situatedness and identity ("home," "tethered," "an identifiable 'somewhere'"). Next, as

TABLE 5.1 Eight lists describing "place" via single words and short phrases.

1. Ontological, embodied, relation, between, emplacement, belonging

2. Belonging, being, expression, home, safe, holding, mother, relationship, ground, base, nourish, renew

3. Home, familiarity, meant space, demarcated, scale, comfort, connection between space and consciousness, presence in space, awareness of surroundings

4. Rich, integrated, whole, alive, positive, heart, center, arrival, discovery, understanding, settledness, desirability, value, beauty

5. Ground, groundedness, home, return, feet, good location, orientation, finding, knowing, somewhere, rainbow, memories, tethered, lost, wandering, gods, genius loci, spirits, beautiful, contour, smell

6. Bounded openness/opening, gathered, unitary/multiplicity, plural/singularity, there/here, happening/event/moment, earth/sky, "those truths the hand can touch" (Camus), near/far, hearth/threshold, horizon, end/beginning, loss and melancholy

7. Home, comfortable, "in place," here rather than there, located, identity, geography, people, specific locale, knowing who I am, knowing who you are, an identifiable "somewhere," centering one's world, always already there, underlying and organizing my life, a part of, belonging, location, known geography, marker needed for living

8. Repose, arresting, anchoring, transforming us, site of encounters – conversations, exchanges that change us and leave their mark, testament to our incarnation and life as body/spirit situated in particular moment in time and space, have local character and personality, have a material and spiritual aspect, inviting us into relation but leaving always more to discover

TABLE 5.2 Some thematic aspects of the place monad.

Thematic aspect	Descriptors (single words and short phrases)
Homelike aspects	Home, attachment, comfortable, holding, mother, nourish, heart, hearth/threshold, intimacy, field of care, settledness, dwelling, care and custodianship, cared for, repose, embodied, habituality and routines, co-habitation of many beings
Identity aspects	Emplacement, identity, knowing who I am, knowing who you are, inextricable, engaging the world, being, inviting a whole-person response, familiarity, meant space, awareness of surroundings, discovery, understanding, space to express agency, makes me feel good, becomes part of my own identity, particularity, distinctiveness, named in some way, unthinkable without humans, intimate connections with others, "those truths the hand can touch" (Camus)
Atmospheric aspects	Many voices, many presences, many gestures, a penetrable mystery, more than human, atmosphere, ambience, character, spirit, rich, alive, positive, value, beauty, charged space, a particular sense of place, an enveloping sensorium, emotional temperature, a particular feeling – safe, calm, threatening, chaotic, arresting, and so forth
Processual aspects	An unfolding process, always present, dynamic, ever-changing, crackling with power (felt but unseen), temporal, accumulating, duration/intensity/dissolution, active and full, appropriation but also control, full of power, fixity/flow, static/fluid, movement/rest, often unexpected, colored by personal anticipations, facilitating encounters/conversations/exchanges, a realm of activity, encounter, participation, communion, dynamic interdependent forces, connecting and interweaving, a joining of what has already happened earlier
Locational/spatial/relational aspects	Belonging, center, in place, here rather than there, located, related, relationship, anchoring, between, arrival, a lived geography, ontological – being is being-in-place, specific locale, an identifiable anywhere, ground, base, here/there, near/far, horizon, groundedness, orientation, finding, somewhere, tethered, stay and go, centering one's world, insideness, organizing my life, known geography, bounded openness/opening, gathered openness/opening, end/beginning, a nesting of different time scales and different physical scales, immediacy, demarcated, a place "to be" inside/outside of/apart from, implies action (to get there, to leave, to enter, to move through), interconnections spatially and temporally, contained, boundaries permeable and flexible, boundaries and limits, unity/multiplicity, plural/singularity, earth/sky, horizon, a configuration with specific sights/sounds/experiences/memories, openness and a vantage point from which to try to make sense of the world

illustrated in Table 5.2, I consolidated the twenty-seven place descriptions by associating specific words and phrases with five broader thematic categories that I have arbitrarily identified as: homelike aspects, identity aspects, atmospheric aspects, processual aspects, and locational, spatial, and relational aspects. One notes in the table that the last category contains the most entries; I assembled these descriptors as one group because environmental and spatial togetherness and belonging appear as a particularly prominent quality in many of the twenty-seven responses. Obviously, the five summary themes might be ordered and identified differently. Other researchers might generate different sets of overarching categories, since ambiguity, overlap, and multivalence are an integral aspect of place experience and meaning. The more significant value of an integrated list is to provide one "sphere of opening" whereby the wholeness of the phenomenon has a space to appear and from which the researcher can begin to locate tentative claims about the phenomenon, which, in relation to place, might include the following:

- Any place is a lived whole unified by its total character.
- This wholeness is not uniform, but characterized by a unity in diversity marking the reality of the particular place and place experience.
- Place is not precisely defined in extent, in material contents, in activity, or in terms of precise experiences, actions, situations, or events, whether related to inhabitation, occupation, or some other manner of human life.
- Specific aspects and elements of a place and place experience can shift without disrupting their constitution, providing the total character of that place and lived emplacement remains more or less present.
- On one hand, any place may incorporate a set of smaller-scaled places; on the other hand, that place may be a part of some set of larger-scaled places. Most places incorporate some sort of lived relationship between themselves and the smaller-scaled places that they contain (e.g., the living room in a house) and the larger-scaled places in which they are contained (e.g., the house in a neighborhood).
- Materially, a place may include a constellation of settings (e.g., residing, working, recreating, and so forth) linked by paths of movement (e.g., corridors, sidewalks, streets, roads, and so forth) that in sum lay out an everyday region of life more or less taken for granted and "permanent" for longer or shorter periods of time.
- Typically, there is a lived appropriateness and fit between specific types of places (e.g., home or work) and specific modes of lived emplacement (e.g., a mode of "being-at-home" or "being-at-work"); different place modes assume different modes of lived emplacement and vice versa (e.g., one typically sleeps in a setting conducive for sleeping or studies in a setting conducive to studying).

The Place Monad and Lived Emplacement

In exploring the monad, the researcher aims to specify some central set of features that points toward the experiential core of the phenomenon. Here, I contend that this core is the way in which place always already conjoins people with the world in which they find themselves. We return to Edward Casey's declaration that "to be is to be in place" (Casey, 2009, p. 16), or, as he explains more fully, "by virtue of its unencompassability by anything other than itself, place is at once the limit and the condition of all that exists . . ." (Casey, 2009, pp. 15–16).

To realize the crucial importance of place in human life it is important to ponder its inexorable presence, to which Casey points. First, he contends that place is "unencompassable" by anything else because there is no thing, living being, event, or experience that can exist without finding itself emplaced in some way, "whether the tiniest locale or the cosmos at large" (Casey, 2009, p. 15). In this sense, place is a limit of all existing things because there is nothing beyond the emplaced thing or situation except another place for some other thing or situation (as in the way, for example, that a person is nested in a chair nested in a room nested in a house nested in a neighborhood, and so forth). Second, Casey insists that, conjointly with its unencompassability by nothing else, place provides a condition for the "being" of all things, living beings, situations, and events: "Place belongs to the very concept of existence. To be is to be bounded by place, limited by it. . . . Place-being is part of an entity's own-being" (Casey, 2009, pp. 15–16).

What Casey suggests is that any manner of specific places and specific place experiences presupposes the primary ontological structure of place and lived emplacement – an inescapable existential situation that subsumes both human experience and the material world in which that experience happens. Philosopher Jeff Malpas (2001, p. 231) makes this point when he writes that

> what we are as living, thinking, experiencing beings is inseparable from the places in which we live – our lives are saturated by the places, and by the things and other persons intertwined with those places, through which we move, in which our actions are located, and with respect to which we orient and locate ourselves.

This contention that human being is always human-being-in-place marks a radical development in environmental and place understanding because it presupposes that "The very possibility of the appearance of things – of objects, of self, and of others – is possible only within the all-embracing compass of place" (Malpas, 1999, p. 15). If the world presents itself only through place, then this lived fact means that human connections with place are not contingent, accidental, or determined by more primary social or political constructs (Malpas, 1999, pp. 29–33). Rather, to be human is always already to be emplaced: "It is through our engagement with place that our own human being is made real, but it is also through our engagement that place takes on a sense and a significance of its own" (Malpas, 2009, p. 23). This lived emplacement means that the quality of human life is intimately related to the quality of place in which that life unfolds and vice versa. As Malpas explains:

> Since life is indeed constituted in and through its relation to the places in which it is lived, so the richness of that life, and the development of a sense of its own unitary character and self-identity, is directly tied to the way in which the lived relation to place comes to be articulated and expressed in that life. In that case, to live in a way that is neglectful of place will be to live in a way that is neglectful of that life itself – it will be to live in a way likely to give rise to an impoverished and perhaps even fragmented mode of existence. To care for and attend to our own lives thus demands that we also care for and attend to place.
>
> *(Malpas, 2001, p. 232)*

In Chapter 1, I defined place provisionally as "any environmental locus that gathers human experiences, actions, and meanings spatially and temporally." In bringing forward lived emplacement as a central dimension of the monad of place, I emphasize that my original definition is partial and, in a sense, erroneous because it highlights the material, spatial, and environmental aspects of place and lived emplacement, whereas both Casey and Malpas emphasize that any specific places or place experiences are presupposed by and necessarily arise from the underlying facticity that human being is always human-being-in-place. To accommodate this existential recognition of lived emplacement, Malpas (1999, p. 32, p. 36) emphasizes that place is "*integral to the very structure and possibility of experience.*" He goes on to explain that, in this way of understanding place, it is neither subjective or objective:

> [I]t is not a matter of the subject grasping something of which the acting, experiencing creature is independent – such a region or place does not simply stand ready for the gaze of some observing subject. Rather, . . . the structure at issue encompasses the experiencing creature itself and so the structure of subjectivity is given in and through the structure of place. Something similar might be said of the idea of objectivity also – at least inasmuch as the idea of objectivity is understood as referring to that which can be present to a subject, rather than to mere physical existence. In this respect, the idea of the object is itself something established only with a place and thereby in relation to a subject, although in saying this it must be remembered that *both* subject and object are thereby "placed" within the same structure rather than one or the other being the underlying ground for that structure.
>
> *(Malpas, 1999, pp. 36–37)*

As Malpas suggests, conventional academic interpretations picture place onto-logically in either an objectivist or subjectivist fashion. On one hand, place is pictured "objectively" as a spatial and environmental "container" in which human life unfolds; on the other hand, place is pictured "subjectively" in terms of individual or group feelings, attachments, cognitive representations, and so forth. A phenomenological understanding of place contends that objective and subjective aspects of any particular place and place experience are presupposed by and only possible because of the inescapable existential fact of an always–already lived emplacement that is one existential grounding of human life. "Who we are very much reflects where we are," writes Casey (2001b, p. 226). Or as Malpas (1999, p. 8) explains, "it is not merely human identity that is tied to place or locality, but the very possibility of being the sort of creature that can *engage* with a world . . . , that can think about that world, and that can find itself in the world."

Modes of Lived Emplacement

Though we are always already emplaced, the particular manner of that emplace-ment incorporates a wide range of specific places and place experiences. Some-times, we are emplaced momentarily – I find myself enmeshed in the streets along which I walk from home to work each day, or I find myself in an unfa-miliar city for three days attending a conference. On occasion, these transitory emplacements can be momentous in sustaining or deadly ways – for example, I serendipitously meet my future life partner in the bar at a Seattle conference hotel, or my colleague is struck by a car because he looks the "wrong way" when crossing a London street.

Beyond momentary emplacements, we find ourselves in lengthier place involve-ments associated with personal life events and situations. I find myself living in Chicago as I participate in a three-week seminar on place. I spend a month in Spain, having attended a conference there and now being the guest of the event's organizers. Through much of my life, however, I am emplaced more or less permanently in a world that, for better or worse, is home. This longer-term permanence of place may remain the same throughout one's entire life. Or one may periodically shift places, depending on family, work, or other life demands. Whatever the time line of a specific inhabitation, this place becomes the taken-for-granted locale of my lived emplacement. Within its horizons is a nested fabric of smaller and larger places comprising my lifeworld – e.g., household, workplace, shopping venues, places of recreation, worship, and so forth. I accept, tolerate, dislike, or enjoy these places because they constitute the world that my life path has given me. Some people get to choose this home world because of wealth, talent, or interpersonal connections. Others may have no choice in their home world, which, on one hand, they may never call into question or, on the other hand, may actively dislike and attempt to escape.

The Commingling of Place and Lived Emplacement

In thinking through the monad of place, one realizes that any manner of place experience presupposes a lived commingling between experiencers' lived emplacement and the particular places where that lived emplacement unfolds. This integral interconnectedness is provocatively pictured by phenomenological psychologist Bernd Jager (1985, p. 219), who writes that any lived emplacement

> cannot be instantaneously accomplished. We are seldom immediately at home in a new place . . . . "To inhabit" refers to a kind of having (*habere*) that permits us a radical access to material objects and allows us to treat these objects as extensions of our own body. To approach inhabitation in this way means to be able no longer to make such a radical distinction between flesh and matter, between bodies and mere things. Bodily existence floods over into things, appropriates them, infuses them with the breath of life, draws them into the sphere of daily projects and concerns. A fully inhabited world is at the same time also a fully embodied world.

Making reference to Merleau-Ponty's lived embodiment, Jager provides a lucid phenomenological explication of the lived body's integral role in facilitating emplacement, inhabitation, and at-homeness. First of all, emplacement incorporates a habitual, taken-for-granted ordinariness sustaining and sustained by the everyday environments of which it is part. Everyday things, actions, events, and places support and depend on a lived extension of our bodily presence, allowing us to do what we need to do in a mostly automatic, unnecessary-to-plan manner. Who we are and what we do ground and are grounded via material, spatial, and built dimensions of human worlds. As Jager explains, place "is a giver of access to a world" (Jager, 1983, p. 169).

Jager points to another crucial aspect of the place monad when he explains that this lived-habituality-in-place is related to particular modes of human being integrally grounded environmentally and architecturally. He writes:

> The home, the factory, the hospital, the laboratory, the city no longer appear in the first place as finished material things, as containers of people and their activities. Rather, these buildings themselves make their appearance as a certain embodied grasp on the world, . . . as particular manners of taking up the body and the world, as specific orientations disclosing certain aspects of a worldly horizon. The first architecture then appears to be that of taking up a particular bodily attitude. Architecture is at first a certain manner of standing or sitting or lying down or walking . . . .
>
> To enter a building, to come under the sway of a certain choreography, means at the same time to become subject to a certain disclosure. Like a certain bodily attitude, a building opens a particular world of tasks, of

outlooks, of sensibilities . . . . In this intimate alliance with the body, the building itself has become a particular access to the world. I no longer am contained within a thing-like construction, no longer remain within the building as one thing enclosed within another. Rather, I have drawn this building into the sphere of my body. I have appropriated it and have drawn it around me like a coat on a windy day to inspect a certain sight or to face a particular task.

(Jager, 1983, pp. 154–156)

In his perceptive interpretation, Jager offers a penetrating account of how the lived body outreaches to accommodate and appropriate its surrounding world, including architectural and place parts. Via lived bodies, selves commingle with worlds in which they find themselves. Drawing on *The Visible and Invisible*, one of Merleau-Ponty's last works (1968), Jager explains how the environment is no longer just something only separate and visible but "a source of vision and light according to which we see" (Jager, 1985, p. 218). In inhabiting place, we automatically find ourselves present and engaged in a particular way that could not be otherwise: "To enter and finally to come to inhabit a house or city means to come to assume a certain stance, to surrender to a certain style of acting upon and of experiencing the surrounding world . . . ." (Jager, 1985, pp. 218–219).

In this sense, the lived body neither envelops its world, nor does that world envelop the lived body. Instead, there is a lived "co-envelopment" and co-constitution supporting or stymying an environmental and place wholeness and fluidity that mark the core of the place monad. Jager's unique interpretive language circumvents the conventional philosophical and practical dualisms of people and world: Two, analytically and instrumentally, are understood as one, existentially and experientially. Jager indicates that, on one hand, we must better understand how the sensory, perceptual, and motor dimensions of the lived body contribute to place making, inhabitation, and human wellbeing. On the other hand, he suggests that we must pay heed to the complementary role of architectural, environmental, spatial, and place elements and qualities.

Having identified some key characteristics of place as a monad, I next consider several of its dyadic dimensions. It is this dynamic unity and communion between place as lived emplacement and place as environmental setting that marks the crux of the place monad and shifts attention to the dyad of place, which is examined in the next chapter via the lived binaries of movement/rest, insideness/outsideness, ordinariness/extra-ordinariness, withinness/withoutness, and homeworld/alienworld.

Note

1 I thank the twenty-seven individuals who provided me with place descriptions. These individuals are listed in the acknowledgements.

6

THE DYAD OF PLACE

In Chapter 5, I considered the monad of place and located several key features, emphasizing that the core characteristic is lived emplacement grounded in the inescapable spatial and environmental commingling of people-in-world. As Malpas makes the point, "Human being is placed being," a claim crucial for environmental thinking, "since it is our own embeddedness in place and the embeddedness of place in us that underpins and should guide environmental care and concern as well as architectural design and practice" (Malpas, 2014, p. 9).

In examining the dyad of place, I consider how the lived wholeness of place and lived emplacement can be further clarified via some set of appropriate binaries and complementarities. These dyads are useful because place experience often involves some aspect of lived opposites, whether relating to modes of action, experience, or encounter. Here, I discuss five place dyads that refer to a range of lived complementarities. These dyads illustrate several essential aspects of place and lived emplacement, though there are no doubt other binaries that one could locate and describe through further phenomenological study (e.g., Wood, 2014). These five place dyads are:

1. Movement and rest;
2. Insideness and outsideness;
3. The ordinary and extra-ordinary;
4. The within and without;
5. Homeworld and alienworld.

1. Movement and Rest

In considering how bodily dimensions of our human constitution contribute to the nature of human experience, one immediately recognizes that our existence as physical bodies involves the typical situation of moving, on one hand, and resting, on the other (Bollnow, 2011; Seamon, 1979; Seamon, 2014c). This lived relationship between movement and rest arises at a wide spectrum of spatial scales (Casey, 2009, pp. 47–70) that range from hand and arm actions while one sits at a table eating dinner to a traveling salesperson's leaving and returning home as she makes her seasonal rounds to the retail businesses that sell her company's products. At their most basic bodily level, movement and rest are experientially grounded in Merleau-Ponty's perception and body–subject: Everyday movement patterns and places of rest are part of a habitual time–space lattice about which, most of the time, one is unaware (Seamon, 1979). Because of the unself-conscious facility of body–subject, life just happens and we follow a more or less regular regimen of actions, experiences, and occasions.

Any situation of movement eventually ends and in turn invokes some situation of rest: I finish my dinner and move elsewhere; the travelling salesperson uses her hotel room as a temporary center of comings and goings but eventually returns home before starting another round of sales trips. In this sense, place experience can be interpreted as a series of shifts between movement and rest within the varied environmental scales of a person or group's lifeworld. In terms of lived emplacement, some of these places, paths, and trips may involve strong emotional attachments whereas others may be taken for granted and deemed an inconsequential but necessary part in everyday life. Phenomenologist Otto Bollnow (2011, p. 80) describes the dyad of movement and rest as "the one basic dynamic of 'there and back again.' [Human beings do] not move arbitrarily in space; rather, all [their] movements are ultimately based on an opposition between going and returning." He writes:

> Going away is not some arbitrary movement in space, but a human being goes forth in order to perform some errand in the world, to attain some goal, in short to fulfil some task or other, but when he [or she] has fulfilled it . . . , he [or she] returns to his dwelling, to his resting point. It is thus at the same time the alternation, of deep significance to [human beings] that expresses itself in this pendulum movement of going away and coming back, from which every phase at the same time has its peculiar, unmistakable emotional colouring.
>
> *(Bollnow, 2011, p. 57)*

Phenomenologically, movement and rest may also be associated with broader existential qualities that often incorporate symbolic and transpersonal significance (Harries, 1997; Lane, 2000). Movement is related to horizon, reach, and unfamiliarity, just as rest is related to home, nearness, and taken-for-grantedness. Experientially and symbolically, movement is typically associated with search, exertion, and exploration, while rest is more often related to security, regeneration, and passivity. Through movement, human beings extend their awareness of distance, environments, and experience, whereas through rest, they invoke at-homeness, comfortableness, and dwelling.

One penetrating evocation of the movement/rest dyad is provided by Bernd Jager, whose work was discussed earlier in relation to the monad of place and lived emplacement. He depicts the dynamic as a lived reciprocity between dwelling and journey (Jager, 1975, 1983, 2010). Drawing partly on Heidegger (1971b), he describes dwelling as the vibrant coming together of individuals, community, and nature in place. He speaks of dwelling as a "round world" that offers a place "where fragile objects and creatures can be tended and cared for through constant, gentle reoccurring contacts" (Jager, 1975, p. 133). In contrast, the world of the journey invokes not only travel, sightseeing, and exploration but intellectual, aesthetic, and transpersonal efforts. The journey moves the person away from his or her secure realm of dwelling and moves one toward some mode of confrontation with new places, ideas, or experiences: "The future makes its appearance straight ahead, making possible *confrontation*" (Jager, 1975, p. 251). Jager emphasizes that lifeworlds can involve a lived excess of dwelling or journey, so that at-homeness can facilitate provincialism and xenophobia, just as an excess of mobility can lead to superficiality and vacuous commonality. Ultimately, the dyad of journey and dwelling is mutually sustaining, with each requiring some lived measure of the other. Jager (1975, p. 249) writes:

> Journeying grows out of dwelling as dwelling is founded in journeying. The road and hearth, journey and dwelling mutually imply each other. Neither can maintain its structural integrity without the other. The journey cut off from the sphere of dwelling becomes aimless wandering, it deteriorates into mere distraction or even chaos . . . . The journey requires a place of origin as the very background against which the figures of a new world can emerge . . . . To be without origin, to be homeless is to be blind. On the other hand, the sphere of dwelling cannot maintain its vitality and viability without the renewal made possible by the path. A community without *outlook* atrophies, becomes decadent and incestuous. Incest is primarily this refusal of the path; it therefore is refusal of the future and a suicidal attempt to live entirely in the past. The sphere of dwelling, insofar as it is not moribund, is inter-penetrated with journeying.

For understanding the dyadic dimension of place and lived emplacement, Jager's discussion of dwelling and journey is important because it suggests that the continuity of place is founded in an environmental and temporal regularity grounded in place as dwelling. On one hand, lived emplacement and place are significant stabilizing qualities in human life, contributing to a regular, dependable unfolding of life characterized by Jager's "round world." On the other hand, through the new places and insights offered by the journey, our environmental attachments and bonds with new places extend themselves. In examining the lived nature of journey more thoroughly, Jager indicates how movement *away from* place can be different experientially from movement *back toward* place. He suggests that we

> metaphorically link an "outside" world that is discovered in adventurous journeys to an "inside" world that is rediscovered in a homebound journey. The coherence of our world ultimately depends on a mutually clarifying interchange between two very different but complementary journeys. The one is an adventurous outbound journey that lights up the distance. . . . The other is a loyal homebound journey that reveals the treasures of intimate and neighborly dwelling. . . .
>
> *(Jager, 2001b, p. 111)*

Because of their dyadic interconnectedness, movement and rest each incorporate aspects of the other. Through movement and journey, people leave the unself-conscious taken-for-grantedness of their place or situation and extend their horizons. Through rest and dwelling, people return to familiar places and collect themselves in preparation for future ventures outward again. For both movement and rest, each requires its opposite in order for itself to be so. In part because of this continual lived exchange of opposites, human beings gain both stability and uncommonness in their ordinary and extra-ordinary lives (Seamon, 1979, p. 134).

2. Insideness and Outsideness

Largely because of geographer Edward Relph's *Place and Placelessness* (1976), the dyad of insideness and outsideness has become a central focus for phenomenological studies relating to place and place experience (Seamon, 2008). Relph defines place as a fusion of human and natural order and any significant spatial center of a person or group's lived experience (Relph, 1976, p. 141). The existential crux of place experience, Relph claims, is *insideness* – the degree to which a person or group belongs to and identifies with a place. If a person feels inside a place, he or she feels comfortable, safe, at ease, *in place*. Relph suggests that the more profoundly inside a place a person feels, the stronger will be his or her attachment to and identity with that place.

The opposite lived relationship with place is what Relph terms *outsideness* – feeling a sense of difference, separation, and even alienation from place. Relph contends that the existential tension between insideness and outsideness is a fundamental binary in human experience. Through different degrees of insideness and outsideness, different places take on different meanings and identities for different individuals and groups. For Relph, *existential insideness* is the foundation of the place concept because, in this mode of experience, place is experienced without any directed or self-conscious attention, yet is laden with significances that are tacit and unnoticed unless the place is changed in some way (Relph, 1976, p. 55). In contrast, *existential outsideness* involves a sense of strangeness, discomfort, and unreality, which might be felt by newcomers to a place or by people who, having been away from their birth place, return to feel like strangers because the place is no longer what it was when they knew it earlier.

Relph uses the experiences of existential insideness and existential outsideness to mark the ends of a dyadic continuum along which he identifies five other modes of place experience (Relph, 1976, pp. 49–55). As with existential insideness and outsideness, these modes do not relate to one's role or social situation in relation to place but, rather, identify the kind and intensity of experience that one encounters via the specific place:

- *Objective outsideness*, a situation involving a deliberate dispassionate attitude of separation from place, which is examined and manipulated as a thing apart from the experiencer (e.g., the typical approach to place often assumed by designers, planners, and policy makers).
- *Incidental outsideness*, a situation in which place is the background or mere setting for activities (e.g., the environments and places along the expressway on which one drives to work each day).
- *Behavioral insideness*, a situation involving the deliberate attending to the appearance of place (e.g., using environmental cues like landmarks and signage to find one's way around an unfamiliar place to which one has just moved).
- *Empathetic insideness*, a situation in which the person, as outsider, tries to be open to place and understand it more deeply (e.g., a researcher's effort to become intimately familiar with an urban neighborhood via participant-observation and community involvement).
- *Vicarious insideness*, a situation of deeply-felt secondhand involvement, whereby one is transported to place through paintings, novels, music, films, or other creative media (e.g., Dicken's vivid portraits of Victorian London or Monet's impressionist paintings of Amiens Cathedral or his beloved garden in Giverny).

These modes of place experience are significant dyadically because they illustrate how existential opposites can become the basis for an integrated continuum of lived meaning. These modes offer a simple language through which can be identified real-world place experiences in terms of the type and intensity of intention and engagement. Through varying degrees of outsideness and insideness, different places take on different identities for different individuals and groups, and human experience takes on different qualities of feeling, meaning, ambience, and action.

These modes of place experience illustrate how the dyad extends monadic understanding. If the monad points to the importance of lived emplacement in understanding the phenomenon of place, Relph's place modes demonstrate the range of ways in which lived emplacement can be experienced in relation to particular places. Though the various modes of outsideness involve various situations of separation from place, they still speak to lived emplacement, though in a lived manner that is limited, partial, uncomfortable, disorienting, or threatening. Relph's place modes also offer a language to describe how the same physical place can, at different times, afford different place experiences for the same individual or group – for example, the house that no longer feels like home because one's spouse has died. In a similar way, these place modes assist in understanding how the same physical place can afford a wide range of contrasting experiences for different individuals and groups related to that place – e.g., the difference in school experience for a new transfer student versus a student who has attended that school her entire childhood and adolescent life (Seamon, 2008).

Relph's modes of place experience are important for understanding lived emplacement because they provide one descriptive language that allows one to separate phenomenologically from the taken-for-grantedness of lifeworld and natural attitude. One example is feminist and cultural-studies research that focuses on negative and traumatic images of place (e.g., Manzo and Devine-Wright, 2014, pp. 178–179; Rose, 1993, pp. 53–55). In emphasizing how family violence generates homes where family members feel victimized and insecure, these researchers sometimes call into question the entire concept of home and place, suggesting they might be nostalgic, essentialist notions that need vigorous societal and political modification – perhaps even substitution – in postmodern society. Relph's modes of insideness and outsideness contribute to a different way of understanding the situation (Manzo, 2003, p. 52). The problem is not home and place but a conceptual conflation for which Relph's language provides a simple corrective: The victim's experience should not be interpreted as a lack of at-homeness but, rather, as one mode of existential outsideness, which in relation to one's most intimate place – the home – is particularly undermining and potentially life-shattering.

Relph's notion of existential outsideness provides a descriptive means to keep the experiences of home and violation distinct. One can say more precisely that domestic violence, whether in relation to women *or* men, is a situation where a place that typically fosters the strongest kind of existential insideness has become, paradoxically, a place of overwhelming existential outsideness. The lived result must be profoundly destructive. The short-term phenomenological question is how these victims can be helped to regain existential insideness. The longer-term question is what qualities and forces in our society lead to a situation where the existential insideness of home and at-homeness devolves into hurtfulness and despair. The dyad of insideness and outsideness offers no direct answers but, in its value for marking out shades of place experience, does offer one helpful language for clarifying the questions.

3. The Ordinary and the Extra-Ordinary

Besides different intensities of insideness and outsideness, lived emplacement as a dyad incorporates a continuum of engagement that ranges from the quotidian and anodyne to the surprising and unusual. Much of place experience is more or less *ordinary*, and lived bodies and place interact via repetitive actions and events that demand minimal attention as a taken-for-granted part of everyday life (Moran, 2011, 2014). Relph (1976, pp. 41–42) describes the lackluster aspect of place as *drudgery*:

> There is a sheer drudgery of place, a sense of being tied inexorably to *this* place, as being bound by the established scenes and symbols and routines. As the ground of our everyday lives, places must partake of . . . tedious tasks, humiliations, preoccupations with basic necessities, its hardships, meanness, and avarice.

This tedium of place can be called a *situation of habituality*, the typical ordinariness of everyday life, which much of the time involves unquestioned repetition and routine that most people, unless required, are unwilling to change (Seamon, 1979, p. 139). In contrast to situations of habituality are *situations of openness*, in which the ordinariness of everyday place in some way becomes *extra-ordinary*. I hyphenate the word because I place the emphasis on "other than ordinary," whether incrementally or dramatically different from usual experience or engagement. In situations of openness, one is suddenly attuned to place in a more alert, sensitive way. One experiences a more intense mode of encounter whereby things taken for granted suddenly seem fresh, startling, or affecting. One example is a revelatory experience described in Southern writer T. R. Pearson's 1985 novel, *A Short History of a Small Place*. As his mother turns on the porch light of their house, the teenage boy who is the novel's protagonist suddenly experiences a bittersweet moment of leaving adolescence and becoming an adult:

> I happened to turn back towards our house just as the porch light came on. Since it was early in the evening yet I don't suppose that single bulb changed the look of things significantly and I probably wouldn't have noticed it was on if I hadn't happened to be watching the bulb itself when it went from grey to yellow. Daddy didn't see it or anyway didn't make like he did and I don't know as it would have meant much at all to him if he had, but I saw it, saw it as Mamma switched it on, and it struck a note with me.
>
> And I said to myself without really saying it but just knowing it right off, this is the sort of thing that sets me apart from Daddy and him from me and both of us from everybody else, not simply that I saw the porch light come on and he didn't and nobody else would care anyway, but more that Mamma could switch on a single bulb and switch on something in me with it, some-thing of sadness and grief and shot through with the melancholy of twilight, something I could not be sure Daddy would know as I knew it, feel as I felt it.
>
> And I told myself how it was probably no more than pure chance and maybe a little grim luck that caused me to turn and look just when I turned

and looked, and I said to myself, this won't ever happen just this way again, not even having to say that either but just knowing it and concluding it right off.

(Pearson, 1985, p. 84)

In capturing an unexpected, blissful moment when an ordinary, repetitive event suddenly strikes one emotionally, Pearson depicts an encounter with place that includes serendipity, sadness, and the melancholy of twilight. Pearson's description is significant phenomenologically because it characterizes impressions embedded in sudden moments of insight – fortuitous, only partly conscious, and often outside the awareness of others present to the same situation. Pearson's account reminds us of those vaguely noticed but emotionally charged moments in which we understand our world and our place more intensely. Partly because of the happenstance of the moment, we engage with the world in a more piercing way through which we deepen our understanding of life, though we may not realize it explicitly, at least in the moment it happens. Pearson pictures the event as "pure chance" and realizes "this won't ever happen just this way again."

Jager (1983, 1985, 2013) envisions the dyadic relationship between ordinary and extra-ordinary experience as a contrast between the *workaday* and *festive* worlds, which he describes as "complementary and dynamically interacting types of relationships that together grant access" to the life of human beings (Jager, 2013, p. 261). The workaday world incorporates the places and situations whereby we "make a go" – employment, household duties, child rearing, and all other practical actions and duties that sustain everyday life. In contrast are the less frequent extra-ordinary moments of festive events and experiences – celebrating holidays and special occasions or partaking in creative or spiritual efforts like dancing, painting, writing poetry, making music, or worshipping.

In pointing to the dyadic constitution of the workaday and festive worlds, Jager (2013, p. 263) emphasizes that each "has its own inherent limits, so that a festive attitude is always followed by a workaday one and vice versa. Neither attitude can be understood in isolation." He argues that both worlds are an integral part of human being and, in some fashion, present themselves in all times and places: "All cultures possess an understanding of what it means to work and to transform a given natural reality so that it will yield needed human resources. They all possess also, to one degree or another, an understanding and a practice of *festive disclosure* in which they are able to witness the un-coerced appearance of heaven and earth and of self and other" (Jager, 2013, p. 263).

For Jager, the bridging of workaday and festive worlds is marked by *thresholds*, which he understands as a distinguishing feature of human civilization because they both separate and join human commonalities and human differences. "A threshold," he writes, "constitutes the ultimate foundation of a human world reflected in all building projects from the most primitive cave or hut to the most magnificent palace or city, all of which we might even consider as mere variations on the theme of the threshold, the essential function of which is to hold separate and distinct worlds together" (Jager, 2009, p. 8). On one hand, the threshold "guards an inhabited domain" and thereby helps sustain the taken-for-granted normality of the workaday world. On the other hand, the threshold relates to the festive world because it is via thresholds that we "come more fully into the presence of self, world, and others" (Jager, 2009, p. 10).

In this sense, a threshold both couples and uncouples in that it both binds and divides human beings just as it both binds and divides worlds of difference (Jager, 2009, p. 10). Though it shelters the thing, place, or situation as it is unto itself, the threshold is also a "place of meeting whose beauty and order inspire hosts and guests to open their hearts and minds to one another" (Jager, 2010, pp. 242–243). Jager's explication of thresholds is significant dyad-wise because it holds the complementarity of workaday and festive worlds together. In terms of place and lived emplacement, the dyad of workaday and festive worlds is important because much of the time these worlds unfold in relation to specific places – the household, the workplace, the theatre, the museum, the dance studio, the recital hall, or the place of worship. One example is the home, which, on one hand, supports the workaday world in the ways in which it provides a place of familiarity, continuity, and other lived qualities grounding an everyday stability and ordinariness. On the other hand, the home can become a place of celebration, creative efforts, and transformative renewal that provokes the extra-ordinary. In welcoming guests from outside, the home bridges difference, transforming its more usual workaday qualities into festive encounter. At least for a time, the ordinary and extra-ordinary are together via place.

4. Inward and Outward Aspects of Place

In describing how the threshold can join worlds within and beyond, Jager points to another place dyad: the inward and outward qualities of place that work in dynamic relationship. On one hand, any place is a world unto itself; the lived nature of that world is largely the concern of that place. On the other hand, almost all places have some relation to the larger world beyond; they rely on that world for various kinds of sustenance, whether material, economic, psychological, social, or spiritual. As one example mentioned earlier, the home is a realm of personal and familial privacy mostly insulated from the larger public world and typically in control of which aspects of that larger world enter that home. At the same time, the home requires a relationship with that larger public world in terms of basic needs and wider social and communal relationships. Referring more broadly to human habitation, Jager relates the inward and outward aspects of place to inside and outside, commonality and difference, and leaving and returning. He writes:

A place of human habitation offers a refuge from a natural world ordered only by brute force. It opens the prospect of a fully human life guided by self-restraint and regard for the domain of one's neighbors. Human inhabitation separates a self from another, while simultaneously drawing a distinction between an inside and an outside, an exterior and an interior. Yet it also creates a new relationship of self to others that takes the form of host and guest. At the same time, it binds the outside to an inside . . . by creating a new dialectic of coming and going, of journeying and returning home.

(Jager, 2001b, pp. 133–134)

There is a lived complexity to the inward and outward dimensions of lived emplacement. On one hand, the inward aspect of any place relates to its being apart from the rest of the world, just as, on the other hand, its more outward, externally-relating aspects relate to the larger world of which it is a part. These two significances of place are often different and may even contradict each other, but both are non-contingent aspects of place experience. One way to consider the inward/outward dyad is to locate situations that exaggerate one aspect or the other – for example, the home that is arranged mostly to impress visitors, or the home that turns its back on the world and is inhospitable. One notes that there may be lived tensions between the inward and outward dimensions of a place – for example, a home comfortable and secure in its inward aspects but unsettling and worrisome in its outward relation to a deteriorating neighborhood that provokes unpleasantness, avoidance, or fear.

One of the most confounding, current-day examples of an imbalance between the inward and outward aspects of place is the insular environmental mosaics springing up today in cities throughout the world and identified by gated communities, sleek commercial developments, and private streets and plazas, all typically monitored by surveillance technology and designed to make a profit by allowing the "insiders" of these places to feel "at home" and undisturbed (Minton, 2009; Zukin, 2010). Often built adjacent to neighborhoods of poverty and dilapidation, these "defensive developments" are artfully constructed to dissuade or deter "outsiders." These places may work as supportive environments for prescreened occupants and users, but as British journalist Anna Minton (2009, p. 179) explains, they make "the city a far more fearful place . . . ." She writes:

So many of today's fractures of civil society have come about as a result of the single-minded approach to extracting the maximum profit from the places we live in. . . . Policies of housing and private places mushrooming in cities are creating a physical environment that reflects the stark divisions of the city, creating homogenous enclaves that undermine trust between people, heightening fear. . . . The consequence is a growing distrust of strangers who are the essence of civility and the undermining of "natural surveillance" that enhances greater collective trust . . . . Smaller interventions, on a more human scale are more likely to bring with them a more diverse and public-spirited culture, which is in tune with local people and creates more successful places as a result.

(Minton, 2009, p. 178, 198)

I highlight these defensive developments because they point toward a problematic dyad in which the inward aspects of place are emphasized to such a degree that any outward interconnections are thwarted or blocked entirely. At the same time, "outsiders" to these developments are "insiders" to their own less-advantaged places and see these fortress-like enclaves as symbols of unfairness, unkindness, and inequity. Rather than gathering social, cultural, and economic differences together environmentally and spatially by integrating inward and outward aspects of place, these developments fracture the lived wholeness of the city and intensify civic dissatisfaction, anomie, and conflict. As Minton indicates, these defensive developments are typically imposing or even intimidating in environmental scale and scope. To draw individuals and groups of difference cooperatively together, Minton suggests that a much more appropriate development model is small-scaled, locally-based place making, a topic I bring forward in Chapters 13 and 14.

One other perplexing aspect of the inward/outward dyad today relates to the experiential impact of digital technology and cyberspace, whereby worlds beyond physical places become readily accessible to those places, at least vicariously and virtually. What happens to lived emplacement if the inward dimension of physical place is largely superseded by the outward pull of virtual places? If virtual places come to be experienced as "real" as their real-world counterparts, does this development mean the eventual demise of many "real" places as we currently know them? On one hand, there is the optimistic argument that virtuality can improve and amplify real lifeworlds in ways impossible before its availability (Greenfield, 2017, pp. 63–84; Kelly, 2016, pp. 216–229). On the other hand, the less sanguine argument is that virtual reality too readily fabricates experiences that might seem real but could never fully happen in actual lifeworlds. As philosopher Albert Borgmann (1992, p. 92) points out, "real" reality must always be existentially different from virtual reality because "real" reality *"encumbers and confines."* Though virtual reality may superficially seem real, it can readily escape from and replace the lived messiness of real lifeworlds with more convenient, vivid, or fantastical situations that require no stakes, responsibilities, or efforts of will.

On one hand, virtual reality holds extraordinary promise in that it may become a welcome means for repairing a good number of the world's problems. Who, for example, needs an automobile if she can simply put on her virtual apparatus and "go to" her virtual workplace, grocery store, or favorite recreation place? Who needs a real house, place of worship, or vacation destination if all these "places" and "experiences" can be reproduced virtually? On the other hand, virtual reality may involve potential risks and dangers, including time wasting, titillation, addiction, and withdrawal from most things real. Why make the efforts that an encumbering, confining real world inescapably requires if virtual reality can provide ease, pleasure, and enhanced vividness without the downside of demands, exertions, obligations, or consequences?

In terms of the inward/outward dyad of place, the central question is whether digital and technological developments will provoke such exclusive attention to virtual places beyond one's actual place that this actual place becomes inconsequential or even disposable. Because we remain physical and lived bodies, one expects that real places, real place experience, and real lived emplacement will continue to remain an integral part of human being. If, however, technology eventually offers a viable means for human beings to "exist" somehow independently from their material bodies and physical environments, then the shift in the manner of human lifeworlds is almost impossible to imagine. What does human being become if lived emplacement and physical places are entirely circumvented technologically and existentially? For example, technology writer Adam Greenfield (2017, p. 83), envisions how virtual and augmented realities might precipitate a destructive erosion in person-to-person place interactions and communal sensibility. He writes:

> If nothing else, reality is the one platform we all share . . . . To replace this shared space with [a] million splintered and mutually inconsistent [virtual and augmented realities] is to give up the whole pretense that we in any way occupy the same world . . . . A city where the physical environment has ceased to function as a common reference frame is, at the very least, terribly inhospitable soil for democracy, solidarity, or simple fellow-feeling.

5. Homeworld and Alienworld

The last place dyad I discuss was first identified by Husserl, who, in seeking to better characterize the lifeworld, spoke of a lived reciprocity between what he called the *homeworld* and the *alienworld* (Husserl, 1970; Steinbock, 1995; Seamon, 2013c). As Husserl defines it, the *homeworld* is the tacit, taken-for-granted sphere of experiences, understandings, and situations marking out the world into which each of us is born and matures as children and then adults. Always, the homeworld is in some mode of lived mutuality with the *alienworld*, which is the world of difference and otherness, but is only provided awareness because of the always–already givenness of the homeworld (Steinbock, 1995, pp. 178–185).

The philosopher Janet Donohoe (2017a, p. 430) explains that the alienworld "reveals to me things about my homeworld that I had taken for granted as simply being the way things are." She pictures the homeworld as "a unity of sense that is manifest in a pregivenness of the things of the world that constitute the norm by which we judge other worlds and by which the pregivenness of other worlds becomes given" (Donohoe, 2011, p. 30). Here, norms and normativity do not refer to some arbitrary ethical or ideological system of right and wrong or better and worse. Rather, they refer to "a foundational standard to which other places are compared in terms of our embodied constitution of the world" (Donohoe, 2011, p. 25). In relation to the homeworld, the alienworld presents norms different from what a person in his or her homeworld takes for granted (Donohoe, 2014, pp. 17–20). The homeworld plays a central role in affording the identity we understand as ourselves:

> A homeworld is privileged because it is that through which our experiences coalesce as our own and in such a way that our world structures our experience itself. This constitutional privilege . . . is indifferent to whether we like it or not, or to whether it makes us happy or miserable. The point is that the norms that guide the homeworld are our norms, our way of life, as that to which we have accrued.
>
> *(Donohoe, 2011, p. 232)*

One crucial aspect of homeworld and alienworld is that they are co-constituted and co-relative in the sense that we always "carry with us the structure of our [homeworld] in the structure of our lived-bodies, in our typical comportment and in our practices" (Donohoe, 2011, p. 164; Donohoe, 2014, pp. 12–15). We recognize the presence of the homeworld when we find ourselves in worlds different from that tacit typicality and normativity. Husserl argues that we potentially grow as persons through two sorts of lived exchanges between homeworld and alienworld – what he calls *appropriation* and *transgression*. In appropriation, we involve ourselves in situations of "the co-constitution of the alien through appropriative experience of the home" (Steinbock, 1995, p. 179). On the other hand, transgression involves situations of "the co-constitution of the home through the transgressive experience of the alien" (Steinbock, 1995, p. 179). In appropriation, we realize qualities of the homeworld through recognizing alienworld qualities as different from those of the homeworld. In a reciprocal way, in transgressive experiences, we encounter the alienworld and, through that encounter, recognize and perhaps accept in our homeworld potentially usable or helpful qualities of that alienworld (Seamon, 2013c). The philosopher Anthony Steinbock (1994, p. 214) describes appropriation and transgression as modes of "critical comportment" that may entail "the renewal of a homeworld's norms, revitalizing and renewing its internal sense; [this process] may even demand going against the prevalent normality, replacing old norms with a new ethical normality in an attempt to realize the homeworld more fully."

For both homeworld and alienworld, the lifeworld is their pre-given, taken-for-granted starting point – their "ground and horizon" as Donohoe (2017a, p. 431) explains:

> [The] homeworld and alienworld are both made possible because of the more fundamental lifeworld. For me to recognize an alienworld trait as alien, it must be within parameters that make sense. Otherwise, I would not even

be able to experience the thing at all. Beneath alienworld and homeworld is lifeworld as ground and horizon making each possible. The lifeworld *a priori* is that which makes us earthlings as opposed to Martians. It is so deeply intertwined with who we are that even if we escaped earth . . . , we would still be earthlings in our manner of constitution and our own way of understanding our place or being in the cosmos.

(Steinbock, 1995, p. 232)

I do not claim that the dyad of homeworld and alienworld is suitable conceptually for describing all manner of places. I do emphasize, however, that it can offer a helpful language for place situations where an individual or group's experience of place and lived emplacement is different from other individuals and groups associated with that place or with other places that must be dealt with (Seamon, 2013c). Especially in today's world of geographical mobility and social and cultural diversity, the dyad of homeworld and alienworld provides one useful means to think through place complexity – the way, for example, socially-different neighborhoods perceive and interact with each other, or a situation of domestic violence or child abuse whereby the homeworld has become a realm of fear, hurt, and cruelty. The crucial lived aspect of homeworld is that places and lived emplacement are integral to its constitution. One's identification with and attachment to place (as well as dislike or discomfort) involves "not simply one's comportment toward this particular place, but simply one's comportment" (Donohoe, 2011, p. 31).

The homeworld's normative significance is important because it means that lived emplacement is typically taken for granted and is regularly out of sight for the individuals involved. This situation points to the lived fact that these individuals may not readily be able to articulate the meaning of place in their lives or even recognize its presence. As with the other dyads of place I have discussed, homeworld and alienworld illustrate the complexity and multivalence of lived emplacement and place experience. This dyadic understanding allows the researcher to locate a field of place binaries, but these binaries remain largely unresolved. This resolution, according to Bennett, is only possible when one moves from the dyad to the triad, which speaks to relationship, process, and reconciliation. In the next two chapters, I introduce the triad broadly and indicate its considerable value for understanding place and lived emplacement.

7

UNDERSTANDING THE TRIAD

Relationships, Resolutions, and Processes

Using Bennett's method of progressive approximation, I have sought in Chapters 5 and 6 to facilitate a fuller understanding of place and lived emplacement. As Bennett emphasizes, progressive approximation involves "the sense of a deepening significance already there" (Bennett, 1966a, p. 78). Toward that end, I began my systematic study of place by considering, in Chapter 5, its constitution as a monad. I concluded that, even though place is a phenomenon of environmental and human complexity, its crux is *lived emplacement* – the existential fact that human beings are always already immersed, entwined, and conjoined with some environmental and spatial portion of the world in which they find themselves. Always, necessarily, and often with little or no choice, human beings are soldered to place, and it is this people–place "soldering" that marks the lived core of place as monad.

To probe place further, I proceeded in Chapter 6 to investigate place as dyad, identifying several lived binaries. I suggested that most places presuppose and invoke a series of complementary structures in tension. As examples relating to place and lived emplacement, I examined the dyads of movement/rest, inside/outside, inward/outward, ordinary/extra-ordinary, and homeworld/alienworld. I argued that, although in one sense they contradict each other, the two natures of these binaries always co-exist; one cannot be present without the other. Because of its non-resolvable structure, however, the dyad offers no means to reconcile the oppositional qualities of place. To locate the possibility of resolution, we must shift our focus to three-ness and the triad, via which the dyad's tensions might be reconciled through an understanding of relationship and process.

The Triad, Three-ness, and Relationship

The triad helps one to understand the dynamic aspects of any phenomenon. Here, I draw on the triad to consider the generative aspects of place. What, in other words, are the various relationships and processes whereby places remain what they are or change for better or worse? The dyads of place say little about how their various lived tensions are to be resolved. What, for example, is the process by which an outsider becomes and insider, or vice versa? Might one establish experientially an appropriate balance between movement and rest? Can a person or group's lived experiences of homeworld and alienworld shift over time?

To move toward answering questions like these, Bennett argues that we must consider the triad and the qualitative significance of three-ness. Three-ness is important because a third element is necessary to resolve the dyad's two-ness: "We must seek a third term for the resolution of complementarity" (Bennett, 1993, p. 102). For Bennett, an understanding of the triad is crucial if we aim to understand a situation and make it better in some way: "Without an understanding of the triad, it is difficult to make any real change in the world" (Bennett, 1993, p. 36). This claim suggests that a triadic knowledge of place is essential if we are to envision design, policy, planning, or advocacy that work to strengthen rather than weaken real-world places.

In its focus on dynamic action and mutual exchange, the triad shifts focus from the monad's hermetic wholeness and the dyad's unresolvable duality. In relation to place, the triad offers a conceptual means to locate its *processual* dimensions, both those dynamics that allow a place to be what it is as well as those dynamics that allow a place to change, both constructively and destructively. One gains a fuller sense of the various processes, happenings, and relationships by which a place and its people survive and prosper, on one hand, or degenerate and flounder, on the other hand. In Chapter 8, I identify six place processes and offer, via systematics, their justification. First, however, the triad must be explained. What, in Bennett's terms, is a triad as a system of systematics? Why does Bennett claim that three-ness is related to process, action, and relationship? If the triad is about three-ness, how can it be that there are six place processes rather than three? These are the key questions addressed in this chapter.

The Triad's Three Impulses

In Bennett's terminology, a system incorporates "some inner connectedness or mutual relevance of its terms" (Bennett, 1956, p. 3). Accordingly, he defines a *triad* as a system of three independent but mutually related terms, each of which he designates by the word *impulse*, to suggest a sense of force or motivation that, interacting with the two other impulses of the triad, leads to a specific action, process, or happening (Bennett, 1993, pp. 37–39). To identify the character of each of these three impulses, Bennett uses the terms *affirming*, for the impulse that acts or initiates; *receptive*, for the impulse that is acted upon or resists; and *reconciling*, for the impulse whereby the affirming and receptive impulses are brought together in an action, process, or dynamic relationship. Bennett simplifies the designation of these three impulses by calling the affirming impulse, *first*; the

TABLE 7.1 The triad's three terms, or *impulses*.

1 – first or affirming impulse (active, initiating, demanding, or forcing)

2 – second or receptive impulse (passive, receiving, resisting, or denying)

3 – third or reconciling impulse (integrating, harmonizing, bridging, or neutralizing)

receptive, *second*; and the reconciling, *third*; or most succinctly, *1*, *2*, and *3* (Table 7.1).

Each of these three impulses can involve a wide range of active, passive, and reconciling expressions. The affirming impulse may be firm, demanding, cajoling, or persistent, just as the receptive impulse may be responsive, needful, resistant, or inertial. Yet again, the reconciling impulse may be integrating, harmonizing, bridging, or neutralizing. The relative force of each impulse can be stronger or weaker and contribute to a lasting or temporary resolution of the three impulses. As Bennett (1956, p. 39) explains,

> [E]ach of the three terms of a triad makes its own specific contribution to the character of the relationship. One of the terms will always have the character of affirmation, or activity; the second will have that of denial; while the third will appear neither as active nor passive, but as the reconciliation of the other two. We may find it difficult to recognize these characters in every situation, because of the many different forms in which they can be manifested. Affirmation is always positive and active, but it can have many different shades; denial can range from violent opposition to inertness and passivity; and within this range there can be such other characteristics as receptivity, response, and co-operation. The third character may be no more than the meeting of active and passive forces, or it may appear as an act of freedom bringing into existence a situation that without it, would not have arisen at all.

The key quality that makes the triad dynamic rather than static relates to Bennett's claim that every action, process, or happening takes place via some mode of conjunction among the three impulses, which in the moment of union, sustains the action or happening. As illustrated in Figure 7.1, Bennett describes this coming-together process as "blending," to suggest that, in the moment of mergence, the three impulses become something other than themselves. They combine synergistically to sponsor some action or happening different from the three impulses as they are in themselves, by themselves. In this sense, the triad helps one to understand "the kind of dynamism present in a given complex structure" (Bennett, 1966a, p. 29).

Whereas the dyad involves two natures linked together by complementary qualities common to both, the triad involves three independent, autonomous impulses differing in character and origin and capable of blending to facilitate

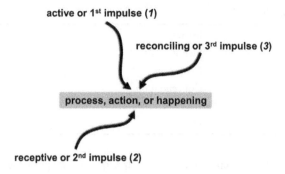

FIGURE 7.1 The triadic blending of the three impulses

appropriate (or inappropriate) actions. One example of the difference between dyad and triad is presented in Bennett's description of the contrasting responses of two "good Samaritans" who encounter a beggar on the street. The first man sees that the beggar is hungry and, acting out of generosity (a dyadic opposite of indifference) gives him money, by which he becomes inebriated and commits a crime. The second man recognizes that the beggar is a drunkard but he also sees that he is really hungry. In this recognition, he establishes a relationship with the beggar, taking him for a meal but giving him no money. Bennett (1966a, p. 93) writes:

> The first situation is dyadic; good and evil are complementary. The beggar goes inexorably to his fate and the generous man is the blind instrument of his downfall. The second situation is triadic. Compassion takes the place of generosity and a relationship is established, the dynamism of which may save the beggar from his fate.[1]

The Triad's Three Positions and Six Resulting Triads

We next must consider how the blending of the three impulses can be related to different modes of actions, processes, and happenings – what Bennett (1966a, p. 29) describes above as "the kind of dynamism present." Bennett pictures the triad figuratively in terms of the linear arrangement of three positions as illustrated in Figure 7.2. In his conception of the triad, there are three impulses, but there are also three positions that each of the three impulses can occupy. It is this threefold combination of impulses and positions that locates different relationships,

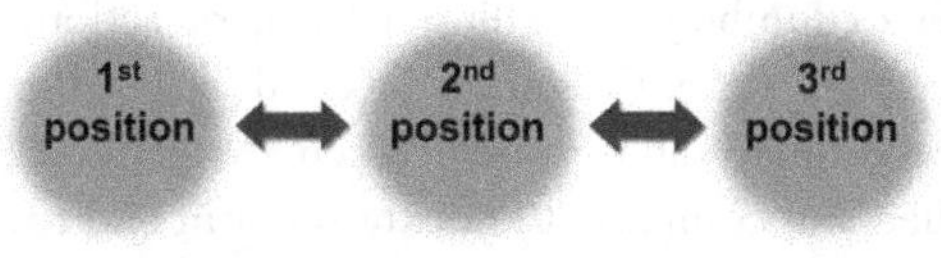

FIGURE 7.2 The triad's three positions

TABLE 7.2 Bennett's six triads.

1–3–2	Interaction
2–3–1	Identity
1–2–3	Expansion
2–1–3	Concentration
3–1–2	Order
3–2–1	Freedom

processes, and actions, depending on which sequence of positions each of the three impulses occupies. The result, generatively, is that the three impulses can come together in six different ways: *1–2–3, 1–3–2, 2–1–3, 2–3–1, 3–1–2*, and *3–2–1*. The order of the three impulses' conjunction marks the essential reason for why each of the six triads relates to a different manner of action and happening. These six triads are summarized in Table 7.2, along with the name that Bennett provides for each.

In claiming an integral relationship between the three impulses and their six possible conjunctions, Bennett establishes an understanding of process that has considerable conceptual and practical power. He contends that the six resulting triads encompass all possible actions, relationships, and situations, whether of the world, of human experience, or of the lived relationship between the two. The implication is that each of these six triads illustrates a unique mode of process, action, or dynamic in the world. Next, I discuss each of the six triads in greater detail, following the order of presentation laid out in Table 7.2.

1. The Triad of Interaction (*1–3–2*)

I begin with the triad of interaction because it describes a large portion of actions, situations, and events that happen in the everyday lifeworld. The *1–3–2* conjunction of this triad can be described as affirming (*1*) and receptive (*2*) impulses brought together processually through some reconciling impulse (*3*). Blending together, the affirming and receptive impulses generate a reconciling impulse that is their resultant (Bennett, 1961, p. 116). Bennett names this triad *interaction* because it relates to "the endless flux of interlocking events going on in the world" (Bennett, 1993, p. 49). These interlocking events include actions in the natural world (e.g., river currents eroding riverbanks or birds making nests), actions between human beings and the natural world (kayakers paddling on a river or lumberjacks felling a tree), or actions between human beings (a nurse dressing a patient's wound or children playing hopscotch). The interactions may be ordinary and entirely taken for granted (reaching for my coffee mug) or skilled and complex (the dexterous arm and hand movements of an experienced machinist shaping an engine bearing on a metal lathe). One simple example of the interaction triad is a boy's tying his shoe, a situation that can be described as the boy (affirmative impulse, or *1*), using the shoelace as an instrument (receptive impulse, or *2*), to produce the action of tying (reconciling impulse, or *3*).

In this triad, the reconciling impulse draws affirmative and receptive impulses together and encompasses "the outer link by which everything is connected to everything else" (Bennett, 1961, p. 116). The interaction triad plays a central role in the automatic unfolding of everyday life and helps explain why so much of typical lifeworld experience just happens without requiring conscious intent, deliberation, or planning. Interaction triads are primary in making everyday life predictable, stable, recognizable, and more or less effortless. Typically, interactions contribute to the ordinary needs and obligations of everyday life and do not produce anything creatively original or dramatically different.[2] Things, energy, and information are shifted around in some way rather than altered or transformed. For example, a moving billiard ball (*1*) strikes a stationary billiard ball (*2*), and that ball moves accordingly (*3*). Although there has been an exchange of energy between the balls, both remain what they are; they continue to be themselves and are not transformed in the way that, say, paper is when burned by fire, or a mathematics student is when she suddenly realizes how to solve a difficult mathematical problem.

Interaction triads play a primary role in allowing the ordinariness of lifeworlds to remain ordinary and mostly uneventful. One illustration Bennett provides is working in his study on a cold winter night. He does not notice that the fire has burnt low until he begins to feel cold. He gets up and uses a poker to reactivate the fire. Once it is burning, he moves back to his chair and continues his work. He explains how this series of simple actions incorporate an interconnected series of interaction triads:

> [This experience] can be broken down into a series of triads, starting with my reaction to the sensation of cold. Here the physical sensation links the fall of temperature with my getting up and taking the poker. The environment is active and my body is passive; sensation is the reconciling impulse. When I get up and poke the fire, my body is active, the fire is passive and the poker transmits the reconciling impulse. When I being to feel warm again, the first is active, my body is passive and the radiation of the fire and the warm air of the room transmit the reconciling impulse. The roles of the different objects – air, body, poker, fire – change from one triad to the next.
>
> *(Bennett, 1961, p. 118)*

The set of triads depicted in this quotidian event is typically unnoticed and taken for granted as the simple experience of "becoming cold and reinvigorating the fire." Underlying its ordinariness, however, is a series of interlocking bodily actions that involve "getting up," "poking the fire," and "returning to work." In the first triad, the cold room triggers a chill, which eventually motivates Bennett to stand and reach for the poker, which, in the second triad, provides the means for reactivating the fire, which, once accomplished, allows Bennett to return to his work. Though these actions and exchanges are unexceptional, they encompass a considerable number of elements and relationships that triadic thinking helps one locate. Much of everyday life is a constellation of interaction triads, some repetitive and integral to lifeworld events, others less usual and requiring conscious intention and decision.

Broadly, the interaction triad refers to situations in which some everyday action or situation happens because, via a reconciling impulse, there is a give-and-take relationship between affirming and receptive impulses. The following are exemplary situations involving the interaction triad:

- A wind turbine's turning: The wind (*1*) strikes the turbine's blades (*2*), which revolve (*3*). Turning is the reconciling impulse resulting from the engagement of wind and blades.
- An accident: I walk out of my house (*1*) on a winter day, don't notice black ice on the sidewalk (*2*), and fall (*3*).
- An annoying interpersonal encounter: I pay for coffee at the local café (*1*), the checkout clerk says, "Have the most wonderful day ever!" (*2*). I respond with irritation (*3*), explaining, "There are few days in one's life that are really wonderful."
- Crossing a busy street involving one triad: I actively look for traffic (*1*), the street is clear (*2*), I cross the street (*3*).
- Crossing a busy street involving two triads: I actively look for traffic (*1*), a car approaches (*2*), I wait (*3*). As I wait, I check for more traffic (*1*), the street is clear (*2*), I cross the street (*3*). In the first triad, one might think the approaching car is an affirmative impulse but, in relation to my action of "crossing the street," it is a *denying* impulse that requires my first action to "wait," followed by my second action to "cross."

Note that, in these examples, the entities marking the impulses of the triads can involve things and actions of nature (the wind striking the turbine blades), people and things (my fall on the sidewalk), or people and people (my café experience). Also note that, in all these examples, my verbal explication of the three impulses is laid out in the presentation order of *1, 2,* and *3* (e.g., wind strikes blades, which revolve) even though the correct triadic explication is *1–3–2*. These two descriptions diverge because the English language does not provide a ready way to express the dynamic aspect of interaction processes. For example, one could write that "The wind (*1*) turns (*3*) the turbine blades (*2*)," but this phrasing is misleading in that its syntactic structure infers that the rotating action is the result of cause and effect – in other words, the wind strikes the blades, which turn. From a triadic perspective, the turning is integral to the interaction process, identifying the third, reconciling factor whereby the active wind and passive blades are brought into relational action via the interaction triad's particular manner of blending.

In terms of place and lived emplacement, we shall find that interaction triads undergird the everyday actions, situations, and events of place, whether regular and taken-for-granted or different from usual and intentionally considered. Whatever their environmental scale or range of impact, interaction triads found the life of places and facilitate their specific presence, ambience, and experiential dynamics.

2. The Triad of Identity (2–3–1)

The **2–3–1** conjunction of the identity triad can be described as a passive situation (**2**), engaged in recurring action through a reconciling impulse (**3**), becoming more capable and whole (**1**). This triad indicates how repetition facilitates actions, skills, routines, and situations that become part of who and what we are – our *identity* as an individual or group. In returning to the example of the boy tying his shoe, we realize that he was not always able to perform this simple action but learned through practice. Here, the receptive impulse is the boy's inability to tie the shoelace (**2**) being transformed, through repetitive effort (**3**), into his mastery of tying, which becomes an integral part of who he is – his identity (**1**).

As in the interaction triad, the affirming and receptive impulses do not act on each other directly in the identity triad. Rather, via the gathering quality of the reconciling impulse, the affirming impulse enables the receptive impulse to *be what it is* (Bennett, 1961, p. 114). In this sense, the triad's reconciling impulse is "the inner bond by which everything is what it is" (Bennett, 1993, p. 49). As a result, the thing, person, or situation is uniquely able to be itself, a manner of being incisively described by British poet Gerard Manley Hopkins when he writes that "Each mortal thing does one thing and the same/ . . . *Myself* it speaks and spells/Crying *What I do is me: for that I came*" (Hopkins, 1953, p. 51).[3]

Bennett (1961, p. 114) argues that the identity triad also incorporates the thing, person, or situation's having a place in the world. He explains that identity includes "'being in one's place'. A thing is 'thus' in a context, and from that context, it derives the power to assert itself. Deprived of its context, it would be mere passivity – a condition of unrelieved negation" (Bennett, 1961, p. 114). A table, for example, is a table only in the context of a particular culture and life-ways; severed from that context, the table is merely a piece of wood: "Inwardly, the table holds together by virtue of its 'tableness,' that reconciles the mere piece of wood to the complex forces that act upon it in its material and human environment" (Bennett, 1961, p. 114).

For most human beings, the triad of identity is greatly shaped at birth as infants inescapably become a part of a time, place, and family over which they have no control – the homeworld as described in Chapter 6. Via the unchangeable, taken-for-granted presence of the homeworld (**3**), the child (**2**) absorbs a way of being that marks his or her identity (**1**), personally, socially, and culturally. As novelist

Penelope Lively (2013, p. 57) explains, "Children do not question their circumstances. You are you, in this place, at this time, with these people – how else could it be otherwise?"

The most common generative process via which individuals extend and strengthen their identity is through learning, practice, and effort. Writer Malcolm Gladwell (2008) examined the process whereby world-class musicians, composers, writers, athletes, and so forth master their craft. The stereotypical understanding is that all these individuals are gifted because of innate ability. Clearly, one must have a propensity for the talent that a person develops, but research indicates that intense, continual practice is crucial – what is called the "10,000-hour rule" because, on average, "ten thousand hours of practice is required to achieve the level of mastery associated with being a world-class expert – in anything" (Gladwell, 2008, p. 4).

The 10,000-hour rule is relevant to the identity triad because it illustrates how a gifted but minimally proficient individual (*2*), through extensive, dedicated practice (*3*), can become much more proficient (*1*), sometimes exceedingly. Though this level of exceptional ability is obviously the exception rather than the rule, one finds the same triadic relationship in any situation where the untrained individual or group (*2*), through practice (*3*), masters some skill, ability, or routine and, therefore, shifts and strengthens the sense of who they are and of what they are capable (*1*), for example:

- The office assistant (*2*) who devotes herself to learning a new software program (*3*) and thus becomes more proficient in her professional tasks and responsibilities (*1*).
- The carpenter apprentice (*2*) who, having been involved in many building projects directed by a master carpenter (*3*), becomes an able carpenter himself (*1*).
- The teenage athlete (*2*) who becomes an exceptional basketball player (*1*) partly because he spends all his free time at the local basketball court and plays every game he can (*3*).
- Members of a rock band, good enough musicians to get regular gigs (*2*), who place themselves under the pressure of performing regularly (*1*) and become exceptional musicians (*3*).[4]

We shall see that, in relation to place, the identity triad is central because lived emplacement provides one lifeworld means whereby individuals and groups gain a sense of self. Who we are is partly where we are, and it is this "where-ness" in relation to self that points to the importance of the identity triad for place and place meanings.

3. The Triad of Expansion (*1–2–3*)

The triads of interaction and identity involve actions, processes, and situations that underlie any lifeworld's typical stability and continuity. The interaction triad relates to why everyday life remains mostly unchanged over long stretches of time, just as the identity triad relates to why entities remain what they are and hold their place in the world, sometimes staying the same through their entire existence. In contrast, the two triads presented next – *expansion* and *concentration* – are associated with processes and actions whereby some sort of transformation or progress takes place. Something in the relationship gains in order, appropriateness, or clarity – for example, a material environment gains in richness and vitality; or a set of seemingly disconnected ideas are integrated into a coherent theory. Because the expansion triad involves some sort of substantive change (rather than the ordinary shifting around of things and energies as in the interaction triad), it is related to creation, generation, transformation, and involution. An active agent (*1*) acts on a responsive ground (*2*) in such a way that some sort of development or improvement results (*3*). For example, an architect (*1*), in studying a nondescript dwelling entry (*2*), envisions ways to make that entry more attractive and welcome (*3*).

Bennett explains that the expansion triad comprises "all self-containing processes in which the affirming impulse requires the co-operation of the denying impulse that constitutes the medium of its activity" (Bennett, 1961, p. 109). The result is a more efficient, workable, or aesthetically striking product arising between the vision of the creator (*1*) and the raw material out of which the product is created (*2*). In this sense, the expansion triad relates to many processes whereby potential becomes real, hence Bennett's designation of "expansion" because the triad's movement is in "the direction of maximum realization of possibilities. . . . The unity of potentiality is broken up in the process of actualization" (Bennett, 1961, p. 137, 138).[5]

The architect, for example, must have the expertise and vision to imagine what a more welcoming dwelling entry could be and to maximize the possibilities of that vision in drawings and plans. There is a closely matched relationship between the architect's creative abilities (*1*) and the nondescript entry (*2*), so that out of this intimacy between affirmative and receptive impulses can arise an effective, appropriate response – a handsome new entryway (*3*). This creative result requires an intimate fit between designer and design problem. In achieving a transformation from featureless to memorable entry, the architect has participated in a process that heightens the reality of the world in a creative way. From a broad range of entry possibilities, one has been fetchingly actualized.

The expansion triad involves situations in which an individual or group creatively increases the order of the world. For example:

- A chef (*1*), having access to only a limited pallet of seasonal ingredients (*2*), produces an exceptional meal (*3*).
- An office assistant (*1*), realizing that the present filing system causes office staff to waste time finding necessary items (*2*), develops a more efficient filing system (*3*).

- An urban designer (*1*) realizing that an urban district is not working well, partly because block size is too large (*2*), produces a redesigned street grid (*3*) to facilitate increased pedestrian movement and a more vigorous street life.
- A high school teacher (*1*), recognizing the exceptional intelligence of a troubled student from a disadvantaged family (*2*), dedicates herself to helping that student develop his intellectual abilities (*3*).

In relation to place and lived emplacement, we shall find that the expansion triad is central because it is the most important means whereby creative individuals devoted to a place can envision ways whereby that place might be made more vital and whole.

4. The Triad of Concentration (*2–1–3*)

The triad of *concentration* (*2–1–3*) is associated with unification, purification, and evolution. In this triad, a receptive impulse (*2*) initiates an action toward an affirming impulse (*1*), and the result, if successful, is new potential (*3*). One example is the situation where I place myself, as receptive impulse (*2*), in front of a challenge (*1*) that I may or may not accomplish successfully (*3*). For example, I know nothing about wood working but want to learn (*2*). I don't know for sure that I'll succeed in the challenge, *but I try* (*1*) and may have positive results (*3*). Like the expansion triad, the concentration triad involves transformative change, but this change relates to a strengthening and transformation *within the receptive agent* (e.g., my wish and effort to master wood working) rather than in the external world as initiated through the active agent of the expansion triad (e.g., the architect designing the new entryway).

The concentration triad may be identified as the foundational process of phenomenological method in that the main phenomenological aim is to activate a receptive mode of awareness in the phenomenologist (*2*) whereby the phenomenon (*1*) reveals its possibilities and aspects (*3*). Heidegger's definition of phenomenology – "to let that which shows itself be seen from itself in the very way in which it shows itself from itself" (1962, p. 58) – is an exceptional description of the concentration triad whereby the phenomenologist works for a kind of naïve openness via which the "thing" becomes ready to be seen. In any situation where we try to allow the world to be, hoping that we might see in a different way, we involve ourselves with the concentration triad, though successful actualization also requires dedication, diligence, and a strong wish to see. Mastering the six triads requires a similar manner of approach: One lets them be, ponders, looks around for possibilities, keeps trying. In time, one begins to see the triads in the fabric of everyday life. The following examples illustrate the concentration triad:

- A guitarist is not very good (*2*) but he asks the members of a local rock band if he can play with them (*1*); performance by performance, he improves (*3*).

- I'd like to play the piano (*2*) and dedicate myself to lessons with an accomplished piano teacher (*1*); over time, I become a proficient pianist (*3*).
- I don't understand the concentration triad but want to. I ponder the *2–1–3* notation. I review past moments when suddenly I have mastered or understood something I had not been able to master or understand before. In all these efforts, I attempt to open myself to the situation (*2*) and allow it (*1*) to penetrate and to show me what it is (*3*).[6]

We shall find that, in relation to place and place making, the concentration triad is key to understanding how qualities of the physical environment, being one way rather than another, can play a crucial role in place experience and thus contribute to a place's life or lifelessness.[7]

5. The Triad of Order (*3–1–2*)

The last two triads relate to *order* (*3–1–2*) and *freedom* (*3–2–1*). Bennett argues that these triads help to explain why, on one hand, the world can only be as it is yet, on the other hand, can become otherwise. The triad of *order* (*3–1–2*) can be interpreted as reconciliation (*3*), acting through an affirmation (*1*), asserting order in receptivity (*2*). Bennett describes this triad as "the custodian of possibility" (Bennett, 1961, p. 148). Because of this triad, "things are kept in their own place as they are, and the world obeys its own laws" (Bennett, 1993, p. 59). He therefore associates this triad with constancy and determinism – with the fact that the world cannot be capricious and arbitrary. The triad of order relates to the question, "Why is it that everything has to be as it is?" (Bennett, 1993, p. 50). Thus, water can never run uphill nor can the sun rise in the west nor can one physical body occupy the same space as another physical body in the same moment. There are certain things about the world that are steady, enduring, and unchangeable. That the world incorporates a good amount of inescapable structure and permanence is the core quality of the triad of order.

The triad of order first of all refers to the aspects of the natural world and universe that maintain perpetuation and pattern – for example, the steady workings of the sun, planets, and solar system whereby we earthlings are guaranteed day following night, season following season, repeating phases of the moon, and the like. Just as important are the innumerable structures arising socially, culturally, and historically that give order to human life – for example, the twelve months of a year, the seven days of a week, the twenty-four hours of a day, the sixty minutes of an hour, and so forth. The order triad plays a primary role in laws and legal systems, units of currency, and cultural traditions such as arbitrary rules as to whether one drives on the left or the right side of a roadway. Other examples include:

- Systems of taxation: As a practical means to sustain a particular jurisdiction economically (*3*), public officials consider the financial situation of their citizens (*1*) and establish an organized method of taxation in which all citizens must partake (*2*).

- Systems of writing: To provide commonality and permanence of written expression (*3*), grammarians over time transform the spontaneity of spoken language (*1*) into an ordered written form supporting clarity of expression and precision in meaning (*2*).

- Musical notation: Because musicians wish to give temporal permanence to ephemeral musical compositions (*3*), they develop a way to convert music as sound (*1*) into a musical notation system (*2*) that represents graphically such sonic elements as time signature, note duration, melody, and harmony via a five-line musical staff in treble and bass clefs.

In relation to place and lived emplacement, we shall find that the triad of order is crucial, since one of its important environmental manifestations is the way that it contributes to the structure and "way of being" of a place.

6. The Triad of Freedom (*3–2–1*)

If the triad of order supports the world's continuity and constancy, the triad of *freedom* (*3–2–1*) allows for the fact that the world *can* be otherwise – that there is something free in both the world and in human beings. This freedom involves those special moments in which there is an opening "through which possibilities happen that otherwise could not" (Bennett, 1993, p. 50). In this triad, reconciliation (*3*), working through the opening of receptivity (*2*), reveals new possibilities (*1*). What was not available in time before – a design inspiration or clarification of an idea – is suddenly at hand.

The triad of freedom incorporates a wide spectrum of human experiences and encounters that range from simple noticing of something in the environment to moments of heightened recognition in which one understands an idea, event, or situation in a way of which she had no inkling a moment before (Seamon, 1979). On one hand, this triad relates to everyday happenstances and surprises. On the other hand, this triad incorporates unexpected moments of discernment, acknowledgement, or revelation. Examples of the triad of freedom include:

- Suddenly noticing the beauty of a hillside garden (*3*) that one has walked by numerous times and taken for granted (*2*) until this moment (*1*).
- Unexpectedly realizing (*3*) that the person she thought she knew (*2*) is someone entirely different (*1*).
- In a moment of spontaneous understanding (*3*), discerning how a set of experiential descriptions (*2*) can be organized and understood in terms of more general phenomenological themes and structures (*1*).

One important human experience associated with the freedom triad is *seren-dipity* – those moments of fortunate happenstance cleverly defined by poet Ogden Nash as "merely the knack of making happy and unexpected discoveries by chance," a line from his poem, "Don't Look for the Silver Lining: Just Wait for It" (Merton and Barber, 2004, p. 95). In their provocative history of "serendipity," sociologists Robert Merton and Elinor Barber explain how the word was first coined by British man of letters Horace Walpole in 1754 and required some 200 years to become an everyday term to describe an essential lifeworld experience.[8] By considering serendipity in terms of the freedom triad, we can say that an unanticipated flash of recognition (*3*), in relation to the ordinary world at hand (*2*), provokes one's realizing some surprising connection or outcome (*1*) not expected or imaginable before the flash of recognition.

We shall find that serendipity and happenstance are an integral aspect of lived emplacement, often provoking unexpected departures from the repetitive ordinariness of place.

Some Key Points about Triads

In understanding the six triads, several caveats need mentioning. First, the six triads are not readily understood by thinking alone. Rather, they need to be looked for and deciphered in one's own experiences: for instance, what is a moment of insight like (triad of freedom), or how do I describe the process through which I have become good at whatever I'm good at (triads of concentration and identity)? Second, one must understand that the three impulses of the particular action or process express themselves through the three terms *but are not the terms themselves*. In the case of the boy's tying his shoelace, for example, the shoelace works as the second impulse only because the boy as active impulse needs a tied shoe and the shoelace becomes the passive vehicle for facilitating that need. Third, the three impulses are relative in regard to context; thus, a term that is second impulse in one situation may work as active or reconciling impulse in another situation (as we shall see in the six place triads). Fourth, as the blending of the three impulses happens in the particular action, they lose their separate identities and something new arises. As Bennett writes: "Although the three [impulses], as they meet to constitute the event, are distinct autonomous elements, within the event itself they are welded into one and abandon their separate identity. It is the emergence of something different, which is not merely the sum of the three [impulses] that constitutes the new event" (Bennett, 1950, p. 9).

Throughout his discussions of the triad, Bennett emphasizes that this system is incalculably complex because human experience is unceasingly dynamic. He writes:

> [The] relatedness [of the triad] establishes a nexus of connections that extends through all possible worlds. These many connections are possible because a term *A* of a triad *X* can also be a term of another triad *Y*, thus linking *X* and

Y together. *X* can also be a term in a superordinate system *Z*. Thus triadic relatedness can comprise coordination, subordination, and super-ordination. For example, we have *A* as husband and father in system *X* but son in system *Y* of the preceding generation. In system *Y, A* fulfills the role of system *C*, the child in *X*. The family (*ABC*) = *X* is a term in the system *Z* consisting of the three generations of grandparents *D*, parents *E*, and children *F*. In this way, *X* fulfills the same role as the link between *D* and *F* as the child *C* fulfills as the link between *A* and *B*. Evidently, the network of triads can be extended in all directions of space, time, and number. It can also be shown that any set of relations, however complex, can be reduced to a nexus of triads. It follows that relatedness is the systemic attribute of the triad, and, conversely, all cases of relatedness can be expressed as systems of the third order – that is, as triads.

(Bennett, 1993, pp. 102–03)

As Bennett illustrates here, the generative relatedness of the world and human life is complex, and the triad provides one conceptual and applied means for sorting out this complexity and making it more understandable. For place and lived emplacement, this dynamic complexity is present both temporally and spatially, since places change over time and smaller-scaled places are often a part of larger-scaled places that are in turn part of yet larger environments.

In the following chapters, I begin by asking how place and lived emplacement can be understood triadically. In Chapter 8, I first identify and justify three impulses of place; second, I consider what these three impulses mean for locating the six triads of place, which I identify as *place interaction, place identity, place release, place realization, place intensification*, and *place creation*. In Chapters 9–14, I discuss each of these six place triads in turn and, in Chapter 15, consider their dynamic relationships, whereby places degenerate or thrive.

Notes

1 Another helpful source for envisioning the difference between dyadic and triadic understanding is the 1993 film, *Groundhog Day*, in which actor Bill Murray plays Phil Connors, an insufferable, self-centered Pittsburgh television weatherman who, covering the annual Groundhog Day celebration in Punxsutawney, Pennsylvania, suddenly finds himself as the only person in town caught up in a time loop and reliving the same day over and over but in vastly different ways – first, through unfettered hedonism and then through a series of suicides. These ways of dealing with the same day over and over, however, offer no solace, and eventually Connors realizes that the most useful thing he can do is to forget about himself and to use the day's repeating events to better the lives of his fellow Punxsutawnians. Instead of writing off these townsfolk as one-dimensional cardboard characters not worthy of his attention, Connors gets to know them intimately and discovers, through trial and error, how he can make their lives better. From one interpretive angle, the film is a masterly presentation of how one person, becoming more engaged with the world, comes to understand that world triadically and thus discovers an existential means for facilitating life-shifting relationships and events that

include short-circuiting accidents and saving lives. Whereas before Connors saw the world dyadically as a self-serving venue for personal satisfaction, he comes to realize that there is a deeper manner of engagement via which he aids others by *really seeing and understanding* who they are and doing the right thing in the right moment. It is this deeper engagement that marks a triadic relationship with the world.

2 Interaction triads can be constructive in the sense that more order is created out of less order. One example is the process of cookie-cutter house building whereby a well-trained construction crew (*1*), making use of standardized designs and building materials (*2*), assembles a standardized house (*3*) in mass-produced fashion. If, however, the house is creatively designed and involves exquisite craft work, then the triad of interaction is supplemented by a different process – triads of creation (*1–2–3*) whereby architect and craftspeople actively engage with design and materials to generate a unique house with aesthetic presence (see note 5).

3 I thank Stephen Wood for directing me to the link between Bennett's identity triad and this line from Hopkins' poem, "As Kingfishers Catch Fire" (Hopkins, 1953, p. 51), which points to the poet's interest in what he called the "inscape," an essential core that makes the thing or living being what it is – in Bennett's language, its *identity*. As critic W. H. Gardner (1953, p. xx) explains, Hopkins "is mainly interested in all those aspects of a thing which make it distinctive and individual . . . . He was always looking for the law or principles which gave to any object or grouping of objects its delicate and surprising uniqueness."

4 As an example, Gladwell highlights the Beatles, who as a mediocre Liverpool rock band, were invited in 1960 to perform in clubs in Hamburg, Germany, where they played seven evenings a week, often non-stop, late into the night. As band member John Lennon explained, "We got better and got more confidence. We couldn't help it with all the experience of playing all night long . . . . In Liverpool, we'd only ever done one-hour sessions, and we just used to do our best numbers, the same ones, at every one. In Hamburg, we had to play for eight hours, so we really had to find a new way of playing" (Gladwell, 2008, p. 49). In other words, the demand of continuous performance in front of a live audience actualized, through inescapable repetition and practice, the group's identity as an exceptional rock band. Obviously, the Beatles possessed unusual creative abilities, but Gladwell's point is that the later opportunities for that creativity might not have arisen if the group hadn't already become exceptional musical performers. I thank Jenny Quillien for introducing me to Gladwell's work and for pointing to connections with the identity triad; see Quillien, 2012, pp. 132–133.

5 As explained in note 2, the interaction triad can also involve the making of greater order, but that order is pre-defined and derivative rather than actualized through creative action and thus new and potentially singular.

6 The lived difference between identity and concentration triads is that, in the latter, the person must consciously wish to improve and find the continuing will to persevere in making that improvement happen. The apprentice carpenter, for example, must follow the instructions of his or her mentor and aim to carry out those instructions with as much skill and craft as possible. For sure, the actual actions – learning to size a beam or working a plane properly – require the repetition of many practical actions, all unfolding as interaction and identity triads. What ultimately is most important, however, is the determination to become a master carpenter and to trust the guidance and tasks that the mentor offers. This willingness to trust one's mentor and follow his or her guidance marks the distinctiveness of the concentration triad. This intimacy of relationship between apprentice and mentor points to the crucial importance of an appropriate, on-going "fit" between the second and first impulses in the concentration triad.

7 A superb personification of the concentration triad is American writer Bret Harte's 1868 short story, "The Luck of Roaring Camp," in which a motherless baby boy is adopted by the miners of a remote mining camp during the California gold rush (Harte, 1961).

Through the sheer force of the baby's helplessness and need of nurture (*2*), the uncouth, hardhearted men of the camp collectively care for the child (*1*) with the result that each man individually and the settlement as a whole become more kindly, refined, and civilized (*3*). "And so," writes Harte (1961, p. 17), "the work of regeneration began in Roaring Camp. Almost imperceptibly a change came over the settlement." Sadly, the camp's shift from communal disorder to order cannot last. A violent flood drowns the infant and demolishes Roaring Camp. Hopeful human possibilities are extinguished by impersonal forces of nature (a destructive interaction triad). Harte's story is a striking instance of the concentration triad in that, at least for a time, order replaces disorder and a situation of "every man for himself" is transformed into a community where individuals discover the value of mutual respect and assistance. The story also illustrates how the fragile, formative action of the concentration triad can readily collapse and fall back into disarray via destructive interaction triads.

8 Walpole was an "inveterate maker of words" and originally coined "serendipity" to mean any fortuitous situation whereby one finds or discovers something that he or she is not in search of (Merton and Barber, 2004, pp. 1–14). He derived the word from a fairy tale, "The Three Princes of Serendip," which described how these men, as they travelled, would discover important things they had not expected to encounter. "Serendip" is said to be an early name for Shri Lanka, known in Walpole's time as Ceylon (Merton and Barber, 2004, p. xiv, pp. 110–120).

8

THE THREE PLACE IMPULSES AND THE SIX PLACE TRIADS

In this and the next six chapters, I consider place as it can be understood through the triad. In Chapter 7, I presented Bennett's six triads broadly. Now I must locate the three impulses that mark place-as-process and ask how these three impulses conjoin to delineate six triads of place. I ask how Bennett's interaction, identity, expansion, concentration, order, and freedom can be translated into six generative modes that clarify the lived dynamics of place broadly and real-world places specifically. In answering this question, I proceed in three steps:

- Identifying and justifying the affirming, receptive, and reconciling impulses that mark place and place-as-process;
- Delineating and naming the six resulting triads;
- Examining the unique manner of actions, happenings, and experiences to which each of these six place triads relates.

In this chapter, I discuss the three impulses of place and overview the six resulting place processes, which I describe as *interaction, identity, release, intensification, creation,* and *realization.* In Chapters 9–14, I discuss each of these place processes individually. First, however, I must locate and justify the place triad's three impulses and then demonstrate how they conjoin to propel the six place processes.

Identifying and Justifying the Three Impulses of Place

How are place and lived emplacement to be considered as a triad? In answering this question, the first requirement is to identify three terms that make sense as *impulses* – in other words, to specify elements that are relatively independent but play a central role in contributing to place happenings, meanings, and experiences. At the start, I emphasize that these terms must address the phenomenon of place directly rather than define place in terms of other phenomena such as community, culture, politics, power, economics, or some similar qualities that in both analytic and poststructural research are assumed to be independent factors shaping the dependent factor of place.

In analytic research, for example, place is typically interpreted as a dependent variable shaped by such independent variables as age, social status, home ownership, or duration of place involvement (Lewicka, 2011; Patterson and Williams, 2005). Obviously, most places incorporate social, cultural, political, economic, and similar dimensions, but my focus is understanding place as a phenomenon *in itself*. I suggest that place can be pictured as an independent, non-contingent phenomenon that actively contributes to that place's social, cultural, and other human-grounded aspects that, in relation to *place as place*, are enmeshed in place and are partially what they are *because of place*. How does one locate three impulses that incorporate both the physical and psychological, the spatial and social, the environmental and cultural, the non-living and living aspects of place? How does one identify three impulses that encompass people and world together via an existential situation in which human being is always human-being-immersed-in place?

I have pondered these questions since the early 2000s and arrived at a tentative solution when attending a conference in Istanbul in 2007. Of all the cities I have visited, Istanbul is the most remarkable in terms of a unique and powerful spirit of place. The geographical locale, the diverse topography and landscape, the teeming street life, the extraordinary range of place activities, the wide range in human types, and the sense of "oldness" that permeates much of the city – all these elements and qualities sustain an environmental character and ambience that are singular and rich. One "feels" the presence of this place viscerally, emotionally, cognitively, and spiritually. There is no doubt that Istanbul is a place vastly beyond its parts and an exceptional example of Malpas's claim, brought forward in Chapter 3, that place is "constituted through a gathering of elements that are themselves mutually defined only through the way in which they are gathered together within the place they also constitute" (Malpas, 2006, p. 29). Or in Bortoft's terms, Istanbul can be understood as a striking example of an environmental "*belonging* together" in which the physical, spatial, and human parts commingle to foster and be fostered by a powerful sense of place (Bortoft, 1996).

For several months before my Istanbul encounter, I had pondered the meaning of place from Bennett's perspective of triads. One morning after breakfast at my Istanbul hotel, I sat reflecting on this matter when suddenly I realized that the triad of place might be considered in terms of three impulses: first, the environmental and geographical foundations of place; second, people of the place; and, third, the relative "togetherness" of the place expressed in a quality of environmental belonging that is both effable and ineffable, visible and invisible, describable and indescribable, objectively present and subjectively experienced. In this

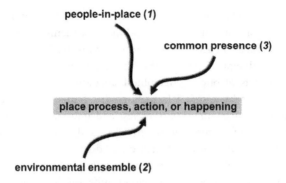

FIGURE 8.1 The triadic blending of the three place impulses

book, I designate these three place impulses as *environmental ensemble, people-in-place*, and *common presence*. Their blending can be schematized by the three-arrowed drawing of Figure 8.1.

As I worked with these three aspects of place as impulses of a triad, I realized that each contributed something different in terms of what a place is – why it seems attractive or unsightly; why it has a strong or weak ambience; how it unfolds as a vibrant or muted environment; how it gains or loses a sense of identity and attachment. Here, I justify my designation of these three impulses and provide a preliminary description. *Environmental ensemble* and *people-in-place* are more or less self-explanatory, but the third impulse – *common presence* – is more difficult to justify and define. After discussing the three impulses, I then describe what their six conjunctions mean as six different place triads pinpointing integral aspects of place experiences, meanings, and events. In following chapters, I explicate each of these six place triads in greater detail and ask what their contrasting phenomenologies entail.

Environmental Ensemble as Receptive Impulse (EE)

The *environmental ensemble* (*EE* as a shorthand label) is the *receptive* impulse of the place triad and refers to the material and environmental qualities of place, including topography, geology, weather, flora, fauna, and natural landscape as well as any human-made elements, including constructions and their spatial configurations – for example, furnishings, buildings, landscape fabrications, pathway layouts, and placement of land uses. There is a wide range of ways to define the environmental ensemble (e.g., Norberg-Schulz, 1980; Tilley, 1994, 2010; Tilley and Cameron-Daum, 2017). One example is French historian Eric Dardel's description of what he calls *geographicality* – the various lived relationships that bind human beings to the earth and contribute to "their way of existence and fate" (Dardel, 1952; Relph, 1985, p. 21). Dardel identifies five dimensions of geographicality, beginning with *material space*, which he relates to physical elements like valleys, hills, and mountains. These geographic features "partake of the character of the surrounding surfaces and manifest themselves directly to us as distances to be travelled in terms of the time and effort needed to climb hills or to drive across cities" (Relph, 1985, p. 25). Second, *telluric space* refers to foundational, steadfast aspects of one's geographical situation: the "depth, solidity, and durability" of stone and geological formations that found the secure, taken-for-granted ground on which human worlds rest and unfold. Third, *hydrologic space* relates to the realm of water that is "formless and filled with motion" and includes the earth's oceans and seas, which offer "distant horizons with their sense of adventure" (Relph, 1985, p. 25). Fourth, *atmospheric space* refers to the realm of air – for example, "skies changing with cloud, mist, sunshine, and rain" (Relph, 1985, p. 25). Fifth, *human-made space* includes buildings, plazas, streets, and any other constructions "that convey human purposes directly through their forms and surfaces" (Relph, 1985, p. 26). Human-made space marks out "human intentions inscribed on the earth" (Relph, 1985, p. 26).

Although any specific place's environmental ensemble is unique, it is integral as an impulse for the place triad because it provides the material foundation for place events, transactions, experiences, and meanings. For this reason, the environmental ensemble is the receptive impulse of the place triad, since it is mostly material, inertial, and normally taken-for-granted and assumed without question to be available for human use. In spite of its passive nature, however, there are situations where the environmental ensemble plays an active role in place processes, sometimes dramatically so (as in natural disasters). In this sense, the environmental ensemble sets the stage for human actions and situations transpiring in one way rather than another. For example, once a building is constructed, human beings must accommodate their movements accordingly, passing through or around the building in the ways that its footprint, layout, form, and pathways allow. A much more dramatic, impinging example is present-day climate change that sooner or later will demand dramatic shifts in places, human life, and environmental and place thinking (Abramson, 2016; Relph, 2008, 2009, 2015).

Paradoxically, human beings' historical success in overcoming, remaking, and controlling the environmental ensemble is now called into question as we transition to a confrontational environmental situation in some ways reminiscent of environmental determinism – the conceptual perspective that the physical environment controls and shapes human actions (Richards, 2012; Sprout and Sprout, 1965). The power of the environmental ensemble to play an active role in lived emplacement must be understood and accommodated if we aim for place making that repairs damaged places, sustains robust environments, and reverses the imminent collapse of the natural world and the earth as our home (Hay, 2002; Abramson, 2016). As we shall see, the active significance of the environmental ensemble is particularly highlighted in the place triad I identify as *intensification*, whereby elements and qualities of the physical environment intensify or weaken place and place making. I discuss place intensification in Chapter 13.[1]

People-in-Place as Affirming Impulse (PP)

People-in-place (**PP**) relates to the human worlds unfolding in the environmental ensemble and is the *affirming impulse* in the place triad, since, typically, people actively manipulate and fabricate their worlds. This impulse refers to the life-worlds, homeworlds, and natural attitudes of people in a place, including their actions, routines, understandings, and situations, whether unself-conscious or conscious, habitual or out-of-the-ordinary. In conceptualizing human beings in relation to place, I move away from a social-constructionist interpretation, which assumes that meaning is generated through human discourse and that representations of reality are therefore partial, arbitrary, and relative (Seamon and Gill, 2016, p. 118). In contrast, I make a phenomenological argument that much of human meaning is grounded in place in the sense that place experience plays an integral role in how human beings know themselves, others, and their worlds. To a greater or lesser degree, human beings are always their place – a situation that Malpas (1999, p. 14) describes as the "place-bound identity of persons."

How people are emplaced plays a signal role in who and how they are as social, cultural, and economic beings. When I speak, therefore, of people-in-place, I recognize that any specific place can encompass a wide range of social, cultural, political, and economic commonalities and differences. That said, my first concern is human aspects of a situation that arise primarily because human beings are always of their place, even if that emplacement is temporary, unwelcomed, or ignored. Obviously, one can consider people-in-place in terms of differences, whether gendered, sexual, social, cultural, political, religious, and the like. But the focus in the six place triads is, first of all, people as they are human beings sharing the lived situation of *emplacement in a particular place*, whether that place is adored, tolerated, disliked, despised, or simply taken for granted and never called into question.

In short, a triadic understanding of place assumes that, as human beings, we are always human-beings-in-place, simply because, wherever, whoever, and however we are, we are always emplaced, regardless of whether we cherish or loathe our emplaced situation. Obviously, not all people in place feel themselves to be a part of that place. Here, however, I assume that any situation of place estrangement is better considered once the six place triads have been understood. In short, I assume that we garner a more thorough understanding of "being-out-of-place" if we first consider "being-in-place" via the six place processes.

Common Presence as Reconciling Impulse (CP)

The most difficult element of the place triad to locate is the reconciling impulse, which I identify as *common presence* (**CP**), defined as the material and lived "togetherness" of a place impelled by both its physical and experiential qualities. The common presence of a place refers to its degree of "life" and its environmental character or *presence* – for example, the "London-ness" of London, or the

"Istanbul-ness" of Istanbul. In this sense, the common presence of place incorporates related phenomena such as "environmental atmosphere," "place ambience," "sense of place," "spirit of place," and its Latin rendition, *genius loci*. From a social-constructionist perspective, the common presence of any place is a result of individual and group discourse defining and sanctioning a specific set of place meanings, actions, and sensibilities. In contrast, I claim that common presence is *a real phenomenon* apart from human subjectivity and at least partly independent of cognitive and affective designations or representations. This claim is contentious, and my justification is as follows.

I draw the idea of common presence from Bennett, who defines it as the "togetherness of entities in a limited region of space" (Bennett, 1961, p. 48). He argues that spatial togetherness induces a "common presence" that "emerges as a recognizable quality shared by all entities in the region" (Bennett, 1961, p. 47). From one perspective, common presence can be related to Bortoft's "*belonging together*," whereby the degree of spatial and experienced cohesion of a place is partly the result of the degree that environmental and human elements "*belong together*" to sustain a robust whole. In contrast, environments that seem placeless or with little sense of place incorporate a weak common presence and fragmented "*belonging together*." Because places range in spatial scale and larger places typically accommodate smaller places, a key feature of common presence is its shifting field of consequence depending on which specific place is given scholarly or practical attention. The common presence of a city as a whole is different from the common presences of that city's unique neighborhoods, which are again different from the common presences of the homes, shops, schools and other buildings in those neighborhoods. Bennett (1966b, p. 6) writes:

> That [place] which on one scale is "at a distance," on another scale is "here." My own house is here and now for my personal life, and other houses are "at a distance." But for my life as a member of a community, all houses in the village and all its inhabitants are here and now.

Significantly, Bennett claims that common presence is one example of phenomena that occupy "a kind of no-man's land between the fields of science, art, and religion" (Bennett, 1961, p. 44). One example he gives is the designer or artist's accepting the "golden mean" as a law of proportion. The special sense of proportional rightness that the golden mean evokes intuitively cannot be demonstrated empirically or proven objectively. Even so, there is a special geometric quality that gives to structures and spaces designed via the golden mean a sense of elegance, beauty, and "rightness" (Doczi, 2005; Lawlor, 1982). Bennett calls this situation *paraesthetic*, by which he means "phenomena that are allied to sensory experience and yet cannot be described in terms of sensation alone" (Bennett, 1961, p. 44).

The common presence of place is one such paraesthetic phenomenon because it cannot be readily grasped directly but only felt and spoken of imprecisely. Most recently in the phenomenological literature, this ineffable aspect of common presence has been discussed via the concept of *atmosphere*, defined as the lived quality of a place whereby it evokes a certain invisible character or ambience that makes that place unusual or unique (Borch, 2014; Böhme et al.,, 2014; Griffero, 2014, 2017; Pallasmaa, 2015). Phenomenological philosopher Gernot Böhme (2014, p. 96, p. 56), for example, relates atmosphere to "spaces with a mood, or emotionally felt spaces" and describes the experience as "that total impression that is regarded as characteristic" of a place. Similarly, architectural theorist Juhani Pallasmaa (2014, p. 20) defines atmosphere as "the overarching perceptual, sensory, and emotive impression of a space, setting, or social situation." He argues that "overpowering atmospheres have a haptic, almost material presence, as if we were surrounded and embraced by a specific substance" (Pallasmaa, 2015, p. 34). In suggesting that all buildings, whether prosaic or monumental, project some degree of mood and ambience, Pallasmaa goes so far as to claim that atmosphere, in contrast to visible building form, is the most important aspect of architectural experience for everyday users: "This unconscious orientation and articulation of mood is often the most significant effect of a space or a building. I believe that non-architects sense primarily the atmosphere of a place or building, whereas an attention to visible form implies a distinct intellectual and theoretical position" (Pallasmaa, 2015, p. 133).

Böhme and Pallasmaa's explications of atmosphere point toward its complex, experiential nature. Atmospheres are invisible, diffuse, and never fully graspable or describable. They are not brought to awareness or identity via vision alone but incorporate a wide range of experiential modalities that include sound, tactility, emotional vibrations, and an active presence of things and spaces. As Pallasmaa explains, an awareness of atmosphere involves "our entire embodied and existential sense . . . and it is perceived in a diffuse and peripheral manner rather than through precise, focused and conscious observation" (Pallasmaa, 2015, p. 133). In many ways, place presence and place atmosphere are related to "spirit of place," or *genius loci* – the unique ambience and character of a place, for example, the "Rome-ness" of Rome, or the "New England-ness" of New England (Norberg-Schulz, 1980; Relph, 2009). As with the discussion of atmospheres, most explications of *genius loci* focus on an ineffable environmental presence difficult to locate or describe completely. For example, British novelist Lawrence Durrell (1969, p. 157) defines *genius loci* as "the invisible constant in a place," and cultural geographer Pierce Lewis (1979, p. 27) speaks of "something intangible in certain places – a kind of quality that makes certain places special and worth defending." American writer Henry Miller points to the impalpability of place when he explains his response to a fellow American who asks why Miller resides in Paris: "It was useless to answer him in words. I suggested instead that we take a stroll through the streets" (cited in Sciolino, 2016, p. 47).

One key concern regarding the common presence of place is how, as an impulse, it differs from environmental ensemble and people-in-place. I repeat Bennett's emphasis on the "togetherness of entities in a limited region of space" (Bennett, 1961, p. 37). The key word is *togetherness*, whereby the environmental and human elements of place are together (or not) in a mode of belonging (or not) that supports (or undermines) the life and wholeness of the place. As novelist Doris Lessing (1969, p. 221) writes: "A whole. People in any sort of communion, link, connection, make up a whole." It is the degree of wholeness, shaping and being shaped by the spatial "togetherness" of the specific combination of environmental ensemble and human-beings-in-place, that defines the common presence of place. The environmental ensemble is the collection of geographical elements making up a place, just as people-in-place are the individuals and groups who live in or are otherwise associated with that place. Common presence refers to the ways that the spatial togetherness of place, associated with both its environmental and human components, contributes to what a real-world place is, especially in relation to its experiences, happenings, meanings and modes of presence. Ultimately, the three place impulses conjoin in varying degrees of intensity whereby each impulse participates in stronger or weaker ways. This range of generative strength or weakness is understood more thoroughly via the six place triads, which I introduce next.[2]

The Six Place Triads

To summarize: I have identified the affirming place impulse as *people-in-place* (**PP**); the receptive impulse as *environmental ensemble* (**EE**); and the reconciling impulse as *common presence* (**CP**). These three impulses can conjoin in six different combinations, each of which relates to a different set of actions, situations, and events that can vitalize or unsettle place. I identify and name these six place triads as follows:[3]

- Place interaction (*1–3–2* or **PP–CP–EE**)
- Place identity (*2–3–1* or **EE–CP–PP**)
- Place release (*3–2–1* or **CP–EE–PP**)
- Place realization (*3–1–2* or **CP–PP–EE**)
- Place intensification (*2–1–3* or **EE–PP–CP**)
- Place creation (*1–2–3* or **PP–EE–CP**)

What do these six triads mean for understanding place and lived emplacement? This question is probed comprehensively in the next six chapters. To help readers get their bearings, I end this chapter by providing an overview of what each triad involves experientially and environmentally. In examining the six triads, one notes that they can be organized in groups of two, depending on the position of *common presence* – in other words, the position of the reconciling, or third impulse. In the first two triads of *place interaction* and *place identity*, common presence as the reconciling impulse is *between* the affirmative and receptive impulses of people-in-place and environmental ensemble; in this sense, common presence *moderates* the exchange between the two other impulses. The first triad of *place interaction* identifies the everyday goings-on of a place – what might be called its "daily rounds." In turn, the triad of *place identity* relates to how people living in a place take up that place as their world; how they unself-consciously and self-consciously accept and recognize that place as part of their personal and communal identity. In both triads, common presence works as a potential bond whereby environmental ensemble and people-in-place are given both outer environmental expression (place interaction) and inner human meaning (place identity).

The next two place triads – *place release* and *place realization* – involve broader qualities of lived emplacement in that these two triads speak to the existential integrity of places themselves as facilitated through common presence. In both triads, the reconciling impulse is now *initiator* of the process. The triad of *place release* incorporates situations and occasions where people-in-place are "released" more deeply into themselves through the serendipity and surprise arising via unexpected happenings in place. Partly because of place, "life is good." In *place realization*, the environmental potential of place is progressively actualized via the potential gathering power of common presence. Place involves a tangible and intangible order that, in a robust form, includes a unique environmental ambience and character. Situated in the first position of these two triads, the common presence of place works in contrasting ways: on one hand, offering an environmental region of spontaneity and freedom whereby the extra-ordinary unexpectedly permeates the everyday ordinariness of place (place release); on the other hand, impelling an ordering process where place becomes more itself materially and experientially (place realization).

In the last two triads – *place intensification* and *place creation* – the third impulse of common presence is *the outcome*. *Place intensification* points to the power of appropriate plans and fabrications to strengthen people-in-place and thereby strengthen place ambience and character. *Place creation* relates to the involvement of dedicated individuals who creatively improve place. Through thoughtful understanding and action (place creation) generating well-crafted improvements in the environmental ensemble (place intensification) the place gains in vitality and atmosphere. Innovative thinking and making boost the common presence of place.

Having described the six place processes broadly, I next consider each in detail. What, in other words, might a phenomenology of each of these six place processes entail? In Chapters 9–14, I discuss each place process in turn. I begin with place interaction and identity because these two processes play a central role in *grounding* place and propelling the qualities that transform an environment into place and lived emplacement.

Notes

1 One of the most significant components of environmental ensembles is technology, which today more than ever plays a determining role in the lived nature of lifeworlds and places. Because my major concern is the larger-scaled, physical environment, I give

minimal attention to technology in this book. But with the arrival of digital communications, driverless vehicles, virtual and augmented reality, and the many other new technologies on the horizon, it is clear that the human relationship with physical places may shift in ways currently unimaginable. A key question is whether physical places will remain integral to human life and continue to provide – via the automatic structuring of lifeworlds – spatial order and environmental identity. Though these new technologies allow human beings to bypass the physical world in many ways, we may find that we must maintain a certain degree of lived anchorage with real-world places, simply because we remain bodily beings and inhabitants in a material environment. If technology eventually allows human beings to dispense entirely with their material bodies, then physical places could well become unnecessary, though one expects that virtual places, virtual worlds, and virtual realities would still be required, since so much of how we understand ourselves as human beings is grounded in spatial, environmental, and geographical sensibilities and meanings (see Greenfield, 2017; Horan, 2000; Kelly, 2016; Miller, 2016; Meyrowitz, 2015; Relph, 2007; Seamon, 2014b, 2018a).

2   In the first iteration of the three place impulses (Seamon, 2012b), I identified the reconciling impulse as *genius loci*. Having pondered the three impulses more thoroughly since that first effort, I realize that Bennett's "common presence" offers a more accurate means to envision the third impulse because common presence relates to the degree of togetherness of a place as well as to the degree to which the togetherness of that place is (or is not) grounded in belonging. Obviously, a place expressing "*belonging* together" manifests a more comprehensive and powerful environmental presence than a fractured place that manifests some physical togetherness but little or no lived belonging.

3   Note that I have partially changed the order of these place triads from the order that I presented the six triads broadly in Chapter 7. I have made this shift because the triads of place intensification ("concentration" in Bennett's designation) and place creation ("expansion") relate to strengthening place and place making and are therefore better discussed last, once one has understood the four triads (interaction, identity, release, and realization) that describe places as they are (their *being*) rather than how they might be made better (their *becoming*). For further discussion of the "being" and "becoming" of place, see Chapter 15, which examines dynamic interconnections among the six place processes. Artist and photographer Sue Michael (2018) provides a provocative effort to illustrate and verify the six place processes in paintings and photographs depicting South Australian places and place experiences.

9

THE TRIAD OF PLACE INTERACTION (*1–3–2* OR *PP–CP–EE*)

In Chapters 9–14, I provide a more thorough description of the six place triads. In generative fashion, these triads work together reciprocally in both place-supportive and place-undermining ways. Before, however, I consider the processual connections and disjunctions whereby the six triads synchronize or collide, I offer introductory phenomenologies for each. Once each of the six triads is considered phenomenologically, I then illustrate potential connections and relationships among them. In this way, one can better locate ways whereby places and lived emplacement intensify, languish, or disintegrate.

The triad of place interaction is vital for place and lived emplacement because, along with place identity, it marks the existential foundation of any place – the lifeworld actions, happenings, and situations associated with that place. I begin by presenting the triad of place interaction broadly. I then provide several real-world examples drawing on newspaper stories and other descriptive sources that illustrate specific place interactions. In the last part of the chapter, I consider some of the more complex aspects of place interaction, including the complicated matter of how individual interaction triads conjoin to invoke larger-scale place processes over time. As a source of descriptive evidence to illustrate how webs of smaller-scaled interactions facilitate larger-scaled places, I draw on urbanist Jane Jacobs (1961), particularly her understanding of urban place ballet.

The Triad of Place Interaction

Broadly, place interaction refers to the typical goings-on in a place.[1] As a triad, place interaction can be pictured as *1–3–2* (*PP–CP–EE*), whereby common presence, as reconciling impulse, facilitates some interaction or exchange between the affirming impulse of people-in-place and the receptive impulse of environmental ensemble.[2] In this sense, place interaction is helpfully visualized in terms of gerunds relating to actions in place – for example, "walking," "sitting," "meeting," "enjoying," "conversing," and so forth. Interaction is important to place because it is the major engine through which the users of place carry out their everyday lives and that place gains activity and a sense of environmental presence. The phenomenon of place ballet, introduced in Chapter 2, is one mode of place interaction whereby individual actions and interpersonal exchanges conjoin spatially through bodily co-presence, co-awareness, and co-encounters grounded in place. Place ballet illustrates one kind of geographical common presence in that it encompasses a network of actions and happenings gathered into a spatial and environmental togetherness that is visible objectively via place behaviors and actions, and known subjectively via place ambience and character.

Place interaction undermines place when actions and situations disrupt the co-presence of users and generate distress, fragmentation, unseemliness, and decline. Typical interactions become fewer, unpleasant, or destructive in some way – for example, a busy stretch of sidewalk and street becomes empty of users; regular interpersonal exchanges in place become fewer and less friendly; informal trust among those associated with the place is reduced or lost; the convenience of daily place interactions devolves into a situation of inefficiency, nuisance, worry, fear, or conflict. Gerund-wise, negative place interactions are described by such situations as "having difficulty 'getting around,'" "being given bad service," "being accosted," and so forth. As I discuss in Chapter 14, a major aim of creative place making is thinking through practical ways whereby vicious circles of place interaction might become virtuous circles.

As a starting point for introducing real-world instances of place interaction, I summarize six newspaper articles that delineate a small portion of the considerable spectrum of interactive situations and happenings associated with place and lived emplacement. I select these entries because they illustrate tangible ways in which concrete aspects of environmental ensemble, people-in-place, and common presence play a role in specific place interactions. I summarize these six newspaper articles and then use them to illustrate some key dimensions of place interaction. Note that the stories are arranged roughly from less to more complex situations and events. The manner of place experiences ranges from temporary emplacement on a bus to long-time residence in a place that is rapidly changing because of climate change and rising sea levels.

- An elderly bus passenger gets up from his seat, comes forward, and uses his cane to fend off a male rider attacking the female bus driver (*KCS*, January 30, 2016, p. 4A).
- A forty-year-old grocery store in New York City's SoHo neighborhood closes because of rising rent, leaving a "food desert" for lower-income and longtime residents whose economic means have not improved as SoHo has

shifted from "a homely enclave to a glamorous address" (*NYT*, December 31, 2017, p. A14, p. A15).

- As digital ride-hailing services like Uber and Lyft become ubiquitous in cities, prospective passengers sometimes misidentify private vehicles for ride-hailing services; unsuspecting drivers are surprised, and would be-riders are confused. Recently, the services have begun providing lighted windshield placards to help customers identify their ride (*WSJ*, February 10, 2017, p. A1).

- In Madrid, Spain, a clergyman has proved himself an innovative entrepreneur by establishing four "Robin Hood" restaurants, which use profits from breakfast and lunch sales to provide free dinners for the homeless (*NYT*, December 20, 2016, p. A8).

- Two inches of snow falls in Portland, Oregon, and the city is badly disrupted, with snarled traffic, abandoned cars, and thirty-minute commutes lasting hours. Because of a particularly hard winter, the city has begun salting its roads, a move that has generated considerable public outcry, since many Portland residents see their city as a model of environmental sustainability (*WSJ*, January 24, 2017, p. A1).

- In Florida's Fort Lauderdale neighborhood of Las Olas Isles, streets and residential properties are flooded by higher tides caused by rising sea levels; homeowners study tidal charts and prepare by parking on high ground, placing garbage cans well away from street curbs, and driving slowly to minimize water splash on wheels and engines, which can be destroyed by saltwater corrosion. A longer-term solution is elevating streets – an expensive effort that costs as much as three million dollars per mile (*NYT*, November 18, 2016, p. A14).

I begin with these news stories because, though each is unique, they point to different ways in which human beings interact with places. First, the stories cover a wide spectrum of place types and environmental scales that range from commercial venues to neighborhoods, cities, and mobility modes. Second, the stories describe place interactions that vary in experiential complexity – for example, the definitive closing of the SoHo supermarket in contrast to the on-going situation of rising tides in Fort Lauderdale. Third, some stories involve people-people interactions in place, and others involve people–environment interactions – for example, the bus passenger striking the assailant and Portland residents coping with snow. Fourth, the stories point to place interactions of varying duration – the vehicle-hailing customers momentarily misidentifying their ride versus the four Rome restaurants regularly serving dinners to the homeless. Fifth, the stories involve specific real-world interactions that cannot be readily envisioned through the three broad place impulses of environmental ensemble, people-in-place, and common presence. If these three impulses are not readily locatable in concrete examples of place interactions, is there not an interpretive problem?

I broach this question shortly, but the broader point indicated by these six stories is that a phenomenology of place interactions is a complex affair that I can only begin to delineate here. In what follows, I discuss four central claims:

- Triads of place interaction incorporate a range of experiential possibilities; here, I describe a threefold typology: *typical* versus *atypical* interactions; *unself-conscious* versus *self-conscious* interactions; and *people–environment* interactions versus *people–people* interactions.
- Specific place interactions must be envisioned in terms of the *specific set* of triadic impulses at work in the specific action or situation; the three impulses of environmental ensemble, people-in-place, and common presence depict the workings of places broadly, but specific place happenings and events involve more focused triads and impulses.
- Individual interaction triads may be part of a longer triad chain whereby more simple place actions and events coalesce into more complex place actions and events.
- Many places incorporate a sophisticated nexus of smaller- and larger-scaled interaction triads, where "smaller- and larger-scaled" refers to both spatial extent and temporal duration.

Types of Place Interaction

Before I consider the question of how specific place interactions can be interpreted triadically, I discuss their typological range. Place interactions involve a wide spectrum of actions, situations and occasions that encompass both human and environmental aspects. Most broadly, these interactions can be conceptualized in terms of three related binaries: first, *typical* versus *atypical* interactions; second, *unself-conscious* versus *self-conscious* interactions; and, third, *people–environment* versus *people–people* interactions. The first binary relates to whether the mode of interaction is usual, regular, and expected, or unusual, infrequent, and unexpected. Regular, taken-for-granted interactions are the lived foundation of place, but less regular or one-of-a-kind events can enhance the attractiveness of a place (for example, a city's hosting a World's Fair) or unsettle and even destroy a place (for example, a city's devastation because of natural disaster or civil war).

In the newspaper stories above, one example of regular place interactions is the Robin Hood restaurants' serving daily dinners to the homeless. In contrast, two articles depict one-of-a-kind or unusual events – the older man rescuing the bus driver or Portland residents coping with an unusual amount of snow. Yet again, two stories illustrate how taken-for-granted interactions with place shift because of external events – lower-income SoHo residents suddenly having no affordable grocery store because a supermarket has closed, or Fort Lauderdale residents, because of higher tides, learning to cope in new ways environmentally and place-wise.

A second interaction binary relates to the ways, attention-wise, that place users engage with place. Is the manner of engagement largely unself-conscious and related to the pre-reflective awareness of the lived body and body–subject described in Chapter 2? Or does the manner of engagement involve some mode of conscious awareness directing the interaction? In the phenomenological literature, there have been few efforts to delineate the range of modes whereby human beings engage, attention-wise, with their world, though in *A Geography of the Lifeworld*, I examined the multifaceted ways in which people make or do not make attentive contact with their surroundings (Seamon, 1979, pp. 97–128). I described several modes of awareness that involve some manner of conscious attention to the world at hand. *Watching*, for example, relates to any experience in which the person looks out attentively at some aspect of the world for an extended time. In *heightened encounter*, one engages with the world in a deeper, more intense way that typically incorporates a powerful emotional cast. In contrast, there is *basic contact*, which I associated with the pre-reflective perceptual facility of Merleau-Ponty's body–subject and "the mode of access through which the body meets the world and the generalized attitude of habit meets the particular environment at hand" (Seamon, 1979, p. 117). In short, place interactions incorporate a wide range of ways whereby human beings attend to the world and thereby interact with that world via awareness, which in turn may propel actions (for example, I notice that a woman in front of me in the café line leaves her wallet on the counter, and I speak up to tell her).

A third binary relates to whether people-of-place interact with each other or with some element of the environmental ensemble. Opening a door, appreciating a café flowerbox, or locating a storefront on an unfamiliar street are place interactions different experientially from enjoying a street musician's performance, hanging out with friends at a café, or apologizing to a person I just bumped into on the sidewalk. Both people–people and people–environment interactions involve a wide range of lived possibilities. For example, people–people interactions may incorporate co-presence (individuals physically present together in place), co-awareness (individuals physically present together in place and mutually aware), and co-encounter (individuals physically present together in place and interacting in some way, for example, waving, conversing, or partaking in common activities). In understanding places processually, both people–people and people–environment interactions are central to place actions, experiences, and meanings. I therefore discuss each in turn, drawing on typologies developed in sociology and urban planning.

Typologies of People–People Interaction

I know of no comprehensive phenomenology of place interactions. Some researchers have generated typologies of interpersonal and group-encounter interactions (Fisher, 1982; Gehl, 1987; Goffman, 1963, 1983; Lofland, 1985,

1998). One of the most thorough examples is urban planner Vikas Mehta's observational studies of three Boston-area neighborhoods (Mehta, 2013) via which he delineates "a typology of social behavior on the street" (Mehta, 2013, p. 98). As a starting point, Mehta identifies a wide range of actions, situations, and events that support opportunities for people–people interactions in place. He notes how basic bodily "postures" like standing, sitting, lying, walking, and jogging set the stage for more intentionally focused events such as eating, reading, smoking, and so forth – a spectrum of place experience that might involve "being left alone," on one hand, or "the close company of others," on the other hand (Mehta, 2013, p. 98). The result is a continuum of interpersonal interactions that ranges "from passive contacts, chance contacts, acquaintances and friends, to close friends" (Mehta, 2013, p. 98).

Based largely on behavioral observations of sidewalk users in his three Boston-area neighborhoods, Mehta identifies three broad modes of place interaction, the first of which he calls *passive sociability* because it involves situations where people enjoy the presence of others but seek no direct contact – for example, reading, using a laptop, eating alone, or people-watching. Mehta's second mode of place interaction is *fleeting sociability* – unexpected interpersonal encounters that sometimes lead to brief conversations, typically with other place users with whom one already has some degree of familiarity. Also relevant for fleeting sociability is *triangulation* (Whyte, 1980, pp. 94–101), whereby interpersonal interactions happen because some thing or event in place prompts strangers to speak to each other – for example, commenting on an unusual street sculpture or discussing the talent of an itinerant sidewalk musician. Mehta's third mode of place interaction is *enduring sociability*, whereby place interactions incorporate an intentional effort to connect with familiar others, whether neighbors, relatives, or friends co-present in the place.

I discuss Mehta's typology of people–place interactions because it is grounded in empirical evidence from three real-world places and because it offers one model for the kinds of place experiences and situations that a phenomenology of people–people interactions might include. Another important guide is the typology of public-place conduct developed by sociologist Lynn Lofland (1998). Her work on the "social life of the public realm" is noteworthy phenomenologically because she identifies lifeworld understandings for strangers' being co-present and behaving normatively in public places (Lofland, 1998, p. xviii). *Cooperative motility*, for example, relates to a taken-for-granted way of moving whereby people traverse space without incident – for example, pedestrians crossing a busy intersection without colliding (Lofland, 1998, p. 29). *Civil inattention* involves situations of co-presence but minimal co-awareness – "co-presence without commingling, awareness without engrossment, courtesy without conversation" (Lofland, 1998, p. 30). Lofland associates civil inattention with "ritual regard" whereby one person openly acknowledges another person visually but then, out of social politeness, withdraws attention so as to make it clear that the other person is not a focus of curiosity or special interest. Lofland also identifies *restrained helpfulness*, whereby individuals, co-present in the same place, provide limited assistance, if asked ("Could you tell me the time?"), and *civility toward diversity*, whereby people of difference in public places are typically respectful and uphold evenhandedness, even for co-present individuals who may be seen to be "out of place" (e.g., the homeless person taking shelter in a pricy café).

Lofland's Typology of People–Place Interactions

In addition to providing a typology of people–people interactions, Lofland's work is significant because she delineates a typology of people–place interactions, which she says are intimately connected with people–people interactions but in ways not thoroughly understood. She writes:

> There is no question but that the connections that humans forge between themselves and places are somehow coupled to the connections they forge between themselves and other humans in those places . . . . But I want to emphasize the modifier *somehow* in the phrase "somehow coupled." We really don't know either the how or the extent or even the necessity of that coupling, so in the absence of such knowledge, it makes sense to try to understand the person-to-place connection in its own right and not simply to subsume it as a by-product of human-to-human involvements.
>
> *(Lofland, 1998, p. 65)*

In providing a "provisional formulation of person-to-place connections," Lofland discusses human interactions relating to three types of places that, in various ways, presuppose and sponsor place interactions but also play a role in place identity, since these modes of lived emplacement involve cognitive identification and emotional attachment. These three place types are:

- *Familiarized locales*, such as paths and spaces that individuals or groups use regularly and with which they "establish a familiar relationship" (Lofland, 1998, p. 66).
- *Hangouts and home territories*, which relate to a region of lived space and place to which an individual or group feels attachment and a sense of identity, even "ownership."
- *Memorialized locales*, which relate to places associated with some significant event that takes on the quality of "sacredness" and often become "lightning rods for feelings of 'community' and the expressions of conflict" (Lofland, 1998, p. 66) – for example, New York City's Stonewall National Monument, which marks events sparking the modern struggle for the civil rights of gay and lesbian Americans.

In terms of the six place triads, these place types are founded in triads of place interactions but also involve triads of place identity, whereby association, familiarity, and attachment to place contribute to an individual or group's sense of selfness. I say more about this dimension of place in the next chapter on place identity.

Deciphering Interaction Triads

Though I began this chapter by describing the place triad broadly in terms of the three encompassing place impulses of environmental ensemble, people-in-place, and common presence, specific place interactions are more precisely envisioned in terms of a *specific set* of impulses at work in the specific action or event.[3] For example, my colliding with another pedestrian on the sidewalk can be pictured as the interaction triad of my oblivious bodily self (*1*), unaware of another bodily self (*2*), bumping into (*3*) that other bodily self. The gerund-describing action here is "colliding." Similarly, the older man's attacking the bus driver's assailant can be pictured triadically as the older man's concern for another human being (*1*), triggered by the assailant's attack on the bus driver (*2*), provoking him to strike the assailant (*3*). The gerund-describing action here is "intervening and protecting."

In picturing the triad of place interaction, one might envision any action as a situation in which the third impulse is the outcome of the encounter between the first and second impulses. For a more accurate picturing, however, one must bracket this cause-and-effect interpretation and envision the action (e.g., "intervening and protecting") as an "event-ing" or "an action-as-it-is-happening-via-the-blending-of-the-three-impulses." One might say that the action is "timeless-in-itself" but happening in time. This phrasing may sound strange, but it is one example of Bortoft's "*belonging* together" in which the three impulses, conjoining in action and inseparable processually, sustain a happening that is outside time yet unfolding in time.[4]

Deciphering the specific impulses generating a specific place interaction requires this synergistic way of envisioning whereby the action is pictured as a single dynamic process rather than as three distinct impulses. One works to picture the specific interaction *as an interaction* (e.g., "colliding," "intervening and protecting," "talking on the street," "washing windows," "driving to the drugstore") without working through precisely the three impulses by which the specific interaction is impelled. Typically, what is most useful in terms of research and practice is recognizing and inventorying the major types of interaction that mark a specific place. In some situations, locating specific impulses that trigger the specific interaction can offer insights otherwise unavailable but, more often, the useful effort is identifying and describing the *particular interactions and their range*, remembering that each involves some triadic set of impulses. At the same time, I emphasize that the three broad place impulses of environmental ensemble, people-in-place, and common presence are the underlying girders of *place as place*, but they are most useful in thinking about a place as it is a *place whole* – in other words, thinking through and identifying the general features and qualities that contribute to the uniqueness of the specific place.

Take, for example, a weekly outdoor market in Varberg, Sweden (Seamon and Nordin, 1980). Most broadly, this place can be pictured in terms of regular interactions like selling, buying, meeting friends, schmoozing, "hanging out," and "having an enjoyable time." There are also less regular or unexpected interactions triggered by less regular participants, such as itinerant "sidewalk" performers or regional vendors who sell at the market only a few times a year. Whether regular or irregular, each of these interactions might be described in terms of a specific interaction triad, but the market *as a place* can be envisioned broadly through a particular environmental ensemble (an open cobblestone space in the center of town that has served as market location for some 400 years); particular people-in-place (sellers, buyers, and visitors, some who are regular, others who are one-time or infrequent); and a particular common presence (a compact spatial togetherness of vendor booths, pathways, sitting places, and users, collectively contributing to the uniqueness of Varberg market as a place). These three impulses conjoin, via the interaction triad, to activate the typical happenings and actions of the Varberg market, just as they conjoin, in other combinations, to express the five other place triads at work in the market.

In relation to how a place might be made more vibrant and whole, the starting point is usually a broad picture of that place's interactions, how they relate to the other five place processes, and how their triadic dynamic might be strengthened via design, planning, policy, and advocacy. This matter is discussed more fully in Chapters 13 and 14, which deal with the place processes of intensification and creation.

Interaction Triads as Chains

Much of the time, specific place events incorporate not one triad but a chain of triads whereby a specific situation unfolds via a series of progressive actions (as was illustrated in Chapter 7 by Bennett's triadic interpretation of his becoming cold and getting up to stoke the fire). My obliviousness to the other sidewalk user with whom I collide, for example, is the result of a preceding triad: my wish to text a friend (*1*), provided for by my cell phone (*2*), leading to my attention given over to texting (*3*) rather than paying heed to the movements of others on the sidewalk. In relation to the older man's attacking the bus driver's assailant, one can picture a much longer chain of interaction triads that ground the progression of events, both before and after the attack:

- The older man riding this bus at this time;
- This bus driver being on duty at this time to drive this route;
- The assailant choosing this bus and this bus driver to attack.
- The bus driver being able to stop the bus and escape the assailant's attack;

- The police arriving, arresting the assailant, and delivering the bus driver to the hospital;
- The older man's continuing on his way after intervening;
- The Kansas City Transit Authority attempting to contact the older man to thank him for his courageous intervention (*KCS*, January 30, 2016, p. 4A).

To illustrate the complexity in identifying and thinking through the specific impulses involved in specific place interactions, I summarize an unusual event in which a New Yorker named Rick locks himself out of his West Village apartment (Alexander, 1997, p. 115). After he waits in the lobby for two hours, his upstairs neighbor Mary Anne comes home. She does not have keys to Rick's apartment, but she does have keys to the apartment of her next-door neighbor Carol, who she knows has keys to Lydia's apartment. Rick has given Lydia keys to his apartment, so Mary Anne uses her keys to access Carol's apartment where she locates a set of keys marked "Lydia." Then Mary Anne and Rick go to Lydia's apartment where Rick finds the keys to his apartment. Shortly after, he is home.

As a place event, we might describe Rick's experience as "the value of trusting one's neighbors as illustrated by being 'locked out.'" Obviously, this event incorporates an interconnected series of interactions, each of which can be worked through in terms of specific interaction triads. For example, Rick's need to enter his apartment (*1*) is stymied by no keys (*2*), forcing him to wait in the lobby (*3*). In turn, Rick (*1*) calls to Mary Anne (*2*) as she returns home, and they work out a way (*3*) to get Rick into his apartment. This plan generates a progression of additional interactions that eventually provide Rick with a set of spare keys. Though one limited event in a single apartment house, this experience is relatively complex as a chain of interactions that coalesce into the more comprehensive place phenomenon of "neighborly trust and assistance." In this sense, a triadic understanding helps one picture the difficult-to-decipher dynamism of place as that dynamism unfolds over time. This possibility is probed in Chapter 15, which considers temporal relationships among the six place processes.

Interaction Triads as Nexus

If place interactions involve chains, they also involve nexuses whereby smaller-scaled triads nest in larger-scaled triads that contribute to the particularity of place and to its specific synergy of environmental ensemble, people-in-place, and common presence. To clarify the nesting qualities of place interaction, I turn to eminent urbanist Jane Jacobs' *Death and Life of Great American Cities* (Jacobs, 1961), which argues that the primary engine of robust urban places is *diversity* – an intricate, close-grained mixture of uses, activities, and environmental elements that mutually support each other, spatially, socially, and economically. Jacobs contends that urban diversity sustains and is sustained by a dynamic place structure that she calls the *street ballet* – an exuberance of place diversity and sidewalk life supported by the regular, everyday comings and goings of many people carrying out their own ordinary needs, obligations, and activities (Seamon, 2012a, p. 142). Out of the independent actions and situations of individuals arises a more comprehensive synergistic structure of urban place with a distinctive ambience and rhythm. Using choreographic imagery, Jacobs (1961, pp. 50–51) describes how each weekday the stretch of Hudson Street where she lives is the scene of "an intricate sidewalk ballet." Shortly after 8 am, she puts out her garbage can, "surely a prosaic occupation, but I enjoy my part, my little clang" as junior high school students pass by on their way to class. As she sweeps her portion of sidewalk, she notes "the other rituals of the morning":

> Mr. Halpert unlocking the laundry's handcart from its mooring to a cellar door, Joe Cornacchia's son-in-law stacking out the empty crates from the delicatessen, the barber bringing out his sidewalk folding chair . . . . Now the primary children, heading for St. Luke's, dribble through to the west, and the children from P.S. 41, heading toward the east.
>
> (Jacobs, 1961, p. 51)

In Jacobs' engaging picture of urban place ballet, one recognizes the partially predictable and partially unpredictable exchanges among Hudson Street's residents, visitors, and passersby. In understanding Jacobs' street ballet triadically, one notes that each participant, in some way, interacts with Hudson Street as a place. In turn, these individual interactions coalesce in a larger-scaled nexus of place interactions sustaining the neighborhood's exuberance and strong sense of place. These interactions vary by participants, purposes, and degrees of regularity, but all contribute to a larger-scale interaction triad that marks the unique liveliness and place presence of Hudson Street. The neighborhood's three place impulses can be summarized as follows:

- Hudson Street's *environmental ensemble* (*2*): A complex mixture of environmental and place elements including a permeable street grid, a range in building types, and a diversity of activities and functions (e.g., dwellings, workplaces, shops, and eateries).
- Hudson Street's *people-in-place* (*1*): a wide range of individuals and groups living in, working in, or passing through the neighborhood; these users include both "insiders" (residents, local employers and employees, and other "regulars" associated with the place) and "outsiders" (passersby and one-time or infrequent visitors).
- Hudson Street's *common presence* (*3*): a unique quality of place ambience grounded in the "*belonging* together" of people-in-a-supportive-environment.

Integrating these three impulses in terms of the interaction triad (*1–3–2*), one can say that, as mediating impulse, the neighborhood's robust common presence

(*3*) sponsors a rich matrix of interactions among users (*1*) as they are present to Hudson Street's environmental ensemble (*2*). First of all, lively urban districts are rich, diverse fabrics of people-and-place *interactions* whereby residents, workers, visitors, and passersby intermingle spatially and environmentally. In turn, these many unpredictable interactions sustain and are sustained by a more comprehensive environmental whole with both effable and ineffable aspects – Hudson Street's common presence.

I began this examination of the six place triads with interaction because actions like moving, encountering, seeing, meeting, participating, and so forth ground the workings of many places. In the next chapter, I consider place identity, which helps explain how individuals and groups become attached to and identified with place.

Notes

1 I use the word "broadly" because, as inferred by the place dyad of ordinariness-extra-ordinariness discussed in Chapter 6, these interactions can also be atypical, unexpected, and out-of-the-ordinary. A large portion of place interactions, however, are taken-for-granted, habitual, and more or less regular.

2 Throughout the rest of this book, I use the designations *1, 2*, and *3* (rather than *PP, EE*, and *CP*) to designate the specific triad because the numbers help one to keep in mind that the first impulse is affirming; the second, receptive; and the third, reconciling.

3 As following chapters demonstrate, this point also applies to the five other place triads of identity, release, realization, creation, and intensification.

4 I am grateful to Stephen Wood, who, in reading an early draft of this chapter, suggested a fuller clarification of how the interaction triad is more than a simple cause-and-effect model. I draw on his phrasing of an action that is both "timeless" yet in time. See Wood's use of the six place triads to examine the experience of "making a new home" (Wood, 2016a, 2016b).

10

THE TRIAD OF PLACE IDENTITY (*2–3–1* OR *EE–CP–PP*)

If the interaction triad involves the typical events and situations constituting a specific place, the identity triad involves ways that place becomes an extended, taken-for-granted part of how an individual or group suppose themselves to be personally and communally. Even in our hypermodern world, we still usually say where we are from when we introduce ourselves in new situations. We may not be satisfied with or attached to that place of residence, but others automatically assume that this place is in some way indicative of who we are. Via actions of identification, we become – fully or partially – the place where we live. For some people, this place is the only one they know. They identify with it their entire lives and accept it as *their* world and *the* world, no questions asked. Other individuals, particularly in today's mobile world, shift places regularly and may feel that the environmental and place aspects of their lives have little bearing on who they are or what their world is. If lived emplacement is an integral constituent of human life, however, a central question is what continuous mobility means, both for the individuals involved and for the places that endure a steady turnover of people.

In this chapter, I introduce place identity broadly and then describe three situations that illustrate varying degrees by which people identify or do not identify with place. The triad of place identity is somewhat different from the triad of place interaction in that the actions facilitating place identity involve repetitive involvements with one's environment whereby that environment becomes a place of positive (or negative) feelings and meanings mostly engrained in the natural attitude. For most people, identification with the place into which they are born is automatically assured via the normative structure of homeworld. Individuals not satisfied with that homeworld may move themselves elsewhere to a lived emplacement more in tune with who they are or who they wish to be.

Many individuals and groups, however, remain bound to the taken-for-grantedness of their homeworlds, whether those homeworlds are supportive or destructive of human wellbeing.

The Triad of Place Identity

As a triad, place identity is expressed as *2–3–1* (*EE–CP–PP*), whereby common presence, as reconciling impulse, facilitates a bonding between the receptive impulse of environmental ensemble and the affirmative impulse of people-in-place. As with place interaction, place identity can be pictured in terms of gerunds, but these gerunds do not so much involve place happenings (e.g., "schmoozing," "watching," "strolling") as progressive immersion and entwinement with place (e.g., "getting to feel a part of," "becoming more attached to," "becoming more identified with this place as *my place*"). For those individuals and groups who never encounter experiences beyond their original homeworlds, place identity is typically intrinsic in the sense that the contingencies of birth, family, history, and geography are normally unquestioned but remarkably powerful and pervasive. Entwined in their homeworlds, these individuals and groups may never or only rarely consider that their lifeworld and place could be otherwise.

Place identity and place interaction are reciprocal processes in the sense that, through place interaction, participants actively engage with place and appropriate it as their own. They come to feel a part of place and associate their personal and group identity with the identity of that place. The result is a virtuous circle whereby place interactions and place identity activate and are activated by firsthand engagement and emotional bonds that are as much pre-reflective as reflective. Place identity as a process undermines place when individuals and groups become isolated from the place of which they are part. People associated with the place become less willing to take up that place as an integral aspect of their lifeworld. They no longer associate themselves with that place. They mistrust or feel threatened by other people or events of the place and may consider moving elsewhere to a safer or more accepting situation. If offensive action is not possible, the person or group may withdraw defensively into minimal interaction with and exposure to the place. Alternately, out of anger or frustration, the person or group may actively work to undermine or harm the place in some way, thereby contributing to a vicious circle of devolving interaction and identity.

As I did with place interaction, I begin by summarizing six newspaper articles that illustrate place identity in various ways. Arranged roughly from smaller to larger place scale, these stories indicate the manner and range of place identity.

- Long Island's beloved Sag Harbor Theatre has been destroyed by fire. A cultural landmark and regional symbol of Long Island's "East End," the theatre was unusual for its single large screen, the breadth of its programming, and a red neon sign intimately associated with the town of Sag

Harbor. One prominent townsperson explained that "Everyone's in tremendous sadness over it. No one has driven by the cinema where it stood and not felt just a tremendous pain and pang of remorse" (*NYT*, December 19, 2016, pp. A18–A19).

- Housed in an 1856 New Hampshire farmhouse, Hope on Haven Hill is a home for expectant mothers who have used opioids. Alone without family support, these women might otherwise be incarcerated, in shelters, or homeless on the street. The aim of Hope on Haven Hill is to provide a safe, nurturing environment where women who are either pregnant or newly postpartum can live while receiving treatment and counseling for substance-use disorders. The hope is that a stable, protective environment will encourage the women to maintain their sobriety (*NYT*, December 12, 2016, pp. A10, A13).

- Once known as a street with some 700 antique dealers, London's Portobello Road is now largely an open market of shops and stalls mostly selling mass-produced souvenirs to non-British tourists. Estimates indicate that some 5.5 million visitors came to Portobello Road in 2016, seeking out the "market experience." The remaining proprietors of authentic antique shops have mixed feelings about the changes in the character of Portobello Road. A dealer of rare books explained that "There's an atmosphere here," and she was happy to cater to the tourists who pass by her bookstall. Another dealer, however, explained that many of his colleagues "are annoyed they're surrounded by fakes." (*NYT*, January 17, 2017, p. C12).

- In a pottery district in southern China's river town of Jingdezhen, young ceramicists are reviving a traditional artisan culture that once produced China's most prized porcelain. The Pottery Workshop, an education center that opened in 2005, has become a magnet for young potters and critical in rejuvenating Jingdezhen's ceramics industry. One young potter explained, "I like the atmosphere here very much. A lot of people with dreams come here. There is a variety of teachers, and they teach all kinds of skills and ideas" (*NYT*, February 1, 2017, p. A9).

- Lafayette, Louisiana, recently held its thirtieth-annual *International de Louisiane*, a five-day music festival featuring the region's Creole and Cajun culture. Marked by the unique musical sounds of accordion and washboard, the zydeco bands attracted some 300,000 listeners and dancers. The festival was originally envisioned as part of an effort to revitalize Lafayette's moribund downtown, which today is vibrant year-round with restaurants, clubs, art galleries, and shops, including an accordion store that makes and sells the special button-style accordions favored by zydeco and Cajun bands. "You just can't find this kind of stuff anywhere else," said one area native who expressed how much he loved the Creole and Cajun culture (*NYT*, April 2, 2017, Travel section, p. 1, p. 5).

- A New England technology center known as the Manchester Millyard is emerging in a district of nineteenth-century brick mill buildings lining the

Merrimack River in the New Hampshire city of Manchester, once a major American textile center. The rehabilitated mill buildings originally housed mechanical looms but are now occupied by some thirty tech companies as well as professional offices and restaurants. One factory tenant, co-founder of a mail-order pharmacy, explains that he has no regrets in locating his start up at the Millyard in 2013; he now has customers in forty-nine states and has expanded his operation to nearly an entire factory floor (*NYT*, March 15, 2017, p. B7).

Several aspects of place identity are illustrated by these news stories. On one hand, two entries describe an identity with place that extends back in time and has become historical – the local fondness for the incinerated Sag Hill Theatre, or newcomers' awareness of Jingdezhen's traditional associations with Chinese ceramics and porcelain. On the other hand, two stories point to newly founded places that may or may not over time be appropriated into a sense of self – the home for expectant mothers and the high-tech Manchester Millyard. Yet again, some stories point to how place identity changes over time, sometimes strengthening (the Louisiana music festival's triggering Lafayette's downtown regeneration) or sometimes weakening (the replacement of Portobello Road's antique shops with souvenir stalls).

As a descriptive means to illustrate the range in intensity of place identity, I draw on three real-world examples, one from an account of an actual person's life, the other two from novels by Doris Lessing and Penelope Lively. The first two situations present individuals who are profoundly identified with their places, to such an extent that they have no wish or will to make those places different, even though, to a sympathetic outsider, these places appear to disrupt or hinder everyday life. The third account describes an individual who moves to a new place with the intent to make that place her home. Ultimately, her efforts are unsuccessful, but her story is important because it illustrates how the triad of place identity unfolds over time, even if ultimately one's efforts at place making fail.

Intense Identification with a House

My first example of place identity is interior designer Jane Barry's personal account of her father's intense attachment to the house he had lived in for sixty-five years (Barry, 2012).[1] In spite of failing health, he insisted that he die at home. For part of the last year of his life, Barry lived with him and attempted to improve his living situation via physical changes like stair handrails, high-contrast step edging, and relocating food items to more convenient locations. Because her father was completely identified with the house-as-his-place, he mostly ignored Barry's modifications and continued to conduct daily actions and tasks as he had before, even though these efforts were now often frustrating or unsuccessful.

Barry offers a heartrending portrait of how his daily life "was deeply rooted in his home . . . . The meaning of [this] place played a strong role in his behaviors and the choices he made, and in his resistance to making changes in his environment" (Barry, 2012, p. 4).

Barry's picture of her father's lifeworld demonstrates a situation of extreme place identification that had been powerfully established in the six decades that he and his family have lived in the house. In her account, Barry (2012, p. 7) highlights what daily life was like as she was growing up. She describes a series of household routines that her father would carry out unstintingly:

> His typical day went like this. The family would awake around 6:45 am, and my parents would go into the kitchen. My mother would light the oven . . . . My dad started a fire in the stove firebox to burn mail, milk cartons, and other discards. He would use the front bathroom getting ready for work while my mother made breakfast. We then went on our ways to work and school. My dad walked to work, only about three blocks away . . . . My dad's spaces [in the house] were the office, the basement, and the detached garage on the north side of the house . . . . There was frequently something that needed fixing: window screens replaced, awnings put up or taken down, pilot lights turned off or on, and so forth. My dad did these things himself, using tools and supplies he kept in the basement or garage. He also made sure cupboards and drawers were stocked . . . . In the basement, he stored bulk sugar, flour, and rice in large jars. From this stock as needed, he would refill smaller jars in the kitchen cupboards.

Here, one recognizes a series of required household tasks and duties that, once mastered via repetition and routine, became habitual and conferred on Barry's father a sense of home identity and attachment. Through tending, being responsible for, and living in, he forged a deep lived relationship with his home, which became an integral part of who he was. One could fairly say that *he was his house*. Even as he aged and became less able to cope with everyday actions and needs, he refused to make changes that might make daily life easier. When, for example, Barry moved canned goods from the cellar to a kitchen cupboard upstairs, he continued to trek downstairs to get similar canned goods still stored there, even though it would be physically easier for him to retrieve equivalent items from the new kitchen storage that Barry had provided. From her objective, professional perspective of interior designer, reconfiguring the home environment would improve her father's situation. But because of his extreme identification with place – what Barry at first assumed to be "stubbornness" – he was unable to understand or to accept these modifications: "He refused to make changes. It seems that he couldn't (or wouldn't) imagine what helpful changes might be possible" (Barry, 2012, p. 5).

Intense Identification with Home

A second example of profound place identity is British-African novelist Doris Lessing's riveting portrayal of character Maudie Fowler, an indigent, ninety-year-old Londoner who faces a life of limitations imposed by circumstances, happenstance, and age (Lessing, 1984).[2] Lessing presents Maudie's situation through the eyes of character Janna Somers, a fashionable, middle-aged magazine editor who befriends Maudie after they meet accidentally waiting in line at a local pharmacy. Place-wise, Maudie's lifeworld is limited in that it includes only her apartment, the street where she lives, and a corner grocery store run by an Indian man with whom she often quarrels because she feels he overcharges. The physical center of her lifeworld is the three-room apartment that Maudie has occupied for over forty years, though her declining health has entirely interfered with efforts to keep the space clean and tidy: "I have never," says Somers of her first impression, "seen anything like it outside of condemned houses . . . . The whole place smelled, it smelled awful . . . . It was all so dirty and dingy and grim and awful" (Lessing, 1984, p. 14).

Over time, however, Somers realizes that Maudie's squalid apartment is an integral part of her identity as a person. Somers' recognizing this fact is crucial to Maudie because it means that, if authorities demand that she move to housing they consider better, Somers will support Maudie's wish to stay in her own apartment. Early on in their friendship, Somers naturally assumes that Maudie would gladly accept new housing with modern conveniences. Once she becomes Maudie's closest friend, however, she understands that the apartment is an integral part of Maudie's lifeworld, which would probably collapse if Maudie were housed elsewhere. As she explains to Somers, "'I've never not paid [the rent], not once. Though I've gone without food. No, I learned that early. With your own place you've got everything. Without it, you're a dog. You are nothing. Have you got your own place?' – and when I said yes, she said, nodding fiercely, angrily, 'That's right, and you hold onto it, then nothing can touch you'" (Lessing, 1984, pp. 18–19).

If Maudie's wellbeing were defined in terms of official social and design criteria, then her moving to better housing would be the appropriate action for which to advocate. In terms of place identity, however, Maudie, like Barry's father, is existentially bound to her dwelling; to propose that she move elsewhere would severely unsettle her sense of self. Somers comes to recognize that more satisfactory material conditions are in the end irrelevant to Maudie, for whom physical difficulty and discomfort have long been taken for granted: "By any current housing standard, [her apartment] should be condemned. By any human standard, she should stay where she is" (Lessing, 1984, pp. 103). Somers realizes that Maudie's identity is inseparable from her apartment and that any improvement in her living situation cannot be had by physical intervention alone:

I've given up even thinking that she ought to agree to be "rehoused"; I said it just once, and it took her three days to stop seeing me as an enemy . . . . I *am* housed, says she, cough, cough, cough from having to go out at the back all weathers into the freezing lavatory, from standing to wash in the unheated kitchen. But why do I say that? Women of ninety who live in luxury cough and are frail.

(Lessing, 1984, p. 86)

The situations of Maudie and Barry's father both demonstrate the potential intensity of place identity. Both individuals define themselves in terms of house or apartment, which are an integral part of their self-worth and personal identity. "I *am* housed," Maudie declares, zeroing in on the nub of place identity. Even though Mr. Barry's house and Maudie's apartment both objectively have their faults as sustaining lived environments, one realizes that these places are taken-for-granted centers of lifeworlds better not questioned or changed. Neither Barry's account nor Lessing's narrative gives a detailed picture of the many everyday repetitions and routines that would have contributed to an intensifying place identity that eventually solders these two individuals to their place. The more important point is that over time, firsthand interactions with place facilitate an impassioned sense of identity with that place. Human being becomes human being in place.

Unsuccessful Place Identity

I next consider a situation in which a person tries but fails at place identity. I draw on British writer Penelope Lively's *Spiderweb*, a 1998 novel that offers a sobering, present-day portrait of one newcomer's effort to become at home in England's West Country (Lively, 1998). The novel is set mostly in Somerset, a bucolic region that, though once perhaps an integrated lifeworld grounded in history and place, has become a diverse mix of contrasting lifeworlds more or less different because of time, happenstance, and varying life paths – in short, "people who have always been there and people who come there fortuitously" (Lively, 1998, pp. 1–2). Lively recounts the efforts of recently retired social anthropologist Stella Brentwood to make a home for herself by purchasing and settling in a cottage near a small, unexceptional Somerset village that Lively names Kingston Florey.[3]

From the perspective of place identity, Stella's story is revealing because she tries to become a lived part of Somerset rather than remain the detached observer she has been her entire professional life, studying lineage and kinship in far-flung places like Egypt and Malta. How, through commitment, involvement, and affection, can she draw this chosen place inside herself so that she is *a part of* the place rather than *apart* as she has always been as a professional anthropologist? Early in the novel, she realizes that, until her present effort to make a home, she has never felt a sense of lived connection to the communities and places she studied, which are little more than "worlds out there, richly stocked and inviting observation" (Lively, 1998, p. 15). She has never really gathered herself up into place and actually *lived* there: "Her professional life has been that of a voyeur, her interest in community has been clinical. She has wanted to know how and why people get along with each other, or fail to do so, rather than sample the arrangement herself" (Lively, 1998, p. 75).

In seeking finally to *enter life* rather than just to observe it, Stella sets herself to engage her retirement place and to embrace its lifeworld: "This is where she would now live, not just for weeks or months but for the foreseeable future. For years" (Lively, 1998, p. 14). She takes long walks, studies maps, drives through the countryside, reads local newspapers, and visits old buildings and places of earlier historical times. She converses with locals, shops in the small village grocery, tries to know her neighbors, and presents a talk to the local historical society. All these actions and efforts involve a chain of place interactions whereby she might become a part of this place and thereby incorporate Somerset and Kingston Florey into her sense of identity. Most broadly, the triad of place identity (*2–3–1*) at work here can be pictured as three impulses: *In-front-of-this-place-that-is-not-me* (*2*), *I-engage-with-this-place* (*1*) *to-engender-in-me-a-sense-of-feeling-part-of-this-place* (*3*). The order of unfolding here is incorrect in the sense that the third impulse arises out of the blending of the first and second impulses and should therefore be pictured as between them. In English, however, there is no convenient way grammatically to express this "between," other than placing the result – a progressively intensive place identity – last. Gerund-wise, the reconciling impulse might be described as "intensifying one's becoming in place" or "reinforcing one's identity with place through efforts at engaging with place."

How one is able or unable to actualize a lasting place identity is a major theme in *Spiderweb*. On one hand, Stella realizes that a genuine identity with place requires putting oneself forward in determined engagement: "Now was the time to prove herself. Even if she could not hope to melt into the ancient levels of this place . . . , there were still slots into which she could fit in the wider context. Join things, she told herself sternly . . . . Participate" (Lively, 1998, p. 76). On the other hand, she faces an unyielding disinterest in engaging this place: "She was comfortable enough with these surroundings, but still not certain how she had gotten here or why. In the past there had been good reason to be wherever she found herself. Now, she was where she was simply because one had to be somewhere" (Lively, 1998, p. 133).

One notes in this description a dyadic tension between disinterest and affirmation: On one hand, Stella is unclear and uncertain as to why she chose Kingston Florey as a place to be: "she was where she was simply because one had to be somewhere." On the other hand, she realizes that if she is to become a part of this place, she must make efforts of commitment: "Participate," she declares. Ultimately, however, her wish to engage with Kingston Florey is not strong enough to accept and come to belong, with the result that Stella's efforts remain dyadic: She is torn between "Yes, I can accept this place" and "No, I cannot accept this place." The triad of place identity remains unactualized in that the third impulse (*engendering-in-me-a-sense-of-feeling-part-of-this-place*) is never brought to presence. She is unable to intertwine her lifeworld with the lifeworld of Somerset. She cannot shift from outsider to insider, never fits in, and eventually leaves.

I discuss the place situations of Barry's father, Maudie Fowler, and Stella Brentwood because they intimate the range of engagement that place identity engenders. On one hand, Barry's father and Maudie Fowler illustrate deep-rooted identification with place, to such a degree that they and their place are inseparable existentially. Literally, *they are their place.* On the other hand, Stella Brentwood has no place but seems to desire one, at least at first. Though she makes well-intended efforts to become part of Somerset and Kingston Florey, she is held back by disinterest, doubt, and inertia. The potential monad of person-in-place remains the bifurcated dyad of person-apart-from-place. Whether Stella eventually "finds her place," Lively does not tell us.

Place Interaction and Place Identity Together

As I mentioned earlier, there is a reciprocal relationship between place interaction and place identity. To provide a real-world example of this lived mutuality, I draw on sociologist Eric Klinenberg's *Heat Wave*, a study of why some 700 Chicagoans, most of them elderly or poor, died in a five-day heat wave in 1995 (Klinenberg, 2002).[4] Though he does not use the language of interaction and identity directly, Klinenberg offers a powerful example of how differences in place interaction relate to differences in place identity, which can be life-saving or life-threatening in times of crisis. Klinenberg's focus is two Chicago neighborhoods and how differences in their street life and people–place interactions "imperiled or protected residents during the extreme summer climate" (Klinenberg, 2002, p. 85). The two Chicago neighborhoods are North Lawndale, a predominantly African-American neighborhood with a 1995 heat-related death rate of 40 per 100,00 residents; and South Lawndale (colloquially known as Little Village), a predominantly Latino neighborhood with a much lower heat-related death rate of less than 4 per 100,000 residents (Klineberg, 2002, p. 87). Even though these two neighborhoods are geographically adjacent and include similar proportions of seniors living in poverty and seniors living alone (the two groups the U.S. Centers for Disease Control and Prevention had earlier determined as most vulnerable in the heat wave), their dramatically different heat-wave mortality rates provoke Klinenberg to wonder whether this difference in deaths might at least be partly related to differences in the two neighborhoods as places (Klinenberg, 2002, pp. 21–22).

As he becomes more familiar with the two neighborhoods, Klinenberg realizes that they are vastly different in terms of environmental ensemble and people–people and people–place interactions. North Lawndale is a neighborhood of derelict buildings, shuttered stores, second-tier fast-food eateries, abandoned lots, deteriorating housing stock, few employment opportunities, and much crime. One result is that Lawndale residents have few neighborhood sites as local destinations or places of employment. As North Lawndale's economy declined, residents able to do so forsook the area, leaving behind empty houses as well as neighbors who had not the will or resources to leave. These remaining residents often withdrew inwardly from North Lawndale by finding social support beyond the neighborhood or isolating themselves. A neighborhood that earlier had supported strong place identity became a place with which these alienated residents no longer identified or belonged.

Klinenberg determines that, during the heat wave, it was largely the place-alienated individuals who died. They had neither the social contacts to assist them nor the courage to seek help in a threatening neighborhood offering few public or commercial establishments where they might escape the heat. There was little collective life that might have protected these isolated individuals, most of whom were older persons living alone "with limited social contacts and weak support networks during normal times" (Klinenberg, 2002, p. 41). Klinenberg (2002, p. 21) points to a collapse of place interaction and identity when he writes that "The heat wave puts into focus the ways that connections made or missed, visible or unrecognized, can determine the fate of the city and its residents."

In contrast, aspects of Little Village's environmental ensemble and people-in-place worked to facilitate positive place interactions and place identity. Though Little Village is just one street south of North Lawndale, its environmental ensemble and people-in-place are much different. Even though it has proportions of poor elderly and elderly living alone similar to North Lawndale's, Little Village incorporates lively retail, bustling sidewalks, and many more intact dwellings, all of which are occupied. Whereas there is little neighborhood activity in North Lawndale, Little Village incorporates "public life and informal social support for residents" (Klinenberg, 2002, p. 109). During the heat wave, this robust place activity was particularly important for older residents living alone because it drew them out of their dwellings into the streets and public places where they made the social contact that isolated individuals in North Lawndale were much less able to establish. In addition, the activity of nearby streets provided shops, eateries, and other places where these individuals could find respite from the heat. Most vulnerable were older white residents remaining in the neighborhood after it had become mostly Latino. For the most part, however, they too were protected. Klinenberg concludes that "the robust public life of the region draws all but the most infirm residents out of their homes, promoting social interaction, network ties, and healthy behavior" (Klinenberg, 2002, p. 110).

In discussing the two neighborhoods, Klinenberg considers social and cultural differences and the contrasting significance of more formal social and cultural institutions, including churches and block clubs. But most of the explanation for the two neighborhoods' dramatically different heat-wave death rates he assigns to the neighborhoods' contrasting place qualities. Most important are Little Village's lively place interactions:

> Many of the [Little Village] elderly I interviewed explained that during the heat wave they sought relief in the air-conditioned stores on Twenty-sixth Street [the neighborhood's commercial core], just as they do on ordinary summer days. Not only did elderly residents in Little Village have less to fear on the sidewalks and streets than did their neighbors in North Lawndale; living in a region with busy commercial traffic and active streets, they also had more incentive to go outdoors and walk to places where they could get relief. The rich commercial resources and a flourishing sidewalk culture animated public areas throughout the neighborhood; and there were always people, including seniors with their pushcarts full of groceries and small bags of goods, in the streets when I did my fieldwork. . . . [T]he sidewalks are primary conduits for social contact and control. The relative security of these public areas makes it easier for residents of Little Village – even the older whites – to engage with their neighbors and participate in community events.
>
> (Klinenberg, 2002, pp. 116–117)

I draw on Klinenberg's research because it demonstrates, in both supportive and undermining ways, the reciprocal relationship between place interaction and place identity. Little Village was a place of lively streets, much commercial activity, residential concentration, and a relatively low crime rate. These supportive features of place contributed to positive place interaction and supportive place identity, especially important for older people, who were more likely to leave home when nearby amenities were safely available. In contrast, North Lawndale was a neighborhood of violent crime, devolving commerce, abandoned buildings, empty streets, and lower density, all of which undermined the viability of public life, setting the stage for fearful older people who rarely left their dwellings. During the heat wave, these dramatically contrasting place identities undermined or sustained "the possibilities for social contact that helped vulnerable Chicagoans survive" (Klinenberg, 2002, p. 91).

An Interdependence of Interaction and Identity

I end this chapter by linking Klinenberg's findings with the urban understanding of Jane Jacobs, who argues that robust urban places are, first of all, a diverse fabric of people and place *interactions* concentrated in the street ballet. She emphasizes, however, that this rich dynamic of place interactions propels and is propelled by a strong sense of place *identity*, which motivates participants to take responsibility and care for their urban place. These people profess an intense attachment to their street neighborhood. It is a big part of their life. They seem to think that their neighborhood is unique and irreplaceable in all the world and remarkably valuable in spite of its shortcomings. In this they are correct, for the multitude of relationships and public characters that make up an animated city street neighborhood are always unique, intricate and have the value of the unreproducible original.

(Jacobs, 1961, p. 279)

Though she does not use the language of place interaction and identity, one recognizes in Jacobs' understanding of the city that the two place processes are interdependent, with a lively street life facilitating place identification, which in turn enriches place interaction. Klinenberg's contrasting neighborhoods of North Lawndale and Little Village are an insightful example of this interdependent relationship. Referring to Jacobs, Klinenberg (2002, p. 94) describes how "commercial institutions draw residents and passersby out into the sidewalks and streets, inviting foot traffic and promoting social interaction among consumers, merchants, and people who simply enjoy participating in or observing public life." When, however, neighborhoods like North Lawndale lose "their animating institutions, they break down, becoming instead the sources of violence, insecurity, and fear" (Klinenberg, 2002, p. 95). The contrasting place dynamics of these two neighborhoods offer a penetrating illustration of how place interaction and place identity can work to strengthen or undermine place.

If interaction and identity mark the core of place and lived emplacement, they are complemented by the four other triads of place – place release, place realization, place creation, and place intensification. Chapter 11 considers place release, which involves environmental serendipity and happenstance.

Notes

1 I also discuss Barry's father in Seamon, 2018d, forthcoming.
2 I discuss Lessing's novel in greater detail in Seamon, 1993.
3 I discuss Stella's situation more fully in Seamon, 2018b, forthcoming.
4 This discussion of Klinenberg's research is largely drawn from Seamon, 2013b, pp. 156–160.

11

THE TRIAD OF PLACE RELEASE (*3–2–1* OR *CP–EE–PP*)

This chapter discusses the triad of *place release*, and the following chapter discusses the triad of *place realization*. I pair these two triads because, for both, the reconciling impulse of common presence *initiates* place actions, though in contrasting ways. On one hand, the triad of place release (*3–2–1*) can be described as common presence (*3*), working through environmental ensemble (*2*), engendering, for people-in-place, some non-expected, surprising action or event (*1*). On the other hand, the triad of place realization (*3–1–2*) can be described as common presence (*3*), working through people-in-place (*1*) engendering, in the environmental ensemble, a distinctive effable and ineffable order (*2*).

Place release and place realization have received little conceptual or applied attention in place research, partly because they point toward aspects of place that are difficult to identify, define, and verify.[1] In this regard, common presence is useful because it offers a means to speak of spatial togetherness as an independent impulse incorporating both tangible and intangible qualities. As I explained in Chapter 8, this spatial togetherness, as Bennett understands it, is the signature feature of common presence because it knits together the entities of any "limited region of space" into a "recognizable quality shared by all entities in the region" (Bennett, 1961, p. 47). In this chapter and the following, I argue that, on one hand, common presence sponsors, via place release, environmental serendipity; on the other hand, common presence sponsors, via place realization, environmental order.

The most difficult and puzzling aspect of place release and place realization is the reconciling impulse's placement in the two triads' initiating position. What does it mean that common presence *initiates* these two triads? What does common presence impel in these two triads? How is it to be identified and described as an initiating quality? Why, on one hand, does it sustain environmental serendipity and, on the other hand, environmental order? These questions have no easy answers, other than Bennett's claim that both freedom and order are integral, non-contingent constituents of the world as we human beings know and experience it (Bennett, 1961, pp. 120–128).

Proceeding phenomenologically, I am largely concerned with explicating and illustrating the *lived aspects* of release and realization as they contribute to the events and happenings of real-world places. How and from where the third impulse arises points to existential and metaphysical questions beyond the range of this descriptive examination. In my own place experiences, I have validated the actions of place release and place realization and recognize them as legitimate phenomena. I would ask readers to look for examples in their own place experiences, giving directed attention to the manner and range of type and intensity. As I have emphasized with all the triads, one cannot understand these six processes by thinking alone. One must look toward direct experience and find firsthand, real-world examples in one's everyday life. In this way, one understands the six triads experientially and existentially rather than intellectually and secondhand.

The Triad of Place Release

Place release involves an environmental serendipity of unexpected encounters and events.[2] In everyday language, these moments of happenstance are described by such words and phrases as "surprising," "coincidental," "accidental," "seemingly random," or "without clear cause." English incorporates a good number of colloquial expressions for these serendipitous events, including "out of the blue," "from left field," "without warning," "all of a sudden," "not bargained for," and "not in the cards." Proceeding phenomenologically, I am largely concerned with explicating some of the lived features of these unusual, unexpected moments.[3]

Real-world examples of place release are meeting an old friend accidently on the sidewalk; enjoying the extemporaneous performance of an itinerant street musician; or becoming friendly with, dating, and eventually marrying the checkout clerk who just happened to take your take-out lunch order each workday. As described in Chapter 8, my Istanbul experience of suddenly "seeing" place triadically is one illustrative instance of place release: the unique life and ambience of the city seemed to "speak" and "point toward" the three place impulses and the six place triads. It was if the city offered me a freedom to see what I had been pondering, and that seeing happened in an instant.

Although my Istanbul encounter is perhaps an uncommon example, place release contributes, in smaller and larger measure, to the pleasure of being alive, particularly in relation to the places with which one is most often associated. Place release as process undermines place when the pleasure of the place becomes unsettled or unsettling in some way. The place less often offers gratifying surprises and no longer contributes to the zest of life in which users delighted before. In a more crippling mode, release as undermining place can involve disruptive, non-expected situations whereby one is upset, frightened, or hurt – for example, one happens by chance to be mugged in front of the apartment house where he or she lives.

As with place interaction and identity, I begin this discussion by offering six newspaper entries that illustrate experiences and situations relating to place release. The common feature is some encounter, event, or situation that is unforeseen, unpredictable, surprising, or seemingly impossible. Most of the examples might be called "happy accidents," though the last two entries describe unfortunate events. The first four entries appeared in the *New York Times'* "Metropolitan Diary," a weekly column depicting "the quirks, foibles, and laugh-out-loud moments of everyday city life" as forwarded to the *Times* by its readers (Alexander, 1997, book jacket). Because many moments of place release are momentary, private, and inconsequent in relation to more momentous life matters, newspapers rarely report their happenings, other than unusual or unbelievable examples (e.g., the stray bullet below). For this reason, "Metropolitan Diary" is a valuable evidential source because it accesses place experiences that otherwise would be known by no one except the experiencers.

- A reader writes that he visited New York for the first time in 1988 to participate in the New York City marathon. Getting off a bus at Forty-Second Street, he noticed a commotion and went to see. A man had set up a table on which there were three shells, one of which hid a single pea. The challenge was to find the pea after the man moved the shells around. The reader watched several rounds, guessing each time the correct shell. Figuring he would win, he waged twenty dollars, but this time the man moved the shells so fast that it was impossible to keep track of where the pea was. The reader guessed incorrectly, and the man quickly gathered his money and shells, folded up the table, and disappeared. "I was awe-struck. I was amazed. I looked around at the other stunned faces and let out a big laugh" (*NYT*, "Metropolitan Diary," December 19, 2016, p. A19).
- A reader writes that, when she was a child, her aunt would send her packages of books, which contributed to her passion for reading. Each book would be inscribed in her aunt's "graceful sprawling handwriting . . . , ending with her familiar signature." Recently, this reader helped at a charitable book sale. She and other volunteers were invited to peruse the books before customers arrived the next day. In front of a table labeled "Jewish music," she noticed a "thin little book of folk tunes." She opened the cover and "there, at the top of the page, in graceful, sprawling handwriting," was her aunt's name (*NYT*, "Metropolitan Diary," April 10, 2017, p. A19).
- A reader describes a Monday morning walk to work: Looking up at the sky for strength to face a trying work week ahead, she sees a flock of geese in V-formation. She smiles as does a lady standing next to her. "How beautiful!" exclaims the lady, who explained that the geese must fly high to keep

in formation. "That's made my day," she says, and the reader responds, "Mine, too." (*NYT*, "Metropolitan Diary," Alexander, 1997, p. 66).

- A reader writes that, some twenty years ago, he went into a store to buy a pair of gloves and promptly lost one the next day somewhere on Sixth Avenue. Since then, it has been a running joke between him and his wife that when he sees a stray glove on the street, he reaches down to see if it is his, a behavior that drives his wife crazy. Recently, he saw a glove "with a bright, neon-green band" and, as usual, said to his wife, "Oh, look, perhaps it's mine." They continued walking and shortly encountered a man briskly headed toward them, wearing one glove with a neon-green band. The reader shouted to the man, "Are you looking for a glove? Keep walking. Midblock – I just saw it." The man profusely thanked the reader, who writes, "I know how he felt and am not giving up hope" (*NYT*, "Metropolitan Diary," March 6, 2017, p. A19).

- One night in 1957, a 1:51a.m. train out of Penn Station bore down on a Queens railroad crossing for which a sleepy gatekeeper failed to close the crossing gate. The train struck a milk truck and killed the driver. Sixty years later, a man haunted since childhood by the milkman's death wrote a poem about the event. The poem was published on a poetry website and caught the attention of the milkman's grandson. "It just blew me away that sixty years later my grandfather pops up in this [poet's] head for no reason," said the man, whose mother was four when her father was killed. The poem, he explained, was "a fire that got me to start researching more about my grandfather," who survived World War II's Normandy Beach landing but then met a senseless death on his home milk route (*NYT*, April 17, 2017, p. A12).

- A forty-five-year-old woman was crossing a street in the Bronx as a bullet improbably traveled two city blocks to strike her dead. The shot had been fired during a running fight between two young men and missed "a maze of telephone poles, streetlights, wires, cars and trees in between." Said the case detective, "Couldn't it have hit a tree? A light pole? A sign?" The woman was going to her grandmother's apartment to drop off a box of sugar substitute before she picked up her sister's daughter from school (*NYT*, November 19, 2016, p. A1).

These six narratives illustrate serendipitous encounters in place, most of them pleasant, whimsical, and life-sustaining, though the last two marked by tragedy and senseless loss of human life. The four entries from "Metropolitan Diary" describe enlivening aspects of place release – small, of-the-moment situations and encounters that spark joy, humor, or surprise: admiring the geese, finding a book belonging to an aunt who loved reading, or helping the man who lost his glove. In contrast are the young woman and milkman's ill-fated deaths, both of which point to a luckless, lamentable dimension of place release. The milkman's untimely death is different from the other examples in that the unfortunate event propels additional serendipitous experiences for the young boy who becomes a poet and for the milkman's grandson, for whom the discovery of this poet's poem provokes his learning more about his grandfather. This example illustrates how one happenstance event can impel other serendipitous experiences not probable otherwise.

Collectively, these six entries point to encounters and happenings that cannot be foreseen or predicted from one's past or present experience. Such events demonstrate that many things in life are unforeseeable and apparently fortuitous. They may be propitious and gratifying; they may be ill-starred and calamitous. A missed train, a chance meeting, a wrong turn – place happenings like these may be momentary disruptions or life-changing events. They offer refreshing or baleful possibilities. As with place interaction and identity, place release demands its own thorough phenomenology, and here I overview three topics that future phenomenologies might explore more thoroughly: first, the moment in which unexpected experiences happen; second, situations in which the unexpected experience triggers a chain of consequential place events, some of which are only indirectly relatable to the original experience; and, third, ways that aspects of the environmental ensemble and people-in-place contribute to situations of place release.

Experiencing Place Release

Moments of place release involve a range of engagement in relation to the relative roles of the experiencer versus the world in which the experience happens. In some instances, something in the world brings forth the unexpected event – for example, the stray bullet strikes the woman; or the book belonging to the reader's aunt appears among the items at the book sale. In other instances, the experiencer plays an active role in how the unexpected experience happens – for example, the woman looks up at the sky for assurance and just happens to see the geese; the milkman's grandson, in perusing the poetry website, by chance discovers the poem about his grandfather's untimely death, which had haunted the poet since childhood.

In other accounts of place release, the experiencer and aspects of the world each appear to play roles more or less equal. The reader drawn to the shell game actively looks to see what the commotion is; once he is involved, the possibility of winning keeps him participating. The unexpected presence of the shell game sets up the potential experience, but the reader's gullibility guarantees that he loses his twenty dollars and, a bit more world-wary, laughs at his naïveté. Similarly, the reader's regularly looking for the glove he lost twenty years ago becomes a trigger for the moment of surprise when he and his wife help the man find his lost glove. If the lost glove were not a running joke between the reader and his wife, the moment of serendipity would not happen.

In the chapter on place interaction, I discussed how, attention-wise, people engage with place, both self-consciously and unself-consciously. In relation to place release, the experience of *noticing* is particularly significant because it happens suddenly and involves a situation where a thing of which we were unaware a moment before flashes to our attention in happenstance fashion. In *Geography of the Lifeworld*, I pointed out that noticing can be either *world-grounded* or *person-grounded* (Seamon, 1979, pp. 108–109). In world-grounded noticing, some atypical or striking feature in the world provokes our attention – for example, the woman suddenly notices the geese. Person-grounded noticing, in contrast, relates to situations where the individual's awareness takes an active role in provoking the awareness – for example, noticing the man searching for his lost glove only because of losing another glove many years earlier.

Regardless of the relative role that experiencers or qualities of the world contribute to a moment of place release, the central point is that this moment is unplanned, unexpected, and typically labelled as "accidental," "random," or "happening by chance." From Bennett's triadic perspective, these moments are possible because there is an action of freedom in the world that allows the improbable and even the "impossible" to appear. These moments can be pleasurable and supportive or hazardous and disruptive.

Place Release and Chains of Place Events

The central quality of place release is all manner of happenstance, which ranges from the momentary and prosaic to the revelatory and life-changing. One author regularly incorporating situations of place release in her writings is novelist Penelope Lively, whose *Spiderweb* I discussed in Chapter 10 as a novel about failed place identity – protagonist Stella Brentwood's unsuccessful efforts at settling in the Somerset village of Kingston Florey. Significantly, Stella's failure is triggered in part by a distressing event relating to place release: Dysfunctional neighbors, out of misplaced spite, shoot and kill a shelter dog she recently adopted as one way to engage with her place. Once Stella loses the dog, her brittle lived connectedness with place is broken, and she leaves Kingston Florey. An unpredictable and unfortunate alignment of serendipity and un-neighborly geography disrupts Stella's hopes for belonging to place. As Lively writes, "Fortune can serve up some strange conjunctions" (Lively, 1998, p. 2).

Here, I draw on two other novels by Lively to illustrate another aspect of place release: How a brief but sudden happenstance can ripple outward to touch the lives of others-in-place, often in ways of which those others have no inkling. One example is in her 2007 *Consequences*, which begins when two people meet by chance on a bench in London's St. James's Park in June 1935. A young woman named Lorna cries because of an unpleasant argument with her mother; a young man named Matt sketches ducks on the nearby pond. Lorna notices Matt's drawing and is fascinated. He soon realizes she is there: "When eventually Matt became aware of her, he looked sideways, and was done for. . . . By the end of the day, both realized that their lives had altered course" (Lively, 2007, p. 1). The resulting love affair and marriage, deeply disrupted by World War II, resounds through three family generations with the novel ending as their granddaughter falls in love.

One of Lively's most penetrating pictures of how moments of place release reverberate through time and place is her 2011 *How It All Began*, which, like *Consequences*, opens with a story of place release as an elderly woman named Charlotte Rainsford, on a beautiful spring day, is mugged and robbed on a London street by a teenage thug. In the attack, she is shoved to the ground and breaks her hip, which forces her to move in temporarily with her son-in-law, Gerry, and daughter, Rose, who, to care for her mother, must miss time at work as assistant to the pompous, aging historian, Sir Henry Peters, who has no recourse but to ask his interior-designer niece, Marion, to stand in and accompany him to give a prestigious lecture in Manchester. Because of this unexpected trip, Marion leaves a last-minute phone message for her lover, Jeremy, explaining that she will miss their tryst, which leads to Jeremy's wife, Stella, discovering the message and the affair and eventually filing for divorce: "The Dalton's marriage broke up because Charlotte Rainsford was mugged. They did not know Charlotte, and never would; she would sit on the perimeter of their lives, a fateful presence" (Lively, 2011, p. 14).

Ultimately, Charlotte's unfortunate accident affects the lives of seven characters, directing them along life paths probably different from what they would have encountered otherwise. Incapacitated and bored, Charlotte asks Anton, a Polish man taking her evening class in adult literacy, to come study with her at Jeremy and Rose's house. There he meets Rose, and they quickly fall in love: "you live twenty years in a London suburb. Husband, children, house, cat – go to the supermarket. Then – something happens. A person happens, that's all. Him" (Lively, 2011, p. 216). Another character affected by Charlotte's mugging is Sir Henry, whose Manchester lecture is a professional fiasco because, in her haste to prepare her uncle's trip, Marion leaves behind his lecture notes. Forgetting his speaking points and humiliated, Henry involves himself in a series of ill-advised machinations to resurrect his professional reputation, including a disastrous venture in television production.

By the end of the novel, very little is quite the same for any of the seven characters, at least partly because of Charlotte's mugging.[4] Interpreted in terms of place release, this one unpropitious event echoes through Charlotte's and the other characters' lives and lifeworlds. Obviously, Lively's account is only a story, and life is never as clear-cut or as decipherable as the serendipitous and integrated way in which consequences unfold for the novel's characters. There is also the question of how Charlotte's mugging can be understood triadically: How can her experience and the other experiences it triggers be related to place release? The answer is in the ineffable dimension of common presence: that the togetherness of place can contribute to an environmental unexpectedness that, in larger or smaller measure, is an integral part of all places. Charlotte and the mugger's just happening to be together (*3*) on a London Street (*2*) accidentally leads to her mugging (*1*). In this case, the intersection of these two characters is a random "belonging *together*" that does not end well: "Thus have various lives collided, the human version of a motorway shunt, and the rogue white van that slapped on the brakes is miles away now, impervious, offstage, enjoying a fry-up at the next services" (Lively, 2011, p. 45).[5]

Place Release, Environmental Ensemble, and People-in-Place

Place release is spontaneous and unsolicited; it rarely can be made to happen intentionally. There are, however, aspects of both the environmental ensemble and people-in-place that potentially enrich the chances of place release, a possibility intimated by sociologist Lyn Lofland (1998, p. 77) when she writes that the most popular public places are typically "associated with enjoyment, with satisfaction, with gratification – in short, with pleasure." She examines several environmental and human features of public places that contribute to this sense of pleasure, including *perceptual innuendo, whimsy, unusualness, people watching,* and *sociability*.

Though Lofland does not refer directly to environmental serendipity, one can argue that the presence of place release has bearing on these modes of pleasure-in-place, including features of both the environmental ensemble and people-in-place. Lofland's perceptual innuendo, whimsy, and unexpectedness relate more to elements of the environmental ensemble. *Perceptual innuendo* refers to alluring partial views of a place that one encounters: One takes pleasure in the visual incompleteness and imagines "an interesting, exotic, weird, enticing . . . world just outside one's range of vision" (Lofland, 1998, p. 80). One of Lofland's examples is narrow streets and alleyways leading away from major thoroughfares; one may be intrigued visually and decide to explore the possibilities that the sightlines of these pathways offer. Lofland relates *whimsy* to environmental features that involve "frivolity, eccentricity, kookiness, nuttiness, capriciousness, oddness." Some environmental feature is so peculiar that one can't help but notice it and be surprised. One of her examples is sidewalk sculpture that generates human engagement – for instance, a popular bench sculpture in Bend, Oregon, that provokes passersby to sit down (and often be photographed) next to a sculpted man and birds.

Lofland's *unexpectedness* is the quality most closely related to place release and involves environmental features that break one free from the familiar and provoke surprising or even shocking juxtaposition. As with perceptual innuendo and whimsy, what is unexpected for one experiencer may be familiar and unsurprising to others. Lofland (1998, p. 82) provides a list of place features that have provoked unexpectedness for her:

> [A] large and extremely fat cat (named "Tiddly") who resided full time in the "ladies loo" in London's Paddington Station; lush rooftop gardens glimpsed from street level in Manhattan and London; a small mews, just off a busy

London traffic artery, which was literally erupting in flowers; prostitutes visible through the "picture" windows of their brothels in Amsterdam (especially astonishing to tourists who just "happened upon" an outer edge of the famous red-light district); and the arrival of a cruise boat at a dock outside a restaurant on the Sacramento River.

As indicated by the Amsterdam prostitutes and cruise-boat patrons, people-in-place also play an important role in place release. Lofland describes this situation as "interactional pleasures," of which she overviews two overlapping modes relatable to place release – *people watching* and *sociability* (Lofland, 1998, pp. 88–96). As pointed out by several researchers (e.g., Gehl, 1987; Whyte, 1980), the most frequent activity of people using public space is *watching other people*. Serendipitous moments happen when a person or group surprises or shocks the watcher, who may creatively imagine who the others are and what they are about: "We oversee or overhear just enough to catch a glimpse of enticing real-life dramas; the filling out of the drama is a work of the imagination" (Lofland, 1998, p. 91). Closely related to people watching is *public sociability*, whereby people-in-place not only watch others but partake in spontaneous interaction, including conversation (Whyte, 1980, pp. 94–101).

Novelty, Place, and Possibility

One specific place type for which place release is a necessary staple is what the sociologist Ray Oldenburg (1999) identifies as *third places* – environments, most often inside, where people socialize to enjoy themselves. If the first place is home and the second place, work, the third place includes enterprises like cafés, taverns, pubs, beer gardens, hair salons, barbershops – any place where people "hang out" to be with others in an easygoing way. Third places refer to "a great variety of public places that host the regular, voluntary, informal, and happily anticipated gatherings of individuals beyond the realms of home and work" (Oldenburg, 1999, p. 16). In terms of place release, third places are significant because they typically involve some manner of novelty that may include a diverse population, a fluid structure, and user participation. The result is an unpredictable mix of interactions and happenings that are regularly pleasurable and sometimes surprising:

> A resulting uncertainty surrounds each visit. Who among the regulars will be there? Will there be newcomers? Will someone not seen in a long while show up? . . . [The third place is] the promise of something pleasantly novel amid the more usual contexts of duty and routine . . . .
>
> *(Oldenburg, 1999, p. 46)*

Finally, I return to Jane Jacobs' understanding of the city, which, though grounded in place interaction and place identity, presupposes the significance of place release in that place interaction and identity support a place regularity and continuity out of which spring satisfying encounters and events contributing in larger and smaller measure to urbanites' appreciation and enjoyment of their city. Successful urban neighborhoods are desirable, says Jacobs (1961, pp. 220–221) because they are "the source of immense vitality, and because they do represent, in small geographic compass, a great and exuberant richness of differences and possibilities, many of these differences unique and unpredictable and all the more valuable because they are." The miraculous result is place unexpectedness, surprise, and freedom:

> [Cities'] intricate order – a manifestation of the freedom of countless numbers of people to make and carry out countless plans – is in many ways a great wonder. We ought not to be reluctant to make this living collection of interdependent uses, this freedom, this life, more understandable for what it is, nor so unaware that we do not know what it is.
>
> *(Jacobs, 1961, p. 391)*

The examples of place release I offer here indicate that environmental serendipity cannot usually be made to happen directly, though the more important question is whether, through design, planning, policy, and advocacy, we can foster robust place interactions and loyal place identities that, in a dynamic environmental synergy, "set the stage" for place release indirectly. Before we speak of making lively places, however, we must consider the triad of place realization, which, in a way opposite to place release, stabilizes places by affording environmental and human order.

Notes

1 One of the few researchers to recognize and examine place serendipity is Lofland, 1998, pp. 77–98. In Chapter 9, I discussed Lofland's typologies of people–people and people–place interactions. Later in this chapter, I review her explication of place serendipity, which she presents under the rubric of "esthetic and interactional pleasures."

2 As pointed out in Chapter 7, "serendipity" conventionally relates to "happy accidents" (Merton and Barber, 2004, p. 95), though I use the word more broadly to describe unfortunate as well as fortunate events. In this sense, my definition relates to Merton and Barber's "a special kind of unintended or unanticipated outcome" (Merton and Barber, 2004, p. 234).

3 The literature on serendipity and coincidence is considerable; one overview is Koestler, 1972. On the relationship between serendipity and creativity, see Johnson, 2010, Chap. 4. On the role that serendipity plays in the course of human lives, see Bandura, 1982. On the role of serendipity in doing research, see Fine and Deegan, 1996. The psychologist C. G. Jung was fascinated by the significance of coincidence in human life, particularly as coincidences happened in a series. He identified a phenomenon he called *synchronicity*, which he defined as "a meaningful coincidence of two or more events, where something other than the probability of chance is involved" (Jung, 1973, p. 104; also see Main, 1997, 2007). Here, I am mostly interested in single moments of

serendipity rather than the serial coincidental events that were Jung's concern. He also claimed an explanation for these clusters of coincidental events: that they were grounded in "the unconscious psyche, the archetypes, which constitute the structure of the collective unconscious" (Jung, 1973, p. 20). My focus is not *why* these events happen but describing them as lifeworld experience through the triad of place release.

4   And what happened to the mugger? Lively (2011, p. 229) explains: "The delinquent – fourteen years old . . . – was himself set upon almost immediately by a hostile gang and relieved of the £67.27, which were distributed among the gang membership and disposed of within the hour. The delinquent was much annoyed at his loss, but recovered within a day or two; so it goes."

5   Readers might wonder why Charlotte's encounter with the mugger is not an example of place interaction in that his accidentally being present (*1*) at the same time and same place as Charlotte (*2*) leads to her being mugged (*3*). Certainly, the actual moment of attack is an interaction triad. Because, however, the mugging has momentous impact reverberating into the future, I argue that the event has a greater significance than that provoked by interaction alone. Many of the examples of place release I offer are much more trivial in their lived significance; I contend that it is the quality of joy and happy surprise (or disruption and unhappy surprise) that seems to set these experiences apart from ordinary interactions.

12

THE TRIAD OF PLACE REALIZATION
(3–1–2 OR *CP–PP–EE*)

As a triad, place realization can be described as common presence (*3*), responded to by people-in-place (*1*), facilitating a specific environmental ensemble (*2*). Via its relative degree of wholeness, common presence works through people-in-place to sustain an environmental ensemble expressing a stronger or weaker environmental character and atmosphere. Place is "realized" as a unique phenomenal presence greater than its environmental and human parts.

Place realization as process undermines place when the ordered wholeness of place deteriorates in some way or is destroyed entirely through inappropriate policy, insensitive design, lack of care, or dramatic events like war or natural disaster. The place may devolve into shabbiness, decrepitude, disorder, distress, violence, or some other entropic quality that works against place interaction and identity. An integrated world collapses into disquiet, discomfort, unpleasantness, or dissolution. This collapse may generate a lackluster place without energy or ambience. In more extreme versions, there may be a complete disintegration whereby the place *as place* no longer exists.[1]

In contrast to the triad of place release, which sponsors serendipity and unexpectedness in place, the triad of place realization sponsors ways in which a place remains consistent in space and time. This triad assures that places maintain a certain order and constancy. As with the other triads, I first present six newspaper entries that point to the range of environmental ordering facilitated through place realization. I then present two contrasting modes of environmental ordering: first, place realization arising *unself-consciously* via everyday lifeworld needs and illustrated by the shop/house, a building type integrating home and business; and, second, place realization arising *self-consciously* through self-directed planning and illustrated by McDonald's, the American fast-food company.

Examples of Place Realization

The following newspaper articles point toward the wide spectrum of place realization. Broadly, they are ordered from larger-scale to smaller-scale places, ranging
from regions and cities to places of business and residence. The entries on Alaska's
dependence on aviation and the ways self-driving vehicles change personal
transportation patterns illustrate place realization as environmental ordering via
movement-in-place.

- An article on the red wines of Corsica suggests that unique environmental
  qualities of place play a key role in whether one type of grape will yield
  "insipid, uninteresting wines" or "wines that astonish and inspire." The article refers to *terroir*, which relates to the claim that "the place where grapes are
  grown and the wine is made imposes a character on that wine." Environmental contributors to the wine's uniqueness are said to include the soil,
  elevation, microclimate, weather, quality of sunlight, and the people who
  care for the vineyards and make the wine (*NYT*, January 25, 2017, p. D4).
- Designated as one of the "Last Great Places" by the Nature Conservancy, the
  Red Hills is a region along the Florida-Georgia border encompassing some
  300,000 acres of pines and rolling, grassy hills. Owners of the region's large
  "plantation houses," some held in the same family for generations, are
  working to keep the Red Hills undeveloped, partly to preserve quail habitats
  for hunting, but also to act as stewards to the land and the region's architecture (*WSJ*, February 3, 2017, p. M1).
- Twice the size of Texas, Alaska is the most aviation-dependent American
  state and relies on planes for commercial, governmental, and community
  needs. Hundreds of towns and villages are beyond the road system, and
  planes provide a lifeline for these difficult-to-reach places. Often, these airlines use planes with nine or less seats, and pilots get to know their passengers
  and their lives. Presently, Alaska faces a shortage of trained pilots, tempted by
  higher-paying aviation work in the lower forty-eight states. Some start-up
  companies are developing pilotless drone aircraft able to deliver supplies,
  medicine, and mail to remote communities (*NYT*, December 29, 2016, p.
  A12).
- Alphabet, the American multinational conglomerate and parent company of
  Google, has announced that its self-driving technology is ready for commercialization. On one hand, driverless vehicles offer advantages that include
  reducing accidents, saving lives, easing congestion, lowering energy consumption, and minimizing pollutants. On the other hand, self-driving vehicles may generate problems currently unforeseen. Accidents may be fewer,
  but because vehicles can move closely together at high speeds, accidents may
  be more violent and involve more vehicles. Millions of truck drivers, taxi
  drivers, and other workers associated with vehicular transportation will lose

their jobs. Vehicle-sharing and app-based car services may reduce vehicle sales, forcing automakers and suppliers to cut jobs. New highway infrastructure will be required, since self-driving vehicles require smooth roads and clearly painted lines for accurate orientation and traversal (*NYT*, December 19, 2016).

- In its home city of Seattle, the on-line retailing company Amazon is experimenting with a new way of grocery shopping where customers buy their purchases online and then drive to a store to pick up their orders, brought to customers' vehicles by Amazon employees. The company is also developing "Amazon Go," a no-cashier convenience store where, to check out, shoppers use sensors and other technology (*NYT*, February 13, 2017, p. B1).

- A Bangladesh man and his two partners operate a halal food cart on New York City's Greenwich Street, near the World Trade Center, throughout the year, whatever the weather. This food-cart operator works five or six days a week in eight-hour shifts. He is one of some 10,000 individuals, most of them immigrants, who earn their livelihood selling food on the city's streets. At 8 a.m. he prepares his cart, which stores vegetables, meats, and other items he needs to serve the day's customers. His menu includes some twenty dishes, most of them cooked to order, though most regulars order chicken biryani. His first customer appears at 9:30 a.m. The lunch rush begins around 11:30 a.m., and at noon, his two helpers arrive. The three men work efficiently around a grill, fryer, and steam table, "finding their rhythm in the surges of orders as clusters of people appear" (*NYT*, April 19, 2017, p. D1).

These six entries illustrate the extensive range of ways in which common presence, working through people-in-place, supports a particular environmental ensemble. For example, the unique "togetherness" of Corsica sustains vineyards producing a unique grape and wine, just as the unique "togetherness" of the Red Hills region sustains a unique natural and human landscape. The manner of presence of a food-cart business, illustrated by the Bangladeshi proprietor's halal food offerings, contributes to Greenwich Street's street-vending scene. An Amazon revisioning of grocery-shopping aims to facilitate new customer behaviors through new kinds of grocery and convenience stores. The examples of Alaskan aviation and driverless cars illustrate how dynamic networks – in this case, differing "webs" of transportation – play a role in lifeworlds and require specific environmental features in which those lifeworlds can unfold.

In all these stories, one notes that some aspect of a place's spatial and lived togetherness – i.e., common presence – works through the people associated with that place to facilitate a constellation of interrelated environmental elements and experiences. To clarify the workings of place realization as a triad, I consider two contrasting examples of place realization in greater detail: first, the shop/house, illustrating what I call *unself-conscious* place realization; and, second, McDonald's fast-food restaurants, illustrating what I call *self-conscious* place realization.

The Shop/House as Unself-Conscious Place Realization

Place realization facilitates environmental order in varying ways. Traditionally and until the twentieth century, most places arose in their own time and manner as particular lifeworld needs sponsored particular place forms, activities, and events. Organized around the everyday requirements and expectations of ordinary people, these places have been variously labelled "organic," "natural," "vernacular," or "folk" because they largely arose pre-reflectively as people, in the course of daily life, made places that worked as supportive but taken-for-granted environments. Geographer Edward Relph (1976, p. 64) explains that this mode of environmental order arises from "a profound and unself-conscious identity with place."[2]

Drawing on Relph (1976, pp. 65–66), I call this mode of place realization *unself-conscious* because it develops spontaneously with a minimum of intentional planning or premeditated intervention. As one real-world example, I discuss the *shop/house* – a mixed-use building incorporating some combination of residence and business. In *Living over the Store*, architect Howard Davis (2012) offers an architectural history and social geography of the shop/house. He demonstrates how this building type is found in almost every culture, geographical region, and historical period, largely because it allows for an efficient lived interconnectedness among architecture, user needs, and the larger communal fabric of which the shop/house is usually part. The shop/house is "embedded in the social and economic life of the urban district" (Davis, 2012, p. vi) and thereby contributes to the wholeness of urban place as well as to the wholeness of life in the shop/house itself.

Much of Davis' study is implicitly phenomenological in that he offers a multi-dimensional picture of the flexible lifeworlds that the shop/house sustains. He illustrates how a building can be an architectural whole that enables lifeworlds incorporating both home and business. Until the early twentieth century, the distinction between dwellings and shops was fluid, with the result that the shop/house could easily be modified for shifting familial, social, economic, and locality needs. This adaptability allowed occupants "to develop businesses in their houses with a minimum of financial investment and to expand and contract space devoted to business as necessary" (Davis, 2012, p. 13). As Davis (2012, p. 89) explains:

> The relationship between the shop/house and everyday life is supple. On a day-to-day basis, work may be easily done in the house or in easy access to the house; workplace and dwelling are sometimes the same, sometimes together, easily intertwined and overlapped. In sustaining an easy movement back and forth between domestic and economic uses, the shop/house may

accommodate functions that readily expand and contract. Economic uses may include the rental of space to people outside the family – a boarder, a student renting a basement room, a rental apartment in a multi-unit building. The family can stay in place by allowing the building to be used in ways that are diverse and easily changeable.

Davis's study is relevant to place realization because it illustrates how the shop/house supports a material and lived order accommodating the contrasting functions of home and work. Davis (2012, pp. 142–70) identifies several building features that integrate residential and commercial needs architecturally and experientially. First, shop/houses typically have narrow frontages that directly connect to the public realm of sidewalk and street. This narrowness allows for many shop fronts per block, which in turn contributes to functional diversity, shopping choice, serendipitous walk ins, and exuberant street life. Second, shop/house spaces are typically arranged to support a workable balance between the contrasting needs and functions of residence and commerce; for example, work-related spaces are often placed at the front of the building, while domestic spaces occupy the building's back portion or the upper floors above sales and work spaces. Third, the kitchen in many shop/houses is an in-between space that helps make the shop a social place, allows family members to tend the shop as they prepare family meals, or, in the case of cafés and restaurants, *is* the shop.

In interpreting the shop/house as a triad of place realization, one can say that the common presence invoked by residence and commerce spatially together (*3*), working through resident-shopkeepers, customers, and the larger place population (*1*), encourages the shop/house as a predominant building type (*2*). The result is an architectural "gathering" of family, clientele, and wider urban neighborhood that unfolds via lifeworld needs, obligations, hopes, and actions:

> The shop/house is useful because it supports everyday life in the most ordinary and common sense. Everyday life – reading the newspaper with a cup of coffee, chatting with a neighbor on the street, putting the key in the front door when arriving home, working hard to meet a deadline, buying bread and a quart of milk, taking children to school, meeting friends, going to the bank on a lunch break, stopping at the dry cleaners on the way home – is the ground of people's experience. It is overlaid with inner lives of thoughts and dreams, and punctuated by the surprising moment, the special occasion, and the beautiful. It is always present, sometimes in the background and sometimes in plain view – and it is lived more than it is thought.
>
> (Davis, 2012, p. 89)

At this point, readers might wonder about another triadic possibility. Couldn't one claim a triad whereby the shop/house (*2*), working through people-in-place (*1*), contributes to a place's common presence (*3*)? In fact, one can speak of this relationship, which marks the triad of place intensification, described in the next chapter. I raise this triadic possibility because it is important to remember that, for any place, all six place triads are present, though not always in equal measure (a point discussed in Chapter 15). For example, note Davis's indirect mention of the place-release triad when he suggests that the shop/house is often the site of serendipitous happenings and encounters: the "surprising moment" and the "special occasion." One can also imagine how the shop/house involves triads of interaction (for family, customers, and sidewalk life of the larger neighborhood) and identity (family attachment for "home" and "workplace" and customer attachment for "favorite shops").

Throughout his study, Davis highlights the integral spatial and lived relationship that shop/houses have with the larger place fabric of which they are part. By integrating complementary functions architecturally, the shop/house contributes to the functional and experiential diversity of city neighborhoods and is a crucial ingredient of the organized complexity that, for Jane Jacobs, is the crux of exuberant urban districts and, like the shop/house, traditionally arose unself-consciously. Davis explains that his book "is partly an extension of Jane Jacobs' argument about the importance of urban diversity," which, he notes, at least until recently, has included "numerous buildings in which families lived above their shops" (Davis, 2012, p. 7). In the last chapter of his book, Davis presents a series of contemporary shop/house designs that he hopes might contribute to a "resilient urbanism" – i.e., robust city districts, neighborhoods, and buildings that can accommodate change without changing their unique character (Davis, 2012, p. 207).

Throughout his book, Davis emphasizes that resilient urbanism relates to Jacob's organized complexity, which, in turn, presupposes a place realization unfolding in an unself-conscious way. Jacobs intimates an environmental ordering that is dense and diverse (*3*), working through the street ballet of people-in-place (*1*) and facilitating a neighborhood fabric that, at least until the recent present, included shop/houses (*2*). The common presence of such vibrant neighborhoods is powerful; their integrated environmental order becomes as real as the human beings who know, encounter, and feel a belonging to that neighborhood place. Jacobs (1958, p. 180) emphasizes that we must better understand this place uniqueness because it is the engine for a neighborhood's vitality:

> What makes a city [neighborhood] magnetic, what can inject the gaiety, the wonder, the cheerful hurly-burly that make people want to come into the city and to linger there? For magnetism is the crux of the problem. All [a neighborhood's] values are its byproducts. To create in it an atmosphere of urbanity and exuberance is not a frivolous aim.

McDonald's as Self-Conscious Place Realization

Davis's shop/house and Jacobs' neighborhoods illustrate how place realization happens unself-consciously, unfolding lifeworld-wise through a progressive give-and-take between everyday human needs and appropriate environmental features. I repeat Davis's incisive point that the shop/house is "lived more than it is thought" (Davis, 2012, p. 89). Another manner of place realization happens deliberately, through reflexive understanding and intentional actions and practices. I call this mode of environmental ordering *self-conscious* place realization, which I illustrate with McDonald's, a premier example of a pre-planned place where nothing is left to chance.[3]

In introducing McDonald's as an example of prearranged environmental ordering, I begin with Relph's *placelessness*, a term he uses to describe the intensifying loss of places in today's world. Placelessness is "the casual eradication of distinctive places and the making of standardized landscapes that results from an insensitivity to the significance of place" (Relph, 1976, p. ii). In explaining the current proliferation of placelessness, Relph identifies several causal factors, one of which is *technique* – the use of rational planning to create self-sufficient environments that are entirely ordered and controlled by bureaucratic or corporate schemes and directives. As an international corporation with franchised restaurants throughout the world, McDonald's is an exceptional example of technique, providing food in Los Angeles and London more or less identical to McDonald's fare in Paris, Moscow, or Tokyo.

Here, I suggest that one mode of technique is self-conscious place realization, which I describe by drawing on sociologist Robin Leidner's insightful study, *Fast Food, Fast Talk* (Leidner, 1993). This book provides an in-depth picture of how McDonald's depends on and effects a place mode in which all aspects of staff and customer decisions and actions are intentionally arranged to promote efficiency, familiarity, and quick customer turnover (Leidner, 1993). The company summarizes its aim in its three-letter corporate credo, "QSC," which refers to "quality, service, and cleanliness." "QSC" is the aim of the thousands of rules and specifications that the company requires its management and employees to follow. The corporate goal is to provide a limited number of food items of uniform quality at low prices and actualized through rigorous, exact standardization.

This standardization begins with employees. McDonald's leaves no part of workers' jobs to their own discretion. The strategy is to determine "the One Best Way to do every task and see that the work is conducted accordingly" (Leidner, 1993, p. 45). An "Operations and Training Manual," known by McDonald's managers as "the Bible," is six-hundred pages long and describes standards and procedures in precise detail – for example, the proper arm motions for salting French fries or the correct placement of ketchup, mustard, and pickles on each kind of hamburger (Leidner, 1993, p. 49, p. 65). Store managers are instructed in a four-step process for training new employees: prepare, present, try out, and follow up (Leidner, 1993, p. 65). Trainees first watch a video of a specific work task and then observe its performance by an experienced employee. Next, trainees do the task themselves as a trainer watches and suggests improvements. Once they have mastered the task, employees work for skill and speed as the trainer evaluates performance, using a "Standard Operations Checklist" as guide (Leidner, 1993, pp. 65–66).

Customers are a second essential component in the smooth functioning of McDonald's, and the company works in a range of ways to prepare and habituate customers' expectations and actions. Media advertisements introduce new products and portray customers purchasing food. Leidner observed that all customers in the McDonald's where she worked were familiar with how they were expected to act: "I never saw a customer who did not know that she or he was supposed to come up to the counter rather than sit down and wait to be served."[4] This familiarity is essential to the automatic environmental ordering in which customers partake, most of the time unknowingly and habitually. Leidner (1993, p. 75) writes:

> Not surprisingly . . . , customers at the McDonald's I studied knew what was expected of them and tried to play their part well. They sorted themselves into lines and gazed up at the menu boards while waiting to be served. They usually gave their orders in the conventional sequence: burgers or other entrees, French fries or other side orders, drinks, and desserts. Harried customers with savvy might order an item "only if it's in the bin," that is, ready to be served. Many customers prepared carefully so that they could give their orders promptly when they got to the counter.

Also important in routinizing employees and customers' behaviors is the restaurants' physical design. Food-preparation and service spaces incorporate an open plan so that managers can readily see that employees are engaged with tasks. In turn, there is considerable visual permeability between work spaces and ordering counters. Awareness of long lines of customers waiting to be served works as an important spur for intensifying employees' efforts, since they recognize that they may become the target of dissatisfied customers: "The arrangement of the workplace, which made window workers clearly visible to the waiting customers as they went about their duties, and customers clearly visible to the workers, was important in keeping crew people hard at work" (Leidner, 1993, p. 78). McDonald's physical design is also arranged to routinize customers' ordering and eating behaviors. Entrances lead to ordering counters rather than to dining areas, making it almost certain that customers automatically get in line. Trash receptacles are prominently displayed to make it clear that customers are to bus tables and remove trash themselves (Leidner, 1993, p. 74).[5]

In terms of place realization, McDonald's is exemplary because it illustrates how technique and planning can envision and arrange an environment where a standardized human and environmental order unfolds in a seemingly "natural" way that is in fact rigidly choreographed and controlled. A common presence dictated by profit generation (*3*), masterly regiments employees and customers (*1*) in the routinized, behavior-shaping environment of a typical McDonald's restaurant (2). Though its motives are driven by global capitalism, I discuss McDonald's because it is an archetypal example of a place type shaped by a predetermined, all-encompassing, environmental order.[6]

The four place processes of interaction, identity, release, and realization help one understand what a place is and how it works. I now turn to the triads of place intensification and place creation, which relate to envisioning and making places that sustain and strengthen human and environmental wellbeing. Chapter 13 considers place intensification, a process demonstrating the central importance of the environmental ensemble in contributing to and shaping place and lived emplacement.

Notes

1 As indicated by the failing French town of Albi described in Chapter 1, many places throughout the world are disintegrating today, partly because of globalization, shifting technologies, and ever-extending corporate forces that undermine local and regional initiatives, enterprises, and employment. My argument is that an understanding of the six place processes offers one means to envision and actualize real-world places with a powerful ambience and "common presence." One means toward this aim is phenomenological explications of vibrant places, drawing on the six place processes as one descriptive and interpretive guide. In relation to the destruction of place in the United States, there has recently appeared a spate of books on the topic, including Alexander, 2017; Goldstein, 2017; Pendergast, 2017; and Timberg, 2015, esp. Chaps. 2 and 5.

2 Today, most buildings and places are designed and constructed by parties other than clients and users. The situation of individuals and groups entirely making their own places is unusual, other than in relation to home interiors – for example, "do-it-yourself" interior design and personal selection of home furnishings. This situation is unfortunate in the sense that an individual or group's active efforts in place making play a significant role in "having a personal stake in place" and thereby contribute to strong place identity. Davis (2012, pp. 89–90) makes a similar point for urban places: "[A] smooth relationship between daily life and its environment has been . . . typical of cities. Until relatively recently, the locus of daily life [in cities] was largely local, not governed by remote economic or political institutions. While larger economic and political forces always affected what happened locally in cities, people's actions, work and decisions were happening within local structures and institutions, and characterized by immediate relationships between individuals. Although life may not have been easy, it was personal rather than bureaucratic."

3 I thank Jenny Quillien for first suggesting fast-food eateries as an archetypal example of self-conscious place realization; see Quillien, 2012, p. 129.

4 In describing the opening of the first McDonald's in Moscow in 1990, Leidner (1993, p. 75, n. 29) points out the crucial importance of customers' taken-for-granted familiarity. In the first weeks of operation, Russian customers had to be persuaded to cue in the shortest counter lines; their taken-for-granted experience was that bona fide goods were available only in long lines.

5 In 2012, McDonald's shifted to a healthier food menu, a change that led to its losing some five-hundred million U.S. orders in 2012–2016. At the start of 2017, the company returned to low-cost fare, hoping to win back core customers who patronized other fast-food chains. The company also introduced self-order kiosks and table-location technology enabling employees to bring orders directly to sit-down customers (Jargon, 2017, p. B5).

6 Though McDonald's as a corporation is an exceptional example of self-conscious place realization, individual McDonald's restaurants contribute to place interaction and place identity. As Relph (1976) points out, the most placeless environments sometimes facilitate a sense of place, and this is often true for McDonald's, particularly in smaller communities where locally-owned eateries have closed and, by default, McDonald's and other corporate eateries become communities' "third places." In 2016, the photojournalist Chris Arnade (2016) made a 58,000-mile trek through the United States, visiting small towns and cities. He discovered that McDonald's is one institution that works to hold people in those places together. He explained that, in many poor and middle-income neighborhoods, McDonald's restaurants "have become de facto community centers and reflections of the surrounding neighborhood" (Arnade, 2016). Arnade also found that McDonald's are often important places for the homeless and for people caught up in addiction: "They have cheap and filling food, they have free Wi-Fi, outlets to charge phones, and clean restrooms. McDonald's is also generally gracious about letting people sit quietly for long periods – longer than other fast-food places" (Arnade, 2016).

13

THE TRIAD OF PLACE INTENSIFICATION (*2–1–3* OR *EE–PP–CP*)

This chapter discusses the triad of place intensification, and the following chapter discusses the triad of place creation. I pair these two triads because, for both, the reconciling impulse of common presence is the *outcome* of place actions, though these actions are considerably different experientially. On one hand, the triad of place intensification (*2–1–3*) can be described as the environmental ensemble (*2*), engaging with people-in-place (*1*) and engendering a stronger common presence (*3*) through a more efficient or enjoyable physical environment. On the other hand, the triad of place creation (*1–2–3*) can be described as people-in-place (*1*), engaging with the environmental ensemble (*2*) and engendering a stronger common presence through creatively envisioning and remaking their place (*2*). Place intensification points to the importance of the physical environment in place making, and place creation points to the importance of innovative design, planning, policy, and advocacy.

Place intensification demonstrates how the environmental ensemble, even as receptive impulse, plays an active role in facilitating place. The result is that environmental entropy is reduced, and the place becomes better or more durable in some way. Its common presence is strengthened because a more appropriate environmental ensemble boosts the lives of people-in-place. Place intensification as process undermines place through poorly conceived designs, policies, and constructions that enfeeble or squelch the life of the place – for example urban mega-structures that provide little physical or visual connectedness to sidewalk and street. An inappropriate environmental ensemble contributes to increasing the environmental entropy of the place. In discussing the process of place intensification, I begin with six newspaper stories that illustrate the wide-ranging expression of place intensification. I then illustrate the process concretely by presenting four examples of how specific aspects of the environmental ensemble play a crucial role in sustaining lifeworlds and places.

Examples of Place Intensification

In each of the following newspaper stories, some aspect of the environmental ensemble plays a role in the life of a place and thereby contributes to that place's strength of presence. The examples move from larger to smaller scale and all, except the first entry on Japanese "forest bathing," relate to some aspect of the built environment, whether city, neighborhood, or building. I emphasize examples of human-made rather than natural environments, since so much of place experience relies on human-made constructions and situations.

- A movement in Japan becoming increasingly popular is "forest bathing," whereby participants immerse themselves in nature, claiming that the chemicals emitted by plants and trees have health benefits. The Japanese government has spent millions of dollars promoting the therapy and funding research on its potential benefits. The Tokyo-based Forest Therapy Society has designated sixty-two forests and woodland paths as "forest bathing" locales (*WSJ*, May 8, 2017, p. A13).
- The city of Rochester, New York, has filled in almost a mile of a sixty-year-old sunken highway bypass and replaced it with a ground-level boulevard and some six acres of prime land for development. The project contributes to the city's efforts to focus on pedestrians and make walkable downtown neighborhoods that intersperse housing, workplaces, and commercial functions. The city mayor explains that the sunken highway was a "moat" and that the reclaimed space "gives people the ability to move easily around. It gives us more space to develop" (*NYT*, November 2, 2016, p. B6).
- Many American cities are removing downtown malls in favor of new streets, office buildings, housing, retail functions, and parks. In Worcester, Massachusetts, a forty-year-old shopping mall that had eliminated "a dense warren of old city streets and downtown buildings" is now being replaced by a hotel, mixed-use buildings, and apartment buildings. Trains to Boston are readily accessible on a nearby rebuilt street. "It's critical," said Worcester's urban manager, "for cities to not just wring their hands about mistakes of earlier eras but to find solutions" (*WSJ*, March 21, 2017, p. A3).
- In Omaha, Nebraska, some paved streets are being ripped out and replaced with gravel. In many American cities, street and road infrastructure has deteriorated badly, and Omaha has chosen a pavement-to-gravel conversion to save public funds and cope with paved streets beyond repair without major resurfacing. "I can't even open my widows on that side of the house," explained a resident who lives on one of the converted streets a block from a busy Starbucks. "During the summer, it's just a dust bowl" (*NYT*, March 8, 2017, p. A11).
- New York City's Building Department has just published a map that identifies the locations of almost eight thousand wood-and-steel scaffoldings

presently in front of city buildings. Though working to protect passersby from debris, many of the scaffoldings have been up for years and are eyesores, generating complaints from pedestrians and business that they impede foot traffic, block light and views, and attract litter and crime. The city council is considering regulations targeting structures that are kept up too long (*NYT*, April 3, 2017, p. A23).

- In many villages of rural France, old, ordinary houses are being stripped of their architectural elements, which are often shipped abroad. There is a thriving market for building parts such as mantelpieces, staircases, moldings, wood paneling, and floor tiles. Antique oak doors may fetch as much as six hundred dollars; mantels, as much as ten thousand dollars. Houses stripped of architectural parts are difficult to sell because of the cost of repair or stabilization. Nearby houses fall in value, and a village "finds it that much harder to retain its population, its attractiveness, and life" (*NYT*, April 17, 2017, p. A4).

In these examples, some element of the environmental ensemble helps shape places that are one way rather than another. In some of the examples, the environmental element – the Japanese forests, Rochester's sunken-bypass infill, or Worcester's removal of the downtown shopping mall – enhances place and place experience. In other instances – the Omaha conversion of pavement to gravel, the deleterious New York City scaffolding, or the stripped French houses – the environmental element undermines place. Whether working in a positive or negative way, some aspect of the environmental ensemble (*2*) allows people-in-place (*1*) to be in one way rather than another, which in turn intensifies or diminishes common presence (*3*).

In the rest of the chapter, I offer four examples of place intensification. The first example illustrates how the major living space in traditional French houses facilitates a complementary style of family living, and the second example draws on the research of urbanist William Whyte to highlight how designable elements of urban plazas and parks contribute to those places' sociability and life. The last two examples illustrate how some aspects of the environmental ensemble are less obvious in the ways they play a role in human life. I draw on architectural theorist Bill Hillier's theory of space syntax to demonstrate how the spatial configuration of pathways is crucially important for whether people meet or stay apart in place. I end by returning to Jane Jacobs' vision of the city and her sophisticated explication of how elements of the environmental ensemble are crucial for facilitating urban diversity and street ballet.

Architecture Organizing Life

In *Village in the Vaucluse*, American anthropologist Laurence Wylie presents an account of daily life in the small southeastern French village of Rousillon, where he and his family lived in 1950 and 1951. They resided in a village house that had electricity, running water, a bathroom with a flush toilet, and a central heating system. These modern conveniences, however, did not work well, and the heating system did not work at all. Over time, Wylie realized that the Matron family, the owners of the house, had rarely used these conveniences and had installed them mostly to enhance the family's community prestige (Wylie, 1957, p. 145).

After living in the house for a few months and preparing for the *mistral*, the region's cold, dry wind that blows December through March, Wylie came to realize that the radiators were incapable of heating the whole house. He turned to other means, which he assumed were the fireplaces in every room and a stove in the kitchen. Determined to keep the whole house warm, Wylie lit daily fires in the stove and fireplaces. He soon realized, however, that keeping these fires burning was a full-time task. More so, wood and coal were scarce and therefore expensive. When the mistral blew, the fireplaces were unable to keep the rooms warm.

Failing in his efforts to heat the whole house, Wylie moved his typewriter and books into the *salle*, the dwelling's main space, traditionally serving as living room, dining room, and kitchen. He discontinued fires in the bedrooms, since heat was necessary there only when the family was dressing and undressing (which they now did in the *salle*). Over time, without realizing it, Wylie and his family adapted themselves to the traditional way of village life in which families, in the colder months, live together in one room:

> Little by little our family life, which at home was distributed throughout the entire house, and which we had tried to distribute throughout the Rousillon house, withdrew from all the other rooms and was concentrated in the *salle*. This change solved some problems: I spent less time keeping the family warm, and the fuel bill dropped gratifyingly. Other problems were raised. I had to learn to work while the children were playing. The children had to learn to play more quietly. I had to learn to pick up my papers from the table so that it might be used as a dining-room table. Most of our meat was cooked over the coals of the fireplace. When one of the children had an earache at night we could not sit in his room and rock him; we brought him down and held him on our lap in front of the fire. The fire of oak logs that burned day and night for six months became the focal point of our family life.
>
> *(Wylie, 1957, pp. 145–146)*

Wylie explains that, in summer, the *salle* is much less important, and fires are lit only to cook food as families spend time outside in the sun. In the winter months, however, the *salle* and its hearth are crucial in the way it gives the family a comfortable place and becomes the day-to-day center of their lives. This intimate lived relationship between the *salle* and the family is a simple but instructive example of an unself-conscious triad of place intensification: The *salle* and hearth (environmental ensemble), gathering the family practically and socially (people-in-place), sustain a supportive everyday lifeworld (a workable common presence).

Architectural theorist Kim Dovey argues that environmental elements providing for and improving everyday life illustrate *appropriation*, which involves responsibility and care for the world at hand. Appropriation refers to "our primary involvement in the world, our concern," which is not only self-serving but incorporates "a respect and preserving of the world in its own right" (Dovey, 1985, p. 37). In addition, appropriation involves a gracious accepting and taking, whereby we incorporate "the world into ourselves" (Dovey, 1985, p. 37). Dovey explains:

> As we open ourselves to the world of things and places, we bring them meaning through our care and concern, and at the same time these things and places lend meaning to our sense of identity. Appropriation is rooted, therefore, in a concerned action through which we appropriate aspects of our world as anchors for our self-identity.
>
> *(Dovey, 1985, pp. 37–38)*

Wylie's example of the *salle* relates to Dovey's appropriation in that, at first, Wylie assumes that his French house works in much the same way as his American house. But as he lives in the French house and attempts to provide a warm space for his family, he realizes that he must better understand what this dwelling is and how it really works. Over time, he and his family *appropriate* the house in that they discover that it works successfully as a comfortable dwelling, provided they understand, accept, and care for it in the particular way it offers and requires. They must set aside their taken-for-granted expectations as to how the house should work and accept the possibilities it offers them, once they realize what those possibilities are. As the family grows comfortable with and appreciates the house, they appropriate it. The resulting lifeworld, though different from their accustomed American experience, becomes taken-for-granted and the new normal.[1]

The *salle* example illustrates how, in every place, all six place processes are at work, though often at different intensities. I have chosen the *salle* example to explicate place *intensification*, but I could also use the situation to clarify the five other processes: By drawing the family together physically, the *salle* facilitates an environmental setting for *interaction*; by holding household members together spatially, it offers a place where they find their *identity* as a family; in opening a space for unexpectedness and surprise, it supports *release*; in ordering a good part of family home life, it fosters *intensification*; in providing a supportive setting for the family to envision novel possibilities, it sponsors *creation*. It is important to remember that the six place processes can *undermine* as well as support the "at homeness" of the house: For example, if family members don't get along, the *salle* may become a place of awkward interactions, disintegrating identity, and a disordered lifeworld.

I highlight the interconnectedness of the six place processes because the *salle* example offers a particularly accessible picture. In Chapter 15, I discuss the synergistic relationship among the six processes further but mention it here because one may become so focused on one place process that he or she forgets that, for robust places, all six triads are at work.

Design Enlivening Plazas and Parks

Having illustrated place intensification through Wylie's encounter with the *salle*, I now turn to three researchers who examine the role of the environmental ensemble in human life and then use that understanding explicitly for practical ends, whether for design, planning, or policy. The first of these researchers is urbanist William Whyte (1980, 1988), whose focus is how plazas and parks contribute to city vitality and an urban sense of place. His work is important because, first, he explains why some city plazas and parks are well used and others not. Second, he demonstrates, in an integrated way, how plannable and designable features play an essential role in why a plaza or park works well or does not.[2]

For Whyte, the best plazas and parks are *sociable* and draw together large numbers of users informally. By "informally," Whyte means that many users find themselves using a particular park or plaza without having intentionally planned to go there. Rather, they have free time available and "stop by" the plaza or park on the way to or from somewhere else. These users attract other users, contributing to a successful plaza or park's common presence, which can be pictured by such descriptors as "activity," "life," "exchanges," "enjoyment," "hustle and bustle," "people watching," and "people 'hanging out.'" In relation to place intensification, Whyte's work is significant because, having identified the importance of sociability for plazas and parks, he next locates three physical features crucial for its happening.

The first and most important of these features is *location*: the plaza or park must be near an adequate pool of potential users, typically associated with high-density areas of mixed uses, especially workplaces, residences, shops, and eateries. In the 1989 film *Field of Dreams*, a voice says, "If you build it, he will come," with the result that a baseball field is constructed in rural Iowa. For Whyte, the phrase is more accurately stated, "If you build it, he *may* come," provided the plaza is within convenient walking distance, which for most users is no more than three city blocks (Whyte, 1980, p. 16). The best plan of action is that plazas or parks be located along streets or at street corners with heavy pedestrian flow.

Provided the plaza or park is well located, a second important physical feature comes into play: the *street–plaza relationship*, by which Whyte means that the plaza should be designed as an extension of the street so that passersby do not notice where the sidewalk ends and the plaza begins. The design aim is to facilitate *impulse use* whereby would-be users are drawn into the plaza or park without realizing it. Physical features contributing to impulse use include *clear sightlines*, whereby users entering or leaving can see who is inside the space or outside on the sidewalk. Whyte is strongly opposed to elevated or sunken plazas because "if people do not see the space, they will not use it" (Whyte, 1980, p. 58).[3] Another useful physical feature for stimulating impulse use is *beckoning devices* – designable elements that draw the user in, such as low, graceful stairs; elegant entrance markings; handsome landscaping; and alluring place elements like water walls or unusual fountains and sculptures. Also useful are attractions around the plaza's rim – for example, shops, eateries, and similar functions that draw users into and through the plaza.

Once users are in the plaza, the aim is to keep them there, most readily accomplished design-wise by *seating*, which should be both physically and socially comfortable. As to the minimum amount of seating that a plaza or park should provide, Whyte establishes an arbitrary requirement of one foot of seating for every thirty square feet of plaza space (Whyte, 1980, p. 112). In relation to *physical comfort*, seating must not be too high, too low, or too narrow. For example, seat fixtures should be no lower than one foot and no higher than three feet; they should be no narrower than sixteen inches and at least thirty inches wide if providing seating on both sides.[4] Also important is *social comfort*, which refers to sitting choice whereby one can sit alone, with an intimate other, or with a larger group. Generally, it is better to design seating for people who "will sit a while," since Whyte finds in his research that the most-used plazas and parks draw a larger number of women, more people in groups, and a higher proportion of couples than in less-used places (Whyte, 1980, pp. 16–39).

In his work, Whyte identifies other significant aspects of plaza and park design such as food sales and the presence of sun and shade, but none of these features is as important for stimulating sociability as location, street–plaza relationship, and sitting. Whyte's work is valuable practically because he demonstrates how different features of the environmental ensemble have different degrees of importance for whether a plaza or park succeeds or fails as a lively urban place. He identifies a hierarchy of design elements that moves from larger to smaller scale and from relationship with the larger urban context (relative location) to the plaza's connections with its immediate surroundings (street–plaza relationship) to the situation within (seating that is physically and socially comfortable).

In presenting these three features in terms of relative significance, Whyte helps one realize that a plaza or park in a poor location can probably not be made successful, just as a poorly performing plaza or park with a good location might be bolstered through better seating or a revamped sidewalk–plaza relationship. In terms of place intensification, Whyte's work is an instructive model because it provides a simple but lucid example of how successfully designed qualities of the environmental ensemble (location, street–plaza relationship, and seating) support a specific manner of people-in-place (sociability) that in turn facilitates an energetic common presence (an environmental exuberance).[5]

Topology Organizing Lifeworlds

Both Wylie's *salle* example and William Whyte's principles for robust plaza and park design illustrate, in an obvious, direct way, how elements of the environmental ensemble play a role in human experiences and therefore contribute to a stronger or weaker common presence of place. There are, however, elements and aspects of place intensification much more complex and difficult to identify and describe. I illustrate these less noticeable dimensions of place intensification by focusing on Bill Hillier's theory of space syntax and Jane Jacobs' conditions for urban diversity and street ballet. Both thinkers delineate physical and spatial aspects of the environmental ensemble that are only seeable and understandable through persistent, self-conscious study.

Though not phenomenological but analytic and instrumentalist, Hillier's theory of space syntax is a prominent example of how some significant aspects of the environmental ensemble are not readily known via lifeworld experience alone (Hillier, 1989, 1996, 2005, 2008; Hillier and Hanson, 1984; Hanson, 2000). Hillier argues that the spatial arrangement of pathways – whether roads, streets, or sidewalks – plays a major role in whether those pathways are well-used and animated or empty and lifeless. His work demonstrates convincingly that different pathway configurations can bring users together spatially or keep them apart.[6]

One central concept in Hillier's theory is *axial space*, which relates to the *one-dimensional* qualities of a pathway and has bearing on human movement throughout a town or city as a whole. Axial spaces are illustrated most perfectly by long narrow streets and are represented geometrically by the longest straight line that can be drawn through a street or other movement space before that line strikes a building, wall, or some other material object. Axial lines are significant phenomenologically for at least two reasons. First, because they indicate the farthest point of sight from where one happens to be, axial lines speak to the lived relationship between "here" and "there" and thus, at the settlement scale, have bearing on environmental orientation and finding one's way in a place. Second, because they collectively delineate the spatial system through which the various parts of a place are connected by pedestrian and vehicular circulation, a settlement's web of axial lines provides a simplified rendition of the potential movement field of a place. Hillier's important discovery is that differently configured pathway webs play a major role in generating different patterns of pathway movement and face-to-face encounter among pedestrians and other users.

An important quantitative measure of axial spaces and pathway webs is *integration*, which Hillier defines as an index of the relative degree of connectedness that an axial space has in relation to all other axial spaces in a pathway system. The assumption is that a pathway connected to many other pathways will be more travelled because users will need to traverse that pathway to get to other pathways and destinations in the town or city. Such a pathway is said to be strongly *integrated* in the movement field because many other pathways run into that well-connected pathway and potentially provide a large pool of users. In contrast, a *segregated* pathway has few or no other pathways running into it – for example, a dead-end street. All other things being equal, a segregated pathway will be the locus of less movement, since it serves a more limited number of users in its immediate vicinity only.

Through integration and other quantitative measures, Hillier develops a compelling understanding of the *global* pattern of a place – in other words, the way the spatial configuration of a place's pathway fabric lays out a potential movement field that gathers or separates co-presence. *Natural movement* is the term Hillier uses to describe the potential power of a pathway network to automatically stymie or facilitate movement and the face-to-face interactions of pedestrians and other place users. With many people present involved in their own regular routines and activities, the result typically is animated pathways and exuberant local places. Hillier recognizes that other place elements like density, building types, and number, size, and range of functions and land uses also contribute to place vitality, but he argues that, ultimately, pathway configuration is most primary and most crucial (Hillier, 1996, p. 161).

In relation to cities, Hillier demonstrates that most urban pathway systems have traditionally been an integrated, interconnected fabric of variously-scaled *deformed grids* – pathway systems in which the most active, integrated streets make a shape that roughly suggests a wheel of rim, hub, and spokes. Typically, each of these deformed grids is associated with some designated neighborhood or district – for example, London's Soho, West End, or City. In turn, the integrated pathway structures of these districts conjoin to shape a much larger *deformed grid* that founds the movement dynamic of the city and London region as a whole. Hillier points out that twentieth-century urban design and planning regularly replaced integrated pathway configurations with treelike systems of segregated pathways that stymied or destroyed the intimate relationship between local and global integration and thereby eliminated much face-to-face interaction – for example, the "cul-de-sac and loop" pattern of low-density, automobile-dependent suburbs or the hierarchical circulation layouts of many modernist housing estates.

From the perspective of synergistic relationality, what is striking about space syntax is that it offers a descriptive vehicle for envisioning how the pathway network of a place works to facilitate or inhibit movement patterns *throughout that place*. In spite of its objectivist framework, space syntax *gathers and holds together the parts of place that sustain traversals within that place*. This synergistic togetherness is grounded in the underlying topological constitution of the pathway structure as a whole – the way that a pathway is more or less enmeshed topologically in the place's overall pathway configuration and, thus, potentially, supports much or little human movement along that pathway. Each line of traversal, in other words, is not interpreted as a separate, disassociated pathway piece but as an integrated, continuous thread of the larger pathway fabric. As Hillier (2008, p. 30) explains, "The configuration of the space network is, in and of itself, a primary shaper of the pattern of movement."

The key phrase is "in and of itself," which intimates the inherent wholeness of the pathway structure. In this sense, space syntax offers a synergistic portrait of the potential pathway-movement dynamic of a place, and this portrait arises, not analytically (from the summation of empirical movement data for each pathway) but synergistically from *the very structure of the pathway configuration itself*, as pictured quantitatively. Via measurement, space syntax provides a descriptive means to identify and evaluate a web of continuous, intertwined pathways "that are themselves mutually defined only through the way in which they are gathered together within the place they also constitute" (Malpas, 2009, p. 29).

In terms of place intensification, space syntax illustrates how one aspect of the environmental ensemble – its spatial and topological features – plays a pivotal role in the movements of people-in-place and therefore contributes to that place's degree of "life" in terms of whether users are drawn together intercorporeally or kept apart. Space syntax offers a superlative example of how environmental spatiality and materiality – though in one sense inert and passive – can actively contribute to making everyday human worlds one way rather than another. Sociologist Thomas Gieryn (2002, p. 341) uses the phrase "agentic capacity of material realities" to describe the independent power of materiality and spatiality to contribute to the specific constitution of human lifeworlds. Space syntax is an exceptional example of this agentic capacity because the approach demonstrates that the physicality of place, via pathway structure, prearranges a spatial field, the nature of which has central bearing on the relative amount of human movement and co-presence in that place.

Environmental Ensemble Supporting Place Ballet

To end this chapter, I return to Jane Jacobs, who argues that the essential lived structure of robust urban places is the exuberance of neighborhood and sidewalk life. Jacobs' work is relevant to place intensification because she identifies key physical and spatial features of the city's environmental ensemble that play an important role in facilitating exuberant street activity. Jacobs (1961, pp. 143–151) contends that efficient urban diversity and vibrant city street life require four specific conditions directly relatable to the urban environmental ensemble: short blocks, a range in building types, a high concentration of people, and a mixture of *primary uses* – in other words, anchor functions like residences and workplaces to which people must necessarily go. In relation to place intensification, one can say that these four features of the environmental ensemble (*2*) set the stage for people-in-place via street ballet (*1*) and generate a unique place ambience and common presence (*3*).[7]

As with Hillier's space-syntax discoveries, these four conditions are not immediately obvious; in that sense, Jacobs' work can be described as an implicit phenomenology of how environmental elements contribute to energetic urban places. Primary uses like dwellings and workplaces are crucial because they provide a regular, guaranteed pool of street and sidewalk users. Jacobs emphasizes that a neighborhood should include at least two primary uses, and ideally more, since different primary uses provide different people on the streets at different times. In turn, these people contribute to the neighborhood's place ballet.

The users associated with primary functions are also important because they provide much of the economic and social support for a neighborhood's *secondary functions* – uses like eateries, cafés, taverns, and shops, for which many patrons are present, first of all, because they are dependent on primary functions like residence, work, schooling, and so forth (Jacobs, 1961, pp. 161–164). Most secondary uses are smaller establishments that can survive only because of another of Jacobs' four key elements – a *dense concentration of would-be users*, provided largely by sufficient primary uses and generating, "in small geographical compass, a great and exuberant richness of differences and possibilities, many of these differences unique and unpredictable, and all the more valuable because they are" (Jacobs, 1961, pp. 220–221). In lively urban neighborhoods, secondary uses greatly outnumber primary uses because many people close together require a wide range of goods, services, and activities (Jacobs, 1961, p. 147).

Jacobs' two other conditions for robust urban neighborhoods are a range of building types and small blocks. In discussing a neighborhood's buildings, Jacobs argues that the district must provide a close-grained mingling of structures ranging in age and condition, including a good amount of smaller, older buildings for incubating new primary functions and risky, start-up secondary enterprises unable to afford high rent. This range of building types becomes "the shelter . . . for many varieties of middling-, low- and no-yield diversity" (Jacobs, 1961, p. 199). Smaller structures are particularly significant because they offer more building units per sidewalk length than larger structures that are monolithic and typically controlled by non-local parties. In this way, smaller buildings contribute to providing a more diverse range of uses, activities, and users, all helping to sustain the visual, functional, and social variety of the neighborhood's street ballet.

Jacobs' fourth element of the urban environmental ensemble is short blocks, which she sees as integral to a district's street ballet because permeable, interconnected sidewalks and streets support intermingling pedestrian cross-use and a longer string of street-front locations than longer blocks provide. Short blocks offer users many more route choices than longer blocks, making traversals more convenient: "[F]requent streets and short blocks are valuable because of the fabric of intricate cross use that they permit among the users of a city neighborhood (Jacobs, 1961, p. 186).

In highlighting the significance of short blocks for robust urban neighborhoods, Jacobs' argument foreshadows Hillier's more recent work on how the spatial configuration of streets and sidewalks plays a major role in whether they are well-used and animated or empty and lifeless (Seamon, 2012a). Like his discoveries, Jacobs' work is a stunning example of how environmental elements play a preeminent role in urban vitality and city place making. She offers conclusive evidence that the environmental ensemble contributes pervasively to human life and to places that sustain a compelling common presence.

In relation to place intensification, the work of Jane Jacobs, Bill Hillier, and William Whyte is elucidating because these researchers probe aspects of the environmental ensemble that are not readily recognized or understood. All three researchers say much about how aspects of the physical and spatial environment play a role in urban lifeworlds and intensify or diminish the common presence of place. In turn, this understanding helps architects, planners, policy makers, or community advocates to better envision an appropriate "fit" between place as environmental ensemble and place as lifeworld. This understanding moves us toward the sixth triad of *place creation*, whereby thoughtful, able individuals and groups partake in innovative place making. This triad is the focus of the next chapter.

Notes

1 Note that Whylie's appropriation of the *salle* is only successful after a series of failed interaction triads in which he attempts to make the house do what it cannot. Through these mistakes, he begins to realize what the house can best offer his family – in other words, he becomes attuned to the ways the *salle* partakes in the intensification of the house as a workable lifeworld and dwelling place.
2 In his studies, Whyte focuses only on plazas and parks in urban districts with high densities and much foot traffic.
3 Though there are exceptions, Whyte (1980, pp. 58–59, p. 114) recommends that generally a plaza should be no more than three feet (about one meter) above or below sidewalk level.
4 Thirty square feet is almost three square meters. Three feet is a bit less than one meter; sixteen inches is about four-tenths of a meter; thirty inches is about three-quarters of a meter. Seating with backs at least a foot high can be as narrow as fourteen inches (about one-third meter) (see Whyte, 1980, pp. 112–116).
5 One of Whyte's most intriguing discoveries is what he calls "effective capacity" – his claim that people have an instinctive awareness for the appropriate number of users in a space: If they sense that a space has reached its optimal number of users, they will not enter the plaza, but go elsewhere (Whyte, 1980, pp. 66–75). As he explains, "capacity is self-leveling" (Whyte, 1980, pp. 73). For New York City officials, Whyte's claim was important, since they were concerned that, if some plazas became highly popular, they might become overcrowded. Whyte concluded that the real problem was not over use but *under* use. Whyte's empirical evidence of effective capacity is limited (a time-lapse study of the north ledge of Seagram's Plaza). As far as I know, no researchers have conclusively demonstrated its reality. Studying the phenomenon more thoroughly, including its phenomenological dimension, is an important research project for the future.
6 Space syntax is also applicable to building interiors; see Hanson, 1998; Seamon, 2017a.
7 I identify "a high concentration of people" here as an aspect of the environmental ensemble, even though one could argue that this condition relates equally to "people-in-place." Since concentration, as Jacobs defines it, is largely an aggregate physical measure of

individuals per areal unit (rather than psychological, social, cultural, or economic characteristics of those individuals), I include it as an element of the environmental ensemble, mostly for presentational convenience. Obviously, concentration relates to density, which has important experiential dimensions as, for example, in the case of overcrowding (see Jacobs, 1961, pp. 205–208).

14

THE TRIAD OF PLACE CREATION
(1–2–3 OR PP–EE–CP)

Closely associated with place intensification, place creation relates to dedicated individuals who, understanding their place and recognizing its needs, envision improvements in that place's environmental ensemble that, in turn, strengthen common presence. Place creation as process undermines place when it produces thinking, envisioning, and making that misunderstand or ignore the real needs of place. The result is arbitrary, inappropriate, or useless policies, designs, and actions that weaken place by misinterpreting what it is and thereby negating its core workings and possibilities.

Pictured as a triad, place creation can be described as committed and knowledgeable people-of-place (*1*) who make creative shifts in their place's environmental ensemble (*2*) that invigorate the place's common presence (*3*). Architectural phenomenologist Dalibor Vesely (2003, p. 144) describes place creation well when he writes that "To create is to bring to existence what was not here before, but in such a way that the result is fully reconciled with everything that is already here." What is central to Vesely's understanding of creation is that its results *fit in with* what is already present and make the situation better. He contrasts this way of creating with what he calls *production*, which is a manner of counterfeit making that interferes with or undermines what is already present. He associates production with "loss of meaning, a confused sense of reality, emptiness of buildings and spaces, the growing room for hallucinatory experiences and growing cultural fragmentation" (Vesely, 2003, p. 144). He writes:

> Production . . . tends to ignore the restrictions of the given reality and moves towards the limits of what can be done, crossing very often and quite deliberately the boundary of the imaginary and hallucinatory level of reality. In

the productive attitude, the hallucinatory quality of products is not seen as problematic or negative but very often as desirable.

(Vesely, 2003, p. 144)

As I speak of place creation, Vesely's production is its negative, destructive side. In this chapter, my extended examples emphasize a *constructive, place-strengthening* process incorporating Vesely's reconciliation of "what is already present" and "what was not here before." I begin with six newspaper stories that illustrate place creation, though one account relates more to a destructive "production" of place rather than to its creative strengthening. I then present five in-depth examples of constructive place creations that include place-based wind turbines, landscape repair, and the fabrication of wholeness.

Examples of Place Creation

The following newspaper stories illustrate place situations ranging from global to local scale and places that are both natural and human-made. The entries point to how "people-in-place" can bolster or enfeeble their place because of appropriate or inappropriate interventions in the environmental ensemble.

- Aiming to mitigate Beijing's chronic air pollution, Chinese officials are planning a "green necklace" of trees around the city. The plan includes five "ventilation corridors" to channel wind and air movement to disperse the city's smog. Each at least 1,500 feet wide (460 meters), these corridors run through the city to improve air circulation (*NYT*, March 24, 2017, p. A10).
- The small Italian town of Soveria Mannelli has harnessed digital technology to its traditional work culture, turning this community of 3,000 into a model for Italy's underdeveloped south. The town has a school furniture manufacturer, a publishing house, and wool mill, all run by families who have maintained their local ties by updating their businesses digitally (*NYT*, December 9, 2016, p. A4).
- Designers are creating a new generation of utility structures that blend in visually with a city's social fabric and that provide amenities and public art. One example is a power substation in Seattle that invites passersby to peer through portholes to see the facility's machinery within. To promote street life, the substation's ground level includes retail space and an outdoor eating area (*WSJ*, April 4, 2017, p. R6).
- Though Detroit's downtown core has been revitalized, many of its surrounding urban neighborhoods are nearly abandoned as residents leave the city or move to its suburbs. The city is currently involved in a range of efforts to restore these blighted areas and to reconnect remaining viable neighborhoods. Solutions to filling the empty space include constructing a range of housing types that might draw newcomers to the city; converting

empty lots into gardens, parks, and cycling paths; developing an urban agriculture; and matching empty storefronts with potential entrepreneurs (*WSJ*, April 17, 2017, p. R3).

- Illustrating "resilient design," a nine-story building in New York City's Chelsea neighborhood will have a main floor above the ground to protect the structure from flooding because of rising sea levels and more intense storms. Users enter the building at sidewalk level and ascend to the first floor by steps or ramps. Floodwaters flow in and out of the lower level through baffles. The building's other storm guards include windows designed to survive high winds and electrical equipment on the mezzanine level rather than in the basement (*NYT*, April 5, 2017, p. A18).

- Greenacre Park, New York City's popular Midtown vest pocket park, may lose much of its sunlight because of a new rezoning plan allowing for taller buildings that would block the park's afternoon sun, threaten its elegant landscape plantings, and make a place that is darker, colder, and much less inviting. A study commissioned by the park's Greenacre Foundation has determined that the six skyscrapers planned nearby would cast the entire space in shadow. To counter the rezoning plan, the foundation has organized a "Fight for Light" campaign (*NYT*, May 23, 2017, p. A22).

In studying these six newspaper accounts, one notes that four stories illustrate creative efforts to make places better – for example, the Italian town's harnessing digital technology, or urban-design efforts to create utility structures integrated with their urban context. Two stories point to inappropriate or questionable policy and designs that potentially weaken place – New York's ill-advised high-rise rezoning that reduces the natural light received by many parts of the city, and architects' controversial efforts to fabricate "resilient" architecture able to cope with climate change.

The story about resilient-building design illustrates how place creation sometimes involves ambiguity. If rising sea levels and more intense storms are a certainty because of climate change, does it make sense to suppose that built environments can be designed to cope with and even overcome environmental consequences? I argue that a key requirement of appropriate place creation is fully understanding one's place and accepting what is possible and what is not. From this perspective, so-called "resilient design" is an uncertain example of supportive place creation and place making, since one wonders how any building could remain usable if higher sea levels become permanent and threatened structures are eventually surrounded by water (Abramson, 2016, pp. 155–156).

In this chapter, my emphasis is on *constructive, appropriate* place making, and the five examples that follow probe the underlying qualities of understanding and envisioning that mark positive place creation and facilitate productive place making. First, I present philosopher Gordon G. Brittan's efforts to envision and build user-friendly wind turbines grounded in place and geographical region.

Second, I review the conceptual and practical efforts of naturalist Paul Krafel to counter the second law of thermodynamics, which claims that the world moves toward progressively more entropy. Third, I consider the pioneering work of Egyptian architect Hassan Fathy, who attempted to build a village for 7,000 displaced Egyptian peasants. Fourth, I highlight the efforts of architect Christopher Alexander to envision and concretize an architectural language that might facilitate a wholeness of place. For my last example, I return to the work of Jane Jacobs, whose extraordinary understanding of the urban lifeworld, now over a half-century old, remains one of the most profound illustrations of place understanding and creation in our time.

I chose these five thinkers and makers because their work illustrates a central feature of genuine place creation: that innovative place making is grounded in an engaged understanding of the place that one wishes to make better. Without a real encounter with the situation one hopes to change, there is much less likelihood of designs and fabrications that make a positive difference. What we make is what we understand, and I argue that the work of these five individuals offers revealing examples of thoughtful understanding and consequential fabrication. These efforts point toward an approach to place making in which environmental ensemble, people-in-place, and common presence are conjoined to facilitate a richness of place, place experience, and place meaning.

Envisioning Wind Turbines Attuned to Place and People

From the 1980s through the early 2000s, Montana rancher and philosopher Gordon G. Brittan, Jr., sought to develop a prototype for a place-based wind turbine adaptable to specific geographical locales and operable by laypersons for whom the device would supply household and neighborhood energy (Brittan, 2001, 2002a, 2002b). Called the "Windjammer," this device was modelled on traditional windmills and incorporated many of their technical features, including slow turning, high torque, and blades made from triangular cloth sails that furl in a strong wind. The Windjammer's machinery was exposed, relatively simple in construction, and repairable by users with a basic knowledge of mechanics and electronics. The turbine's gearbox, brake, and generator were at ground level, and the twenty-five-foot-long rotor blades did not require a tower or crane for installation or repair as do the much larger, corporate-utility wind turbines that can be as high as 700 feet (200 meters), have wind blades 400 feet (120 meters) long, and produce power for as many as 4,000 homes (Pasqualetti et al., 2002).

The key design aim of Brittan and his development team was a wind turbine "small enough and simple enough and cheap enough (under 1,500 dollars) that almost anyone could install it, unaided" (Brittan, 2001, p. 184). The Windjammer's manageable size, low cost, and ease of installation and maintenance meant that units could be locally owned and potentially organized into community co-operatives providing surplus power to the larger regional energy grid. In addition, Brittan's aim was to produce different Windjammer models for different geographical locales, taking into account both natural and human variations relating to such place features as terrain, climate, seasons, dominant winds, environmental aesthetics, and social and cultural traditions and lifeways (Brittan, 2002b, p. 15).

As a philosopher, Brittan described the Windjammer as a *thing* rather than a *device*. Drawing on philosophers Martin Heidegger (1971b) and Albert Borgmann (1992, 1999), Brittan (2002b, p. 11) defined a thing as an object in the world that engages users and offers them a sense of self-worth – for example, a tool, heirloom, or musical instrument. In contrast, a device is a machine that remains apart from its users, who need not know how it works or how it might be repaired if broken – for example, a personal computer or cell phone. Many of today's devices are designed not to be repaired and to be discarded if they fail. Other devices are so complex that when they do break, they can only be repaired by experts with specialized equipment – for example, a jet aircraft or digitally-sophisticated automobile.

Whereas the conventional three-blade wind turbines promoted by corporate utility companies are devices, Brittan's Windjammer is a thing that can be appropriated, whereby users feel a sense of care and obligation, which in turn supports a sense of personal and communal autonomy. To take full advantage of local winds, both the Windjammer's design and its operators must be attuned to qualities of regional geography, particularly daily, seasonal, and annual variations relating to weather and climate. Operators must also be attuned to the wind turbine itself, feeling a sense of responsibility for running it properly and for knowing when it is working sub-optimally. In this sense, devices like the Windjammer relate people to their place and facilitate both place identity and place interactions that might sustain human community and a stronger sense of place.

I draw on Brittan's work as an example of place creation because his efforts offer a perspicacious example of one group of committed individuals who work to envision one new element of the environmental ensemble that might strengthen place, place experience, place actions, and place meanings. Brittan's creative efforts to design and fabricate (*1*) a wind-turbine prototype (*2*) might instill care and concern that connects local people and places, thus strengthening common presence (*3*).

Healing an Eroded Landscape

I next turn to Californian naturalist Paul Krafel, whose writings and practical efforts are a major contribution to a lived environmental ethic, whereby individuals might come to revere and heal the natural world through deepening understanding and invigorative practical actions. Krafel's *Seeing Nature* (Krafel, 1998) can fairly be described as a phenomenology of the two laws of thermodynamics: First, that energy is neither created nor destroyed; second, that all activities left to their own devices tend toward greater disorder and fewer possibilities. In thinking through the lived implications of the second law, Krafel asks a question crucial for our times: Can human beings do nothing but consume and undermine the Earth? "I despair," writes Krafel (1998, p. 198) "at not being able to do more than live at the expense of the world."

In finding conceptual and practical ways to counter the second law, Krafel presents remarkably creative ways to look at and contribute order to the natural world. He calls his approach *shifting*, whereby one works to see from a new perspective and thereby understands the world differently. This manner of engaging with the world might help actualize intentional, caring actions whereby human beings increase, rather than decrease, the possibilities of the world. As illustrated in Figure 14.1, one of Krafel's examples is shifting his perspective so that he sees the earth–sun relationship in a new, more experientially accurate way:

> One evening I saw the earth turning. Before that night, I had always seen the sun *setting* toward a stationary horizon [upper drawing]. But when I saw the sun, instead, as stationary, then I saw my horizon *rising* toward the sun [lower drawing]. In the first view, the sun moves. In the second view, my world moves. My eyes see the same thing – the gap between sun and horizon closing. But what is moving? My brain must make an assumption. Shifting that assumption changes the world I see.
>
> *(Krafel, 1998, p. 13)*

One of Krafel's most rousing efforts to shift his understanding and thereby facilitate constructive change is the work he does to heal an overgrazed California field badly eroded by gullies. During rain storms, he takes a shovel out

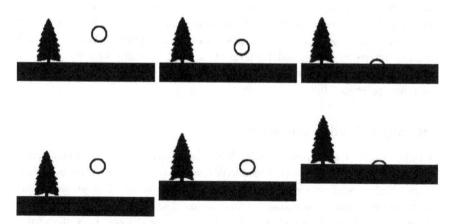

FIGURE 14.1 Seeing the sun move and seeing the earth move
Source: from Krafel, 1989, p. 12, and used with permission of the author.

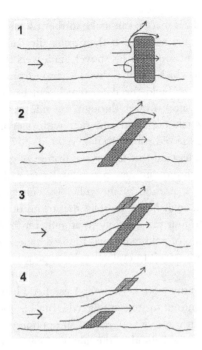

FIGURE 14.2 Krafel's four stages in gully repair
Source: from Krafel, 1989, pp. 147–149, and used with permission of the author.

to the ravaged property and builds mini-dams to split the rain torrents and weaken their erosive power. As illustrated in Figure 14.2, his understanding of how he might heal the gullies shifts as he becomes progressively aware of how rainwater moves. His understanding and consequent repairs proceed in four steps.

1. When Krafel initiates the project, he shovels sod directly into the gully's channel to form thick dams that must be high enough to deflect the rainwater along a sideward path. These dams quickly erode, however, because they force the water to stop, pool up, and then move in a sideward direction. This effort successfully diverts and reduces the flow of water in the eroded gullies but leaves a pockmarked field because of the considerable amount of sod required for the thick dams.

2. As Krafel becomes more familiar with the gullies, he realizes that he only needs to deflect *some* of the water onto a new path. Recognizing that water flows more readily along curves, he now places the dams at an oblique angle so that the momentum of the water that earlier eroded the dams now becomes a positive force deflecting water from the gully into the new side path.

3.   Next, Krafel realizes that he can make further use of the water's momentum
     by offering it a new path rather than using the dam to oppose its original
     path. Scooping out sod with his shovel, he lowers the bank to make a side
     channel through which water is diverted away from the gully. He uses the
     scooped-out sod to build the dam, which can be smaller because a good
     portion of water now moves through the side channel. Krafel notes that
     "This discovery felt profound and rich with allegory. Offer a new path
     before opposing the old path" (Krafel, 1998, p. 147).

4.   In coming to understand that the pivotal feature of gully repair is to turn the
     rainwater's momentum into new pathways, Krafel realizes that he need make
     dams across only a portion of the gully. By cutting the side pathway and
     building a partial, angled dam, he splits the stream of water and diminishes its
     erosive power. In four years, his efforts at gully repair show significant results,
     and "mini-marshes of wild radish and mustard appear where there was noth-
     ing but bare, hard earth." In evaluating his experience, he writes:

> When I began my work in the field, I assumed I had to work in the eroded
> gullies and confront the torrents directly. But I learned that helping the soil
> absorb the rain was more effective than opposing the concentrated power
> of runoff. If the soil absorbed the rain, the power of erosion never formed
> in the first place. The most powerful place for healing was not in the gullies
> but where raindrops first touched the Earth.
>
> *(Krafel, 1998, p. 158)*

For a lived environmental ethics, Krafel's work is exemplary because it illustrates a manner of encountering the natural world that geographer Edward Relph
calls *environmental humility* – a way of seeing and understanding that is responsive to
the best qualities of the Other and might foster a compassion and gentle caretaking
for places, people, and the things of nature. As Relph (1981, p. 187) writes, "The
call is for guardianship, for taking care of things merely because they exist, for
tending and protecting them. In this there is neither mastery nor subservience, but
there is responsibility and commitment" (Relph, 1981, p. 187).

Krafel's account illustrates the close relationship between environmental
humility and place creation: His growing awareness and understanding (*1*) perfect
a process of repair (*2*) that in turn heals and renews common presence – the
field's ecological viability (*3*). His experience points to the crucial importance of
an intimate engagement between person-in-place and environmental ensemble,
actualized in Krafel's case by going out in the rain with his shovel and carefully
looking, seeing, and realizing how he can most effectively redirect the rushing
water. In Relph's terms, he "becomes" the Other. Krafel's success demonstrates
that the most useful envisioning and making is grounded in an empathetic
understanding whereby the situation to be bettered is given full attention,
carefully engaged, and *always put first*.

Designing and Building an Egyptian Village

Another inspiring effort at place creation is Egyptian architect Hassan Fathy's efforts to design and built a village for some 7,000 Egyptian peasants living in Gourna, an Upper Nile village located in the Cemetery of Thebes, a site of ancient tombs and holy relics. A principal Gourni livelihood was robbing the cemetery tombs and selling their contents on the black market. Concerned that irreplaceable archeological artifacts were being lost, the Eyptian government decided in 1945 that the Gournis must be relocated. Fathy was commissioned to organize this relocation, which he describes in his inspirational *Architecture for the Poor* (Fathy, 1973). This book has become a seminal text for self-help housing, sustainable dwelling, and design-build place making.

Although New Gourna, the village Fathy planned for the Gournis, was never completed, his work is central to place creation because he illustrates a way of designing and building that attempts to understand the Gournis' needs and to draw on that understanding to fabricate an environmental ensemble that maintains and enhances the Gournis' lifeworld. Fathy argues that, before the coming of Western influences, traditional Egyptian building was founded on the needs of people-in-place, facilitating a building style that integrated "the imagination of the people and the demands of their countryside" (Fathy, 1973, p. 19). He contends that modern housing in the developing world, strongly influenced by Western architectural styles and construction methods, has too often broken with traditional building. The poor too often reside in "rows of identical houses" that negatively affect their residents: "The people will grow dull and dispirited like their houses, and their imagination will shrivel up" (Fathy, 1973, p. 31).

To revitalize traditional building, Fathy realizes that he must thoroughly engage with the Gournis' lifestyle in a way that is implicitly phenomenological: "We should have to uncover the everyday life of the Gournis and reveal it, perhaps even more minutely than they themselves knew it" (Fathy, 1973, p. 50). In turn, this thorough, empathetic effort to understand the Gournis provides the impetus for appropriate design. One example is his using traditional construction materials and methods common to the Gourna region, particularly mud brick, which can be made economically from local materials and produces buildings that work well experientially, ecologically, and aesthetically. Building comfort, for instance, depends largely on the thermal qualities of walls and roofs. As a poor conductor of heat, mud brick remains cool during the day and radiates heat at night. In the hot, arid climate of Upper Egypt, with its widely fluctuating daytime and nighttime temperatures, residents can live downstairs by day and move up to the roof to sleep in the cool night air. At the same time, mud brick is inexpensive and leads to buildings of human scale that are handsome aesthetically: "[Mud brick] cannot help being beautiful, for the structure dictates the shapes and the material imposes scale, every line respects the distribution of stresses, and the building takes on a satisfying and natural shape" (Fathy, 1973, p. 11).

In designing New Gourna, Fathy pays close attention to the Gournis' social structures of family, extended family, and tribe. Houses are not freestanding but share common walls in neighborhood blocks to support the *badana*, a tightly related group of ten to twenty families with a recognized patriarch. Families of the badana live in adjoining houses that enclose a shared, semi-public courtyard for receiving guests and for conducting social gatherings like weddings. The badana collectively form a larger social unit – the tribe, of which in Old Gourna there were four, each living in its own village quarter. In his plan for the new village, Fathy duplicates these quarters, using functions traditionally associated with each tribe to locate public facilities. The *Hassassna*, for example, were traditionally thought of as pious and learned; Fathy groups their quarter around buildings related to religion and education – the mosque and the girls' and boys' schools. In contrast, the *Horobat* were traditionally known as the "warriors" and the tribe most active in tomb robbing. Fathy plans their quarter to include the market, village hall, crafts school, and police station. In making these linkages between social and spatial order, Fathy seeks to respect the Gournis' lifeworld and to provide for its continuity in the new village.

One of the most praiseworthy and hopeful aspects of Fathy's efforts is his insistence that every village element integrate a range of practical and lived functions. One example is the courtyard, an architectural element that he makes work environmentally, experientially, socially, and spiritually. The courtyard is formed by the enclosure of houses turned inward. First, the courtyard works environmentally, providing shade, keeping out the harsh desert, and serving as a collector of cool night air that moderates daytime temperatures. Second, the courtyard incorporates a spiritual dimension, drawing down the sky, which reflects the oneness of Allah: "The sky is . . . pulled into intimate contact with the house, so that the spirituality of the home is constantly replenished from heaven" (Fathy, 1973, p. 56). Third, the courtyard holds an important social function, providing a space for children's play, informal gatherings, and family celebrations. Fourth, the courtyard contributes to the unique atmosphere of each house, supporting a "certain quality that can be distinctly felt and that carries a local signature as clearly as does a particular curve" (Fathy, 1973, p. 55). Fathy also uses a courtyard arrangement to organize New Gourna's neighborhood blocks by widening the central portion of street running through them, thereby creating a sizeable social space for badana events such as weddings and funerals (Fathy 1973, p. 55). In a similar way, he uses a larger-scaled, "courtyard" arrangement to center the village spatially, providing a main square around which he places the mosque, village hall, exhibition hall, and several other public buildings (Fathy, 1973, p. 70, p. 76).

Though Fathy grounds his village design in the Gournis' traditional lifeworld, he recognizes aspects of that lifeworld that might be improved. He realizes, for example, that the traditional ovens used by the Gournis to heat their homes are inefficient (Fathy, 1973, p. 97). He looks for a more effective device, which he finds in the *kachelofen*, an easily constructed Austrian stove that directs the hot gases from combustion back and forth through a system of partitions and thus allows more time for heat to radiate into a room. Fathy finds an old woman who makes the traditional Gourni ovens and teaches her to make the kachelofen with traditional oven materials. The woman learns the fabrication method and produces stoves as cheaply as the older ovens. In this case, Fathy aims to develop a new domestic technology that might eventually become part of the Gournis' older building traditions (Fathy, 1973, p. 24).

Fathy also realizes that New Gourna cannot succeed as a place unless he provides the Gournis with viable ways of livelihood to replace their dependence on illegal tomb robbing. He designs the village to support farming and rural crafts, particularly those common to life in the old village, such as weaving, dying, and potting. He insists that the Gournis build New Gourna themselves, since village construction will teach them additional building crafts, especially vaulting and dome construction. When Fathy visits New Gourna several years after the resettlement experiment has ended, he finds that the forty-six masons he trained still work in the district using the building skills they learned at New Gourna (Fathy, 1973, p. 192).

Although Fathy's New Gourna experiment ultimately failed, partly because of a hostile government bureaucracy, Fathy's work is an outstanding example of place creation. Fathy's New Gourna effort is first of all concerned with rural rehabilitation of the developing world's poor. It is also, however, a signal illustration of one committed individual, working with people-in-place (*1*) to construct the environmental ensemble of New Gourna (*2*) and facilitate a strong common presence via a thriving village life (*3*). Though Fathy has been criticized for partially misunderstanding the lifeway needs and wishes of the Gournis, his New Gourna experiment is relevant to place creation because it demonstrates the architect's sincere wish to understand the Gournis and thereby improve their village life through architectural design. His work is a stellar model for place making grounded in the needs of people and place.[1]

Understanding and Making Wholeness

In considering place creation, one of the most challenging questions is whether the spontaneous place making of the past can, in our hypermodern world, be regenerated intentionally (Relph, 1976, 1981). Fathy's work is one important attempt to offer an affirmative answer to this question as are the efforts of architect Christopher Alexander, who I discuss next.[2] Though Alexander does not describe himself as a phenomenologist, one can argue that his work is implicitly phenomenological because he attends to the experienced qualities of buildings and places and to the lived process of architectural and environmental design. For example, his efforts to create a "pattern language" (Alexander et al., 1977; Alexander et al., 1987) can fairly be described as an implicit phenomenology of design elements that contribute to a sense of place. Similarly, his four-volume *The Nature of Order* (Alexander, 2002a, 2002b, 2004, 2005) can be interpreted as an implicit phenomenology of a manner of architectural and environmental order that Alexander calls *wholeness*, which, whether in nature or human-made, is "the source of the coherence that exists in any part of the world" (Alexander 2002a, p. 90).

Phenomenologically, one can say that Alexander aims to understand and make places grounded in *"belonging* together." In all his writings and building designs, his central concern is understanding how the parts of a designed thing – whether an elegant doorway or a gracious building or an animated city plaza – belong together and have their proper place in the whole (Alexander, 2005, 2012; Alexander et al., 1977). He asks how architectural and environmental wholeness comes into being and how an ever-deepening reciprocity between understanding and designing might allow for more and more wholeness to unfold. His aim is "an architecture in which every part, every building, every street, every garden, is alive" (Alexander, 2002b, p. 2). To design the built environment well is to *make life* in the sense that the designed environment can, on one hand, be comfortable, beautiful, robust, and whole; or, on the other hand, be disconcerting, unseemly, moribund, and fractured. As Alexander writes, "Our wellbeing originates in large part from the spatial ordering of the world" (Alexander, 2012, p. 382).

At different times, Alexander has applied different labels to the wholeness he seeks – "the quality without a name," "the timeless way of building," "creating pattern languages," "density," "degrees of life," "fundamental properties sustaining wholeness," or "wholeness-extending transformations" (Grabow, 1983; Alexander, 2007). In his efforts to generate a "pattern language," for example, Alexander sought to gather examples of buildings and places throughout the world that evoke a sense of order, robustness, and comfort. These examples then became a real-world basis for identifying and explicating underlying physical qualities, or "patterns," that might be a model for conceiving future buildings and places (Alexander et al., 1977).

Significantly, these patterns are not architectural elements or material things but constellations of environment–experience relationships that sustain, through architectural and place qualities, a sense of human and environmental wellbeing – for example, "identifiable neighborhoods," "degrees of publicness," "main gateways," "entry transition," "window places," "balconies at least six feet wide," and so forth (Alexander et al., 1977). In explicating "main gateways," for instance, Alexander suggests that urban designers should highlight important urban districts with some form of entry marking "where the major entering paths cross the boundary" (Alexander et al., 1977, p. 278). Or, in emphasizing the importance of "entry transition," Alexander refers to the psychological transition from street to building entry: "[B]uildings with a graceful transition between the street and the inside are more tranquil than those that open directly off the street" (Alexander et al., 1977, p. 549). He discusses how entry transitions can be strengthened design-wise through gateways and through shifts in pathway direction, level, surface, light, view, and so forth.

Eventually, however, Alexander became dissatisfied with pattern language as a design approach. He realized that the pattern language process alone was not sufficient for producing life-sustaining buildings or places. He recognized that his theory of wholeness needed to incorporate a design-and-construction process whereby wholeness is not just envisioned but made to happen. This concern led Alexander to his most recent work on the nature of order, by which he means an ever-intensifying making and unfolding of life, which, depending on the design aim, might refer to poise, exuberance, happiness, solace, holiness, awe, sense of community, or some other lived quality supporting place (Alexander, 2002a, 2002b, 2004, 2005, 2012).

Alexander's major purpose in *Nature of Order* is to establish a contemporary design method for generating wholeness and life through an incremental intensi- fication whereby each step in the design process becomes a pointer for the next step. This process can only unfold rightly "when the response of each act of building has been fresh, authentic, and autonomous, called into being by previous and present circumstance, shaped only by a detailed and living overall response to the whole" (Alexander, 2005, p. 22). His way of working illustrates place creation in that Alexander carefully engages with the design needs of people-in-place (*1*) and thereby envisions appropriate elements of the environmental ensemble (*2*) that strengthen the common presence and wholeness of place (*3*). Alexander offers a practical method of "making" whereby activities, experiences, buildings, and spaces might be designed in an integrated, coherent way to create places that work well practically and evoke life, sustenance, pleasure, and wonderment. The broadest aim is *healing*, whereby every new construction is designed and fabri- cated in such a way as to make the environment and place *more whole* (Alexander, 2002b, pp. 249–266; 2007).

Alexander's work says much about place intensification, since he deeply believes that the designed environment plays a central role in human life and human wellbeing. He assumes that, by realizing the importance in everyday life of architectural and environmental elements and qualities that we normally take for granted, we will be better able to envision and design future places, whether they be rooms, buildings, neighborhoods, cities, or regions. Through its percep- tive explications of the lived nature of architecture and the design process, Alex- ander's work is an exceptional example of place intensification, place creation, and their intimate reciprocity.

Discovering a Phenomenology of the City

One of the most remarkable twentieth-century examples of place creation is Jane Jacobs' *Death and Life of Great American Cities* (Jacobs, 1961). Though Jacobs herself played no direct role in designing or planning urban places, the ideas in her book have been a powerful impetus for how many urban designers and planners envision better cities today. I use Jacobs' work as an example of place creation because it illustrates one researcher's ardent wish to thoroughly understand a phenomenon – citiness and urban experience – and to use that understanding as a practical guide to generate exuberant city environments. In this sense, Jacobs' work is an applied phenomenology of the city and urban place making (Seamon, 2012a). Methodologically, her major aim is to allow citiness to reveal itself in everyday, taken-for-granted life and to use these firsthand discoveries as a starting point for identifying more general principles and structures that make the city what it is essentially.

As explained in earlier chapters, Jacobs says much about urban-place-as-process. Her hopeful city vision is "ever more diversity, density and dynamism – in effect, to crowd people and activities together in a jumping, joyous urban jumble" (Martin, 2006, n.p.). In *Death and Life*, she argues that mid-twentieth-century urban design and city planning undermined American cities because professionals understood the phenomenon of city not as it is but as these professionals wanted it to be – for example, Le Corbusier's "towers in the park," Louis Mumford's network of new towns in the countryside, or Robert Moses's mega-block urban renewal policies and massive highway construction (Laurence, 2016). Engaged in an arbitrary manipulation of place that illustrates Vesely's "production," described at the start of this chapter, urban practitioners and researchers have

> ignored the study of success and failure in real life, have been incurious about the reasons for unexpected success, and are guided instead by principles derived from the behavior and appearance of towns, suburbs, tuberculosis sanatoria, fairs, and imaginary dream cities – anything but cities themselves.
>
> *(Jacobs, 1961, p. 6)*

Architectural historian Peter Laurence (2011, 2016) has traced Jacobs' growing disenchantment with post-World War II urban planning and design. As a writer on urban issues for *Architectural Forum* in the early 1950s, she felt more and more guilty about supporting urban-renewal projects that, she realized through firsthand visits, were dramatic failures as livable places and communities. In 1959, as she was writing *Death and Life*, she described her growing cynicism to landscape architect and friend Grady Clay:

> I had a pervading uneasiness about the way the rebuilding of the city was going, augmented by some feeling of personal guilt, I suppose, or at least personal involvement. The reason for this was that in all sincerity I had been writing for *Forum* about how great various redevelopment plans were going to be. Then I began to see some of these things built. They weren't delightful, they weren't fine, and they were obviously never going to work right . . . I began to get this very uneasy feeling that what sounded logical in

planning theory and what looked splendid on paper was not logical in real life at all, or at least in city real life, and not splendid at all when in use.

(quoted in Laurence, 2011, p. 35; originally written March 3, 1959)

On one hand, therefore, Jacobs' understanding of citiness developed through her seeing, directly in the field, the failure of post-war urban renewal. On the other hand, she was busy identifying and observing real-world urban neighborhoods and districts with an animated, diverse street life – particularly her Hudson Street neighborhood in Greenwich Village. This mode of inductive observation and interpretation would eventually lead to her claim in *Death and Life* that her understanding of urbanity was grounded in what the city and urban experience *actually are*: a lived diversity of place that sustains personal and group identification and attachment. In a description of her method that could serve as instruction for urban phenomenology, she wrote: "The way to get at what goes on in the seemingly mysterious and perverse behavior of cities is, I think, to look closely, and with as little previous expectation as is possible, at the most ordinary scenes and events, and attempt to see what they mean and whether any threads of principle emerge among them" (Jacobs, 1961, p. 13).

Just as important as her substantive urban discoveries are the affection and hope that her heartfelt explication provokes. Through Jacobs' sympathetic understanding, readers may be motivated to involve themselves in place creation as it might happen in *their own city*. Jacobs' work is a lucid example of how better understanding place experience and life can foster ways to make that place more livable and vibrant. As urban historian Christopher Klemek (2011, p. 75) explains about his own personal experience of Jacobs' work: "[Reading *Death and Life*] was paradigmatically transformative, and I have hardly framed an urban observation since that day that is not somehow indebted to her ideas. *Death and Life* is simply that kind of book; once you read it, you seem to forever encounter the urban world on its terms . . . ."

As Klemek indicates, Jacobs felt an absolute loyalty to the urban lifeworld and to elements of the environmental ensemble that mark the essence of citiness and urban life. She understood urban place as a complex, interconnected environmental and human whole that presupposes "the unencompassability of place by anything other than itself" (Casey, 2009, pp. 15–16). In terms of place creation, what is central about Jacobs' understanding is that the parts of urban place only work together when they facilitate and are facilitated by an appropriate "*belonging together*" of people, activities, situations and environmental elements unfolding in a dynamic place synergy.

Jacobs' work on the city is one of the great examples of place creation. Through her unceasing efforts to understand the city as an urban lifeworld (*1*), she recognizes the central importance of various elements of the environmental ensemble (*2*) and thereby delineates an understanding that might practically foster city exuberance and a powerful sense of urban place (*3*). Her work is a superb instance of how a careful, extended engagement with the phenomenon leads to conceptual and practical understandings that in turn offer a way of creating that is grounded in lifeworlds and lived emplacement. She exemplifies Vesely's articulation of creation, highlighted at the start of this chapter: "To create is to bring to existence what was not here before, but in such a way that the result is fully reconciled with everything that is already here."

In the five examples of place creation I have presented in this chapter, readers may have noticed that the affirming impulse is not "people-in-place" *per se*, but one creative individual who envisions innovative possibilities that he or she concretizes practically – Brittan's Windjammer, Krafel's landscape healing, Fathy's village plans, Alexander's environmental wholeness, or Jacobs' conditions for urban diversity. The fact that these examples involve creative individuals rather than ordinary, committed people-in-place leads to an important question: Can place creation be successful without the help of perceptive, creative persons who "see" the central needs of place and envision changes that make that place stronger? A related question is the relative significance of the environmental ensemble in place and place making. Some readers may see my emphasis on environmental elements as a kind of environmental determinism whereby I claim that appropriate environmental change effects appropriate human change.

These two questions are important and I discuss both in the last chapter. Before they are addressed, however, I offer a summary of the six place processes and their interconnections. Drawing on J.G. Bennett's systematic concept of *event*, I argue that the six place processes illustrate synergistic relationality and offer one integrated way to locate and evaluate the strengths and weaknesses of specific places.

Notes

1 For discussions of Fathy's New Gourna project and criticisms leveled against it, see Miles, 2006; Pyla, 2007. Concerns relating to the project include, first, the questionable propriety of Fathy's importing masons from Nubia, a region geographically and culturally different from New Gourna and associated with mud-brick vaulting and dome making, two building skills unknown to the Gournis. A second concern is that the house courtyards Fathy incorporated into the New Gourna dwellings were not part of Old Gourna's traditional house architecture but were adapted by Fathy from Egyptian urban dwellings and therefore may have been inappropriate for the Gournis' rural situation. Even if these two criticisms are correct, one does not know how the Gournis would have responded to these novel architectural interventions, since the Gournis ultimately refused to relocate to New Gourna, which, over time, "squatters" occupied.

2 My discussion is partly drawn from Seamon, 2016, which examines more fully Alexander's understanding and making of wholeness.

15

INTEGRATING THE SIX PLACE PROCESSES

In this chapter, I review the six place processes and examine interactions among them as a conceptual means to understand how places change over time. In discussing synergistic relationality in Chapter 3, I emphasized that places are constituted dynamically, continuously shifting physically and existentially. To probe more exactly how places flourish or languish, I return to J. G. Bennett's systematics and draw on his concept of *event*, which refers to any consequential happening that makes life unfold one way rather than another. Whether large or small, of long or brief duration, places can be understood as events in that they provide organized, non-contingent worlds instrumental in people's lives. To think about places as events offers one conceptual means for integrating the six place processes as they unfold in space and time as a physical and lived expression of synergistic relationality.

The Six Place Processes as Strengthening and Weakening Place

Table 15.1 summarizes the six place processes as, on one hand, they maintain and buoy places; or, on the other hand, as they undermine and shatter places. In thriving places, the six processes mutually support and invigorate each other at a wide range of generative levels and environmental scales. Robust places give pleasure to their users, who in turn feel attachment to those places and may wish to preserve and strengthen them through responsible, well-considered actions, plans, and constructions whereby robustness is intensified further.

One must emphasize, however, that the six processes can *weaken* place. For example, American post-war urban-renewal programs exemplify a mode of place creation in which policy makers and planners, partly out of ignorance as to how places work, imposed an inappropriate mode of place intensification that

TABLE 15.1 Sustaining and undermining aspects of the six place processes.

Place process	Sustaining aspects	Undermining aspects
Place interaction (1–3–2)	The goings-on in a place, both ordinary and day-to-day *and* out-of-the-ordinary and eventful; "a day in the life of the place"; the daily, weekly, and seasonal "rounds" of a place.	Typical interactions of place become fewer or destructive; the pleasure of being part of place is undermined through discomfort, stress, nuisance, inefficiency, fear, and so forth.
Place identity (2–3–1)	Taking up place as a significant part of one's world; accepting and recognizing place as integral to one's personal and communal identity.	People associated with a place feel uncomfortable with taking up that place as a part of their world; one mistrusts or feels threatened by the people and events of the place; one loses her unself-conscious sense of belonging to the place; one feels a lived separation from a place that before was an essential part of who one was.
Place release (3–2–1)	An environmental serendipity of unexpected encounters and events; people are "released" more deeply into themselves through gaining pleasure from surprises-in-place.	Serendipitous events unfold that make one anxious, unsettled, or fearful; unfortunate surprises undercut people's sense of security and safety.
Place realization (3–1–2)	The power of place to generate an environmental order with a special ambience and character.	The physical and lived order of place deteriorates or disintegrates; the ambience of the place becomes unpleasant, negative, or non-existent.
Place intensification (2–1–3)	The ways that the physical, material, and spatial environment works as an independent agent for strengthening place; the active role played by architecture, design, planning, and policy in making place one way rather than another.	Arbitrary, imposed plans, designs, and policies upset and undermine the place; inappropriate constructions and interventions squelch the life of the place.
Place creation (1–2–3)	People-in-place, out of concern and attachment, imagining and reshaping place in ways whereby it is sustained and strengthened.	Individuals and groups misunderstand place and impose unsuitable policies, designs, and actions that weaken place and ignore its unique qualities and character.

unsettled or destroyed the animated street life and *genius loci* of many American cities and their neighborhoods and districts (Fullilove, 2004; Rae, 2003; Simms, 2008). Similarly, many of today's "gated communities" are premised on a mode of exclusionary place identity that interferes with place interactions that might otherwise connect those communities to the larger environmental fabric of which they are a part (Low, 2003a). Another example is superficial modes of place intensification that incorporate inappropriate environmental designs contributing to an erosion of place rather than to its invigoration – e.g., public plazas that include no seating; megastructures that turn their backs to the sidewalk and street; or a hierarchical pathway structure that interferes with ease of pedestrian movement (Whyte, 1980; Hillier, 1996).

In examining the six processes as they unfold in lived relationships, one notes that the first four (interaction, identity, release, and realization) relate more to the *being* of a place: What that place is, how it maintains itself, and how and why people are attached to that place. The processes of place interaction and place identity might be called the *generative foundations* of place and place experience, since they point to the everyday actions, meanings, and identifications that presuppose and ground robust places. Through place interaction, participants identify with place and feel partiality, affection – even devotion and profound loyalty. In turn, this lived reciprocity between place interaction and identity sustains place release in that environmental serendipity offers the surprises and pleasures of place unexpectedness. Yet again, a supportive reciprocity among interaction, identity, and release energizes place realization and a distinctive atmosphere and character that, though largely ineffable, become an integral place quality.

If the first four processes contribute to a synergistic understanding of what places are and how they work in day-to-day fashion, the two remaining processes (intensification and creation) speak to the *becoming* of place: How robust places might be envisioned and actualized via empathetic understanding and action (creation) and well-crafted improvements in the place (intensification). Place creation requires dedicated, well-informed individuals who thoughtfully improve place, whereas place intensification identifies the independent power of appropriate designs and fabrications to revive and strengthen place by being one way materially and spatially rather than some other. The result is that place becomes better or more durable in some way – for example, increasing sidewalk traffic by creatively redesigning street fronts; or enhancing street activity by making an urban district's pathway grid more connected and permeable for pedestrians.

The Six Place Processes as Event and Place Tube

As illustrated in Figures 15.1 and 15.2, one can envision the interfused constitution of the six place processes as a synergistic structure incorporating a continuous, give-and-take interconnectedness. Figure 15.1 illustrates a simplified rendition of this processual interplay, and Figure 15.2 illustrates a more lifelike rendition with the six place processes intermeshing in an unpredictable, overlapping unfolding. None of the six processes is more significant than the others, though for specific places and historical times, the real-world dynamic of the six processes may incorporate different generative combinations and varying degrees of duration, vigor, and relatedness. In their constructive, place-supportive modes,

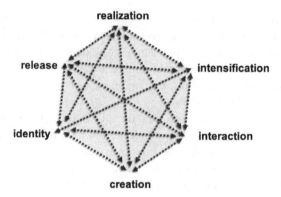

FIGURE 15.1 Simplified rendition of give-and-take linkages and dynamics among the six place processes

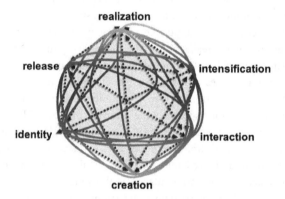

FIGURE 15.2 A more lifelike rendition of give-and-take linkages and dynamics among the six place processes, which proceed in an unforeseeable, interlocking unfolding

the six processes mutually sustain each other at a wide range of generative intensity. In synergistic fashion, each process potentially activates and is activated by the others. One can argue that, in robust, well-used places, all six processes are present and involved in an intricate reciprocity that is largely unpredictable.

I next ask how a temporal dimension might be incorporated into the inter-weaving, folding-over structure of Figure 15.2. Returning to J. G. Bennett's systematics, I draw on his discussion of six-ness and the *hexad*. Bennett claims that, when all six triads are working cooperatively in a situation, there is the possibility of an *event* – a durable, influential happening that plays a larger or smaller role in making the future other than what it would be without the event. Bennett (1993, p. 107) describes an event as an accomplishment that "asserts itself and reverberates through time and space. As the event occurs, it gains in concreteness." In this sense, an event refers to a situation whereby what is potential becomes actual in a lasting way that has bearing on the future. Clearly, places are integral to human life, and the founding and historical unfolding of a great city like London or the smallest of villages can be interpreted as events playing a larger or smaller role in human life and human history.[1]

The dynamic interconnectedness pointed to in Figure 15.2 suggests that, if we are to resuscitate and strengthen real-world places, all six processes must be present and active; they must be given thoughtful attention and provided openings in which to happen continuously and robustly. Thinking about places as events offers a way whereby the lived complexity of place *can be placed*: places are sites of interaction and identity, potentials for being shaped and shaping; worlds that provide taken-for-granted environmental and spatial order as that order can offer moments of surprise and freedom. Who we are is how we are emplaced, and thinking about places as events helps one to understand lived emplacement and to envision ways whereby it might be strengthened and made more hardy and resilient.

How might place-as-event be described temporally and historically? As illustrated by the two meandering "streams" marked **A** and **B** in Figure 15.3, one possibility is what quantum physicist David Bohm calls a *world tube* – "an

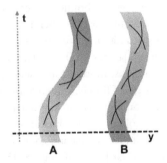

FIGURE 15.3 Physicist David Bohm's graphic rendition of two world tubes (**A** and **B**) in temporal flux (**t**) – "an infinitely complex process of a structure in movement and development" (Bohm 1980, p. 10). The **X**'s inside the two tubes represent the interconnected, overlapping actions, happenings, and situations unfolding in the two tubes over time. The line marked by **y** indicates one moment of time in the two tubes' temporal progression. In a similar way, one might envision the nested, interconnected environmental and temporal relationality of place. As a shifting constellation of people, things, situations, and events, place can be understood processually as one mode of "world tube"; the six place processes might be represented as the give-and-take connections and exchanges unfolding in the "tube" over time as a place event (see Figure 15.4).

Source: Figure redrawn and based on Bohm, 1980, p. 10.

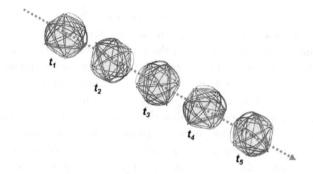

FIGURE 15.4 Place as event and temporal process (the arrow representing time). The six place processes interweave environmentally and unfold temporally with the result that the place becomes stronger, weaker, or remains more or less the same. Suggested by Bohm's world tube, this environmental–temporal structure could be called a "place tube" and reflects Bohm's conception of "the unbroken wholeness of the totality of existence as an undivided flowing movement without border" (Bohm, 1980, p. 172). From J. G. Bennett's perspective, the place tube points to the relative power of a place to unfold as a more or less significant event.

infinitely complex process of a structure in movement and development which is centered in a region indicated by the boundaries of the tube" (Bohm, 1980, p. 10). Bohm envisions any world tube as "a coherent whole, which is never static or complete, but which is an unending process of movement and unfoldment" (Bohm, 1980, p. ix). The irregular **X**'s inside the two world tubes of Figure 15.3 represent these interwoven actions, motions, interactions, and situations.

Making use of Bohm's image of flowing, interconnected processes unfolding in time and space, one can envision any place as a *place tube* and *place event* – a shifting time–space constellation of people, things, situations, and happenings, all linked through temporal and spatial limits but having some degree of connectedness to other places, whether nearby or farther away. Figure 15.4 portrays, through time, one place tube as it "events" historically. This drawing is partial and artificial, since it represents only one place tube arbitrarily severed from the integral fabric of other places and worlds of which it is always part. A more comprehensive rendition would imagine the places of the world as an incalculable number of overlapping, interconnecting and interacting "tubes" and "events" in which a continuously shifting web of the six place processes work reciprocally to strengthen, undermine, or maintain place. One pictures an inestimably complex weave of variously scaled places, some nested within others; some colliding in destructive conflict; others coalescing in constructive integration; others never or rarely engaging.

Though even today there remain remote places without contact to the larger world, most places have practical and lived relationships and exchanges with other places. This larger-scaled environmental relationality suggests that there must be another set of generative processes underlying the actions, encounters, and associations unfolding *between* and *among* places, a topic beyond the range of discussion here.[2] In addition, all actual places have a beginning and end in the sense that, at some point in time, a place comes into being and at some other point falls into demise – the story of ancient Babylon, for example. Other places face potential collapse but recover – Chicago after the 1871 fire; or New Orleans after Hurricane Katrina in 2005.[3]

When speaking of the beginnings and endings of place, one moves toward both a "phenomenology of place founding" and a "phenomenology of qualities of the founding site that contribute to the site's being chosen as 'the place'" (Seamon, 1985). One could also consider how places come to an end and what that experience of demise entails for which experiencers in what ways. One thinks, for example, of Fried (1972) and Gans' (1962) accounts of Boston's West End residents' losing their long-time Italian neighborhood to 1950s urban development; Erickson's study (1976) of the destruction of West Virginia's Buffalo Creek community by flood; Rae's investigation (2003) of disintegrating urban lifeworlds in New Haven, Connecticut; or Fullilove's research (Fullilove, 2004, 2011) on the collapse of African-American neighborhoods because of American urban renewal in the 1950s and 1960s.

Place, Synergistic Relationality, and Caring for Place

In this book, I have sought to demonstrate that places enable worlds. To probe this enabling power, I have drawn on the six place processes as they offer one means for envisioning place as synergistic relationality. What, however, is the relationship between place as synergistic relationality and caring for and tending place? If care for place, whether through thought, feeling, or action, presupposes such positive emotions as affection, concern, responsibility, devotion, and love, how are these feelings to be given sufficient recognition in terms of the six place processes?

In relation to healthy, robust places, one might envision "virtuous" spirals whereby a dynamic interweave among the six processes supports an unfolding place tube intensifying the wellbeing of place and working against environmental and human entropy. Supportive interactions strengthen personal and group identities that vitalize sense of place and life-enhancing serendipities. In turn, this *joie de vivre* progressively enlivens place interactions and place identities as well as responsible place creation and intensification. In contrast, faltering places can be pictured as "vicious" spirals with tangled, collapsing linkages that agitate devolving interactions and identities that in turn undercut place release, realization, creation, and intensification. Without some entry of constructive interactions and creative interventions, whether from within the place itself or from some outside agency, this floundering, entropic place tube may well end in place unrest, violence, disintegration, or demise.

Whether in relation to evolving or devolving place tubes, care for place or lack of care for place appears largely to be a *byproduct* of place-as-process. For sure, place identity can incorporate strong attachment and devotion to place. If, however, care for place relates to taking responsibility for that place and finding ways to make it better, then this care seems more reliant on a wholesome dynamism among the six place processes because *the vibrant life of a place calls care to it.* In other words, care for place can probably not be made to happen directly or all at once. Rather, it comes about progressively in auxiliary fashion because *already the place calls out for care as it receives care in turn.*

Humanistic geographer Yi-Fu Tuan speaks of a *field of care* – a place only known through prolonged experience – for example, a cherished home, a favorite park, a revered neighborhood, or a beloved region (Tuan, 1974a). In relation to place and care, the crucial phrase is "prolonged experience." In other words, via individual and group's extended lifeworld involvements through the six place processes, a positive emotional bonding unfolds in a fortuitous, unplanned way, including a pre-predicative, unmediated ethos of *caring for this place.* This impulse to care does not happen directly or intentionally through willed feelings, thoughts, or actions. Nor can it be instituted arbitrarily by external, imposed fiat. Rather, this impulse to care arises matter-of-factly alongside a synergistic relationality envisioned here via the six place processes as they intensify environmental and human wholeness. Care can be an integral part of lifeworld and place but it arises, mostly unself-consciously, via extended, active engagement with place.

Place, Place Making, and Synergistic Relationality

Urban designer Stephen Marshall (2012) suggests that an integrated theory of place making requires three components: First, a conceptual understanding of how the world works; second, a position on how that world should work; and, third, a practical means for translating that normative vision into actual places. In this book, I have argued that a synergistic understanding grounded in the six place processes provides one means for envisioning these three components. First, the six processes offer an insightful, process-grounded picture of what place and lived emplacement experience entail; second, they provide a helpful vision for how places might be made to work better; and, third, coupled with design approaches like those discussed in Chapters 13 and 14, the six place processes point to ways in which place making might better unfold in terms of planning, policy, design, and advocacy. In that they offer an understanding whereby the undivided wholeness of place and place making remains intact, the six place processes contribute to Marshall's call for an integrated theory of place making.

Throughout this book, I have argued that how we understand the world is how we interpret and make that world, both in our everyday lives and in our scholarly and professional efforts. In terms of place making, this situation means that what we know about the world largely sets the bounds for how we design and otherwise reshape that world. In this regard, the differences between analytic relationality and synergistic relationality are far-reaching because the two perspectives assume dramatically contrasting understandings of what places are and how they are to be studied and fabricated. As Wiggins, Ostenson, and Wendt (2012, p. 210) explain, "the assumptions that we make about relationships can have profound implications for the way we theorize about, empirically investigate, and intervene in the relationships between humans and the natural [and human-made] world."

The perspective of analytic relationality demonstrates that place can be understood via static, fragmented, predefined parts that are then reconnected arbitrarily via measurable, fixed relationships. In contrast, the perspective of synergistic relationality demonstrates that place can be understood as an indivisible, shifting whole, the parts of which can only be understood as they are in an intricate, integral relationship always in flux. For studying and designing real-world places, the perspective of synergistic relationality offers many advantages because it cleaves more closely to the lived reality of place, place experience, and lived emplacement.

I have argued for an understanding of place that is multivalent, dynamic, and synergistic. In Chapter 16, I respond to potential criticisms and concerns. I begin with the criticism that my point of view is essentialist and presupposes an environmental and architectural determinism. I then discuss the question of how my perspective on place might respond to the obvious fact of differences and conflicts within place. Finally, I address a poststructural and social-constructionist concern relating to places: that in our hypermodern era, places are no longer independent entities but nodes in a global structure grounded in networks, digital connections, and ever-shifting parts, interfaces, and webs.

Notes

1   As indicated by Table 4.1, "event" is associated with six-ness and the system that Bennett calls the *hexad*, which I do not discuss in detail because its explication is not essential for thinking about the six place processes as they coalesce to make place. Bennett contends that, through the hexad, the potentiality of a thing or activity (which Bennett associates with five-ness and the pentad – see Table 4.1) is given concreteness and real-world influence. In this sense, "the act of realization is dynamism transformed into substance" (Bennett, 1966a, p. 44), and "the dynamism of every possible event is given by the six fundamental triads" (Bennett, 1966a, p. 46). Thus, the hexad is "the system most appropriate for studying [phenomena] in process of realizing their significance as events" (Bennett, 1966a, p. 49). Here, I suggest that the life of a place over time is one kind of event and that in robust places there is a continual, vitalizing unfolding of the six place triads.

Readers may wonder why, in drawing on Bennett's systematics, I do not discuss place as four-ness and the tetrad and five-ness and the pentad. Bennett claims that the systems become progressively more concrete as their number increases; the first three systems of monad, dyad, and triad describe place as it can be understood broadly as a non-contingent feature of human life and experience. Beyond the triad, however, each system is more appropriately usable in relation to specific places – for example, the tetrad of a specific school or plaza or the pentad of a specific neighborhood or city. Readers should note that this specificity is also the case for the hexad: In drawing on the hexad and event, one can best apply the six place processes as they manifest in a specific place – for example, New Orleans, London's Regents Park, or Jane Jacobs' Hudson Street neighborhood. To hold to the non-contingent dimension of place, I keep the discussion of "event" general and conceptual, though it is worthwhile for the reader to think through the interconnected dynamics of the six place processes in relation to specific places with which he or she is familiar.

2 A triadic understanding of relationship *between* places requires its own detailed phenomenology that is not attempted here. In some cases, the relation between places remains dyadic, and a stronger place overwhelms a weaker place. Two-ness becomes one-ness at the expense of the weaker place (military defeat is the most obvious example). Relationship requires some third impulse, which most broadly might be described as "exchange," though the question becomes in what ways is exchange possible between places? For example, a stronger place's demanding some sort of exchange from a weaker place is a much different relationship than the stronger place helping the weaker place to facilitate an exchange that is useful to both places; see Bennett, 1993, pp. 41–45.

3 In her thought-provoking study of human altruism during disasters, journalist Rebecca Solnit (2009, p. 24) quotes California writer Mary Hunter Austin's description of living through the devastating 1906 San Francisco earthquake and how San Franciscans became homeless but not without place: "[T]hey discovered the place and the spirit to be home rather than the walls and the furnishings. No matter . . . what landmarks, what treasures of art are evanished, San Francisco, *our* San Francisco is all there yet. Fast as the tall banners of smoke rose up and the flames reddened them, rose up with it something impalpable, like an exhalation." In her image of an "impalpable exhalation," Austin intimates the impressive staying power of common presence, which, in the case of San Francisco, assured that the city would rebuild. Though it does not use phenomenological language, Solnit's study is an important contribution to the phenomenology of place disaster.

16

LIFE TAKES PLACE

Criticisms, Concerns, and the Future of Places

Drawing on synergistic relationality and J. G. Bennett's progressive approximation, I have offered one phenomenology of place and place making. I have argued that place and lived emplacement are complex, multivalent phenomena incorporating a generative dimension whereby places, place experiences, and place meanings shift over time. I have used Bennett's method of systematics to examine place and lived emplacement from three different perspectives:

- The wholeness of place and peoples' inescapable immersion-in-world;
- The dyadic aspect of place, including such lived complementarities as movement and rest, dwelling and journey, and insideness and outsideness;
- The triadic nature of place, described as the six different processes whereby places are what they are and what they become.

I have suggested that, for any place, the six processes are present, and their degree of intensity and interchange ground the relative robustness or fragility of that place. I have argued that place making is related most directly to the two processes of place intensification and place creation, through which a dedicated reflective effort to understand a place leads to appropriate ways of generating designs, plans, and policies for that place.

In this last chapter, I consider some criticisms and concerns regarding the phenomenology of place I offer here. First, I consider the social-constructionist contention that my perspective is essentialist, claiming non-contingent features of place and lived emplacement that are present, regardless of personal, social, cultural, or historical differences. Second, I consider the question of environmental and architectural determinism – whether I claim too much independent power of the physical environment to shape place and people-in-place. Third, I respond to the obvious, lived fact that places can be sites of individual and group differences, often in ways that provoke antagonism and conflict. Last, I respond to the postmodernist contentions that places are either obsolete exclusionary structures in our hypermodern world, or that they are little more than flickering nodes in a larger global structure of ceaselessly shifting networks and interconnections.

Place, Lived Emplacement, and Place Processes as Essentialist Concepts

For social constructionists and poststructuralists, my conceptual approach in this book is more than likely labelled *essentialist* – i.e., that I presuppose and claim an invariant and universal human condition to be revealed only when all "non-essentials," including historical, cultural and social qualities, are stripped away, leaving behind some inescapable core of human experience centered on place and lived emplacement (Cresswell, 2013, 2014). The social-constructionist concern is that, in focusing on the phenomenon of place and lived emplacement as a foundational existential structure, I ignore the specific temporal, social, and individual circumstances that shape individuals and groups' situations in relation to place and lived emplacement.

I respond to this essentialist charge by emphasizing the basic phenomenological recognition that there are different dimensions of human experience and existence that all must be incorporated in a thorough understanding of human and societal phenomena, including place and lived emplacement. These dimensions include:

1. One's unique personal situation – e.g., one's gender, sexuality, sexual identity, physical and intellectual endowments, degree of ableness, and personal likes and dislikes;
2. One's unique historical, social, and cultural situation – e.g., the era and geographical locale in which one lives; his or her economic and political circumstances; his or her familial, educational, religious, and societal background; the technological, communications, and media infrastructure that contribute to the person or group's particular lifeworld;
3. One's situation as a typical human being immersed in a typical human world, of which an integral lived aspect is human-being-in-place.

It is this third, universal and non-contingent dimension of human being that is my focus of concern in this book – in other words, giving central attention to the lived qualities that presuppose and contribute to place, lived emplacement, place experience, and place meanings. I agree with the poststructural concern that, if we shift to the dimensions of cultural, social, or personal experience, then places and lived emplacements for the group or person may vary and sometimes be in conflict. Any phenomenological investigation must describe and interpret these variations and differences as they relate to the specific real-world cultural and social patterns, processes, and power structures. I argue, however, that the broad themes and structures identified phenomenologically might provide one useful conceptual means around which to examine and understand specific lived emplacements and place experiences.

My broader point is that there is no conceptual right or wrong here – rather, the poststructural and phenomenological differences in emphasis can be recast in terms of the interrelated dimensions of phenomenological investigation: (a) typically human, or "essential"; (b) cultural and social; or (c) individual and personal. Each of these three lived dimensions lead to different phenomenological topics and results, though in all there are common threads as, for example, the significance of lived emplacement, or the presence of some version of the six place processes in the workings of actual places. In short, each of these three dimensions of any lifeworld is a legitimate arena for phenomenological investigation, and one does not displace or supersede the other.

Drawing on this multivalent perspective, one might say that a poststructural perspective is more interested in explicating the social, cultural, and uniquely personal dimensions of place and lived emplacement, whereas I, as a phenomenologist, am more interested in these phenomena as they arise and unfold in their inescapable, invariant, universal, essential typicality. Ultimately, all these dimensions of place can be examined, and discoveries regarding one aspect should offer understandings regarding others. For example, in-depth studies of the six place processes as they are present in specific places or for specific individuals and groups should provide additional insight and clarity as to these processes more broadly. But the reverse is also true: that using the six processes to understand specific places and specific human-lives-in-place should point to understandings not available otherwise.

Place, Lived Emplacement, and Environmental Determinism

A second criticism of my approach to place is that it gives too much causal weight to the physical and spatial environment – what I have identified as the environmental ensemble. There is a large, conflicting literature on the relative role that physical, designed, and built environments play in human life (Hay, 2002; Sprout and Sprout, 1965). On one hand, architect Christopher Alexander declares, without reservation, that environmental design contributes to "the comfort of belonging to the places where we live and work" (Alexander, 2005, p. 66). Similarly, architectural writer Sarah Williams Goldhagen (2017, p. xiv) argues that "the built environment shapes our lives and the choices we make. . . . It affects our moods and our emotions, our sense of our bodies in space and in motion. It profoundly shapes the narratives we tell ourselves and construct out of our daily lives."

On the other hand, art historian Simon Richards (2012, p. 1) questions the claim that "the right kind of building can transform us into happier, healthy, better people." He disputes the assumption that the built environment plays a central role in human worlds – what he describes as "the belief that architecture and planning are capable of transforming the world and everyone in it for the better" (Richards, 2012, p. 1). He argues that this claim is used to justify practical, political, and ethical arguments that often conflict and provide little conceptual justification or real-world evidence:

> [These arguments] should be handled more responsibly, with a greater awareness of the prejudices and value-judgments that often they represent, especially since no other profession [i.e., architecture] seems quite so eager to proclaim itself ready, willing and able to save the world and everyone in it.
>
> (Richards, 2012, p. 157)

Here, I agree with Alexander and Williams Goldhagen that the designable environment plays an important role in human life, but I also agree with Richards' call for an accurate understanding of the specific ways in which environmental influences work. In this book, I have argued that place and lived emplacement are an integral part of human being. In turn, I have argued that an integral feature of place is the environmental ensemble, which, particularly through the process of place intensification, works in an active way to make life-in-place one way rather than another. In the chapter on place intensification, I overviewed three examples of how the physical environment definitively contributes to lifeworld actions and experiences: urbanist William Whyte's criteria for successful urban plazas; architectural theorist Bill Hillier's space syntax theory; and Jane Jacobs' four conditions for urban diversity and exuberant street life.

I chose these three examples because each offers convincing evidence for clearly identified ways in which physical, designable qualities play a role in human life, place experience, and place making. For example, Jacobs' argument is persuasive because it demonstrates how an interplay of human and environmental qualities sustain and are sustained by place. Primary uses like dwellings and workplaces are crucial because they provide a regular, guaranteed pool of street and sidewalk users. In turn, these people contribute to the neighborhood's place ballet and provide "eyes on the street" and an informal policing structure that facilitates community order and neighborhood safety. Similarly, Jacobs demonstrates that short blocks are important because permeable, interconnected sidewalks and streets support intermingling pedestrian cross-use and many more street-front locations than larger blocks can provide. In addition, short blocks offer many more route choices than longer blocks, making traversals more convenient. One understands how primary uses and short blocks contribute to place interaction, identity, release, and realization. With that understanding in hand, designers and policy makers can creatively envision and reconfigure urban districts and strengthen their place character.

One of the most comprehensive efforts to demonstrate the importance of physical design in robust place making is *Responsive Environments*, an urban-design manual written by designers Ian Bentley, Alan Alcock, Paul Murrain, Sue McGlynn, and Graham Smith (Bentley et al., 1985). Close in character to Jacobs' ideal neighborhood, a "responsive environment" is a diverse, walkable neighborhood providing users "with an essentially democratic setting, enriching their opportunities by maximizing the degree of choice available to them" (Bentley et al., 1985, p. 9). Bentley and colleagues identify seven designable qualities essential for generating and sustaining a responsive environment: *permeability, variety, legibility, robustness, richness, visual appropriateness*, and *personalization*. For example, *permeability* parallels Jacobs' short blocks and Hillier's emphasis on pathway configuration; it relates to the way that street and sidewalk layout determines where people can go and cannot go within a city district. Bentley and colleagues insist that urban designers must always consider permeability first because it involves pedestrian and vehicle circulation within the whole city district. The greater the number of alternative routes through an environment, the greater users' freedom of movement and, therefore, the greater the potential responsiveness of that place.

Once designers have worked through a permeable, interconnected street arrangement for the site, they must then carefully think through *variety*, the range of uses that the place will provide – housing, workplaces, shopping, recreation, and so forth (equivalent to Jacobs' primary and secondary uses). Easily accessible places are of little use if their choice of place experiences is limited. The design aim is to determine the widest mix of uses feasible economically and functionally and then to locate them carefully on the site in such a way as to maximize pedestrian flows among the various functions. With functional variety in place, designers then turn to *legibility*, working through ways that physical elements might be formed and placed to make the site more imageable and memorable (a signature building or striking landscape element, for example). In turn, designers work to facilitate the smaller-scaled environmental qualities of *robustness, richness, visual appropriateness*, and *personalization*. Moving from larger to smaller scale in a way paralleling Christopher Alexander's pattern language, Bentley and colleagues recognize that all seven qualities are important to urban place making, but they emphasize that larger-scale qualities like permeability and variety must be put in place first before smaller-scaled qualities are envisioned and fabricated. Creative possibilities for place creation and place intensification are guided by these seven designable features of successful real-world places.

Like the work of Jacobs, Hillier, Whyte, and Alexander, *Responsive Environments* provides a set of designable qualities grounded in understanding place as a dynamic interplay of environmental elements and human possibilities. Bentley and colleagues assume a synergistic relationality in that people and place are understood as integrally interconnected and conceptualized together. Any claims that "the environment shapes people" or "people shape the environment" are beside the point. Rather, there is an implicit phenomenological recognition that people and place are indivisible, and place making is grounded in a dynamic environmental synergy. The place-making approach of *Responsive Environments* offers a powerful, practical example of Malpas's claim, cited earlier, that places are "constituted through a gathering of elements that are themselves mutually defined only through the way in which they are gathered together within the place they also constitute" (Malpas, 2006, p. 29).

Places as Sites of Difference and Conflict

One of the most questionable aspects of my argument in this book is that, in emphasizing place as the central phenomenon, I ignore the fact that places are often sites of disagreement and conflict: Different individuals and groups associated with the same place may understand, in competing ways, what that place is, who controls it, and how it should be planned for and managed politically and economically. Though I have not highlighted them here, I collected many newspaper articles that dealt with place conflict as illustrated by the following headlines:

- "Expand the museum, but open the park: A fair trade is possible over a tiny patch of green space" (*NYT*, January 30, 2017, p. C5).
- "Westchester gets a new gun store, and a battle of ideas" (*NYT*, November 16, 2016, p. A22).
- "Solar projects sow tension: As solar panels supplant crops on more farms, states weigh limits on big renewable fields" (*WSJ*, March 9, 2017, p. A3).
- "Coal giant and Native Americans spar over coal-mining expansion in Arizona" (*NYT*, December 30, 2016, p. A14).
- "Iraqi Christians fight for ancestral lands: Force of mostly Assyrian-Christian troops form militia to fight Islamic State" (*WSJ*, December 7, 2016, p. A8).
- "Earthquake propels competing visions for restoring Myanmar's temples" (*NYT*, May 12, 2017, p. A4).

Obviously, individual and group differences can provoke place conflict. The possibility I address is whether place might also be a site for drawing differences together in such a way that *the place is put first.* Can the power of place, especially the presence of strong place realization, offer an opening for common values and actions? In examining this possibility, I turn to the work of political philosopher Daniel Kemmis (1990, 1995), who considers the value of place as it might have meaning for urban politics and citizenship: "[T]he refocusing of human energy around the organic wholeness of cities . . . promises a profound rehumanizing of the shape and condition of our lives" (Kemmis, 1995, p. 151).[1] Kemmis describes a way of life that involves individual citizens' feeling a part of their urban place because it provides one mode of belonging. He works to answer the difficult question of how the practical steps of constructive place change are to be decided by the various parties involved. For Kemmis, this decision-making process is through-and-through political, whereby he means the realization of a place's possibilities through a civility among the views of the individuals and groups associated with the place. He writes that "politics emerges as the set of practices which enables . . . people to dwell together in [their] place" (Kemmis, 1990, p. 122).

Kemmis discusses the relationship between politics and place most thoroughly in *The Good City, the Good Life* (Kemmis, 1995), which explores in considerable detail how a citizenship grounded in place might be applied at the urban scale. Early on in this book, Kemmis discusses what he calls the "good life," which "makes it possible for humans to be fully present – to themselves, to one another, and to their surroundings. Such presence is precisely opposite of the distracted-ness – the being beside – that is so prevalent in our political culture" (Kemmis, 1995, p. 22). For Kemmis (1995, p. 177), the city is synergistic in the sense that it "organizes in its own terms a certain portion of the world." For this reason, Kemmis argues that city dwellers do not always initiate an active interest in their city; more often, the city, in its liveliness and attraction, activates the attention and concern of its dwellers, who then contribute to the city. In this sense, place wholeness begets human wholeness and vice versa. This mutual interplay of part and whole, person and world, dweller and city is, for Kemmis (1995, p. 12), the foundation of civilization: "This fundamental connection between human wholeness and livability and the wholeness and life of the city are all contained in . . . the word 'civilized.'"

What Kemmis discusses here, implicitly, is the phenomenological principle of lived emplacement whereby people and place are not separate but intimately interconnected as one aspect of human-being-in-world. This relationship reflects one mode of "*belonging* together" and synergistic relationality. It is elusive and difficult to give grounded significance because it is a holistic structure that becomes other than itself when conceptually broken apart. One of Kemmis' strengths is his ability to explore and describe this person–place intimacy through his own political experiences as former mayor of Missoula, Montana, and former Speaker of the Montana State Legislature. For example, he discusses Missoula's lively farmer's market, which provides a place for the city to work on its citizens by bringing them together and providing economic and social exchange. This "gathering role . . . enables people to come away from the market more whole than when they arrived" (Kemmis, 1995, p. 11).

Kemmis' central question is how citizens' sense of responsibility for their place can facilitate a civilized politics. All politics, Kemmis (1995, p. 153) emphasizes, is about power, but the politician who can make the good city happen must always remember that his or her power "is only a form of stewardship on behalf of those whose power it really is." Kemmis argues that good politicians remember they are stewards of power, which they barter to make a better city, through listening to what citizens say but also listening to the city itself. The need is to meet with many different people, to get them to talk to each other, and – when the moment seems right – to make the best decision possible on behalf of the city. In the end, says Kemmis (1995, p. 177), the mark of the good politician is "knowing when to let the world work, and when to work on the world." For Kemmis, the good politician is open to the needs of both people and their place so that, as the right moment arises, he or she can use power to make the next step toward healing the city:

> [I]f the city is constantly responding to what it has already created and to what fortune brings forward, then the next act of creation must always be some paradoxical blend of will and acceptance . . . . This blend is precisely the defining characteristic of the good politician . . . .
>
> *(Kemmis, 1995, pp. 178–179)*

At the same time, however, this practical openness to what the city might become cannot happen if ordinary citizens do not partake in the political process. Unfortunately, today, community involvement too often becomes special-interest groups fighting for power. The need, says Kemmis, is to draw into the process people who can be civil and take responsibility for mediating extremes and finding a middle point of possibility. To be a citizen involves "the ability to teach or encourage one another to speak so that you can actually be heard by others who do not already share your view" (Kemmis, 1995, p. 192).

Though this process of motivating citizens and healing place is not necessarily easy, immediate, or guaranteed, Kemmis believes that, if citizens sincerely look at and listen to their place, then it can "say" what it needs. For example, he discusses the development of a riverfront park system along the Clark Fork River just south of downtown Missoula, which in the 1980s had been largely destroyed economically by retail competition from outlying suburban malls. To stimulate an economic renaissance, Missoula's leaders implemented tax-increment financing, which leveraged private investments in downtown improvements and store renovations. This early success spawned additional downtown investments, which in turn stimulated the creation of a downtown riverfront park that would eventually spur, on both sides of the river, the creation of additional parks connected by walking trails.

Kemmis emphasizes that, at the start, neither citizens nor politicians could have imagined the chronological order or physical shape that Missoula's downtown revitalization would take. The success of the original risk that Missoula's leaders took in implementing the tax-incentive program led to private entrepreneurs and public and private agencies taking additional risks, many of which also proved successful. In describing the incremental, serendipitous piecing together of Missoula's downtown and riverfront, Kemmis (1995, p. 171) refers to Christopher Alexander's aim to facilitate environmental healing, whereby "every new act of construction . . . must create a continuous structure of wholes around it" (Alexander et al., 1987, p. 22).

Toward the end of his account of downtown Missoula's redevelopment, Kemmis explains that the riverfront parks and trail segments are still not connected in one complete walking loop allowing users to experience Missoula's river district as a whole. Yet he trusts (as would Christopher Alexander) that there are enough environmental parts in place so that now Missoulians feel the lack of an appropriate environmental whole. He predicts that eventually this feeling will generate the public will to complete the riverwalk system. He explains:

> The riverfront trail literally reaches out to join itself, putting pressure on the intervening parcels that prevent it from doing so, and then whenever it succeeds in filling in one of those gaps, it encourages whatever touches it to a greater wholeness as well.
>
> *(Kemmis, 1995, p. 171)*

Though Alexander and Kemmis agree that healing the city is a central need, their understanding of how this healing happens is considerably different. Kemmis – as a politician and political philosopher – sees urban healing fostered largely through civil discourse among citizens and politicians who put their place first. In contrast, Alexander – as an architect – insists that, before any such discourse can begin, there must first be a basic understanding as to what environmental wholeness is and how it can be strengthened or stymied by qualities of the physical–spatial environment and urban and architectural design.

For sure, both aspects of the healing process – physical and human, material and communal – must be considered and carried out, though I concur with Alexander that a knowledge of how the physical city grounds and stimulates the healing process must inform civil discourse. In this way, I answer the question I raised at the end of my discussion on place creation in Chapter 14: Place making cannot simply happen, but must be grounded in an empathetic understanding of place and a knowledge of how qualities of the environmental ensemble can strengthen or weaken place. Citizens' aiming to make their place better is crucial, but this commitment must be complemented with thoughtful understandings as to how that place improvement can be facilitated practically via the environmental ensemble. The work of Alexander, Bentley, Brittan, Fathy, Hillier, Jacobs, Krafel, and Whyte all offer invaluable guidance.

Kemmis' work is important for place making because he points to a practical middle way whereby people-in-place, putting their place first, might set aside conflicting differences and become constructively involved in understandings and actions that might make their place better. Though he does not use phenomenological language, one can say that Kemmis marks the start of a phenomenology of the way by which individuals and groups come together to envision and make the "good city," or more broadly, "the good place." He writes:

If public life needs to be revitalized, if its renewal depends upon more conscious and more confident ways of drawing upon the capacity of practices to make values objective and public, if those practices acquire that power from the efforts of unlike people to live well in specific places, then we need to think about specific places, and the real people who now live in them, and try to imagine ways in which their efforts to live there might become more practiced, more inhabitory, and therefore more public.

(Kemmis, 1990, p. 82)

Places as Exclusionary or Shifting Nodes in a Globalized Network

It is currently fashionable in poststructural and social-constructionist theory to criticize place and lived emplacement in two contrasting ways.[2] One group of critics contends that phenomenological interpretations have too readily emphasized the centered, static, limiting, and parochial aspects of place.[3] This criticism is partly accurate in that the first phenomenological studies of place in the 1970s and 1980s drew on first-generation phenomenological work of philosophers like Gaston Bachelard (1964), Otto Bollnow (1967, 2011), and Martin Heidegger (1962, 1971b), who largely pictured place as static, bounded, and thus exclusionary.[4] Critics of this conservative place perspective speak instead of a "progressive sense of place." They ask how places relate and respond to their larger social, economic, and political contexts. For these critics, places remain important, but the more urgent practical and conceptual need is delineating ways whereby the specific place becomes more connected and permeable in relation to the wider, surrounding world. How, in other words, might place incorporate diversity and the integration of differences? As geographer Doreen Massey (1997, p. 320) asks, "Can't we rethink our sense of place? Is it not possible for a sense of place to be progressive; not self-enclosing and defensive, but outward looking?"

A second group of critics contends that, because of current trends toward globalization, cyberspace, and virtual realities, real-world places are, in many ways, becoming increasingly irrelevant and obsolete.[5] Motivated in part by the work of poststructural thinkers Gilles Deleuze and Félix Guattari (1987), these critics dispute the rigid, centered stasis of place. They speak instead of shifting movements and flows "between identities, between nation–states, between ideas, between places, between peoples, and so forth" (Kogl, 2008, p. 1). A central concept is Deleuze and Guattari's metaphor of *rhizome*: a spatial structure of free, unpredictable flows and movements generating centerless networks that abjure boundaries or containments (Deleuze and Guattari, 1987, p. 8; Kogl, 2008, pp. 57–77). Political philosopher Alexandra Kogl (2008, p. 1) summarizes this poststructural criticism of place:

The early twenty-first century appears to be an era of radically shifting geographies: from the space of place to the space of flows, from the space of the nation–state to global space, from a round world to a flat one. Places, as the tangible, distinctive spaces to which peoples and states attach meanings, and in which people live their everyday lives, appear to be overwhelmed by flows of values, people, information, capital, pollution, ideas, technology, culture, language, and diseases.

Though Kogl appreciates this poststructuralist critique, she points out that the perspective is simplistic, partly because, even as globalization and flows undermine some places today, these same processes strengthen other places and facilitate new kinds of places (for example, exporting–processing zones and global cities) (Kogl, 2008, p. 1). More significantly, places retain their importance because "the human body is always local, living a particular life in a particular place, with others, for better or worse" (Kogl, 2008, p. 143). Even in the mobile United States, almost forty percent of Americans have never left their hometown and another twenty percent have never left their home state (Cohn and Morin, 2008). British residence patterns are similar in that some one half of British adults live within five miles of where they were born (Morley, 2000, p. 14). In terms of global patterns, the number of migrants voluntarily leaving their home place to take up residence elsewhere varies from country to country, but the total percentage has remained relatively stable as a share of the earth's population, increasing only slightly from 2.9 percent in 2000 to 3.1 percent in 2010 (UN DESA, 2010; IOM, 2010). A 2017 United Nations study estimates that the global population of displaced people, including refugees, asylum seekers, and people forcibly separated from their home place, was almost sixty-six million in 2016, about one percent of the world's population (*NYT*, June 6, 2017, p. A5). In sum, about ninety-six percent of the world's population continues to live in their home country.[6]

In this sense, place remains one of the great stabilizing constituents of human life in that it automatically "places" and holds lived bodies spatially and geographically. Because of this "bodily placement through place," human beings are automatically provided one mode of spatial order and environmental belonging that in this book I have described through the place processes of interaction, identity, and realization. Unless human life becomes entirely virtual, non-material, and secondhand because of continuing developments in digital technologies and robotics, places will remain a part of human being. Though not all individuals are equally identified with and attached to the places of their lives, those places are still inescapable in the sense that they provide the everyday, taken-for-granted spatial and environmental context for each person and group's lifeworld, at least in terms of body–subject and environmental corporeality.

This inescapable corporeality of place is often ignored by the first group of place critics who seek a more progressive sense of place. These critics are correct that, in our postmodernist age, we must locate ways whereby the stasis of a place might be invigorated and in turn invigorate other places through a vibrant interconnectedness that facilitates diversity and contributes to the acceptance of difference (Kogl, 2008; Massey, 1997, 2005, 2009; Morley, 2000). But much of such dynamic exchange will remain grounded in the habitual regularity of body–subjects commingling with place. Nor can these critics discount the reality that a dynamic interchange among places presupposes a robust integrity of each place itself; this robust integrity is at least partly founded in the inertial regularity of lived bodies in material space. In this sense, the integral role of places in human lifeworlds provokes questions such as the following:

- If an unavoidable part of place is inertia and bodily regularity, how can these lived qualities be used via planning, policy, and law to facilitate robust places and to generate mutual support and understanding among places, especially places that are considerably different (e.g., different ethnic neighborhoods or regions)?
- Might a phenomenological education of lifeworld, place, and environmental embodiment assist citizens and professionals in better understand the workings and needs of real-world places and thereby contribute to their envisioning and making?
- Is it possible to speak of human-rights-in-place or place justice? If so, would such a possibility move attention and supportive efforts toward improving the places in which people and other living beings find themselves, rather than focusing only on the rights and needs of individuals and groups without consideration of their place context?

Place, Lived Emplacement, and Place Justice

In relation to my argument in this book, all these questions are significant, but I want to devote my conclusion to the last: Can a phenomenological approach have relevance for what might be called *place justice*, by which I mean the use of environmental design, public policy, and place-grounded advocacy to protect vibrant places and to invigorate moribund environments? What does a phenomenology of place and lived emplacement contribute to this task? Perhaps its most important recognition is that human life is always human-life-in-place. Especially because of body–subject and environmental embodiment, everyday life for many people *simply happens* because of habits, routines, and the taken-for-granted inertia of day-to-day living. Unless ordinary life shifts dramatically and one is forced to do other than usual, most human beings rarely question the taken-for-granted inertia of their world or suppose that world can change.

Because of the natural attitude, people habitually accept their lifeworld and place as the only way the world can be. I return to Klinenberg's research on the isolated Chicago elderly who died in the 2005 heat wave (Klinenberg, 2002; see Chapter 10). These individuals took their social and environmental isolation for granted and had little will or active means to shift their situation in time of crisis.

If the inertia of lifeworld is an integral part of place and lived emplacement, then positive change whereby one becomes more free and more whole may sometimes be most effectively supported by place creation and intensification whereby thoughtful, constructive engagement with place envisions and fabricates changes in the environmental ensemble that strengthen the common presence of place and thereby enhance place experiences, actions, and meanings.

In short, the need is to reconfigure places that facilitate lifeworlds in which people feel a part rather than apart. This approach to human rights is indirect in that helpful change arises, not by formally allotting power, through legal and political means, to powerless individuals, but by making their place better materially and spatially so that qualities of the place contribute to these individuals' wellbeing as they simply live their everyday lives. We return to Daniel Kemmis "good life," whereby people are fully present to themselves, to others, and to the places that make up their world. He speaks of "a politics that rests upon a mutual recognition by diverse interests that they are bound to each other by their common attachment to a place" (Kemmis, 1990, p. 123).

The perspective I offer here has much in common with law scholar Conor Gearty's insightful integration of human rights and environmental protection. He writes:

> Once we see human rights and environmental protection as forms of activism driven by a desire to make the world a better place, both for its own sake and for the lives of all who live in it . . . , we can see that there are in fact close bonds between the two fields, and that human rights are a help rather than a hindrance to progress in the environmental field.
>
> *(Gearty, 2010, p. 15)*

Though I agree with Gearty's call for integration, he and I might partly disagree on the definition of "activism," which conventionally is interpreted as individuals and groups self-consciously working to make positive changes in their world through willful, self-directed efforts relating to law, politics, economics, and so forth. I certainly am not opposed to self-conscious, autonomous initiatives and believe them to be an integral part of place making as Kemmis demonstrates in his work. I do, however, want to repeat that much of the lifeworld and natural attitude is *unself-consciously grounded*, partly because of body–subject, environmental embodiment, and place. This sphere of pre-predicative, unreflected-upon life points to a complementary dimension of human rights and environmental justice: thoughtfully devising ways whereby inequitable or life-devolving lifeworlds are transformed indirectly through creative spatial and material changes like those argued for by Alexander, Jacobs, Whyte, Bentley, and others who thoughtfully probe the significant role of environmental ensembles for places and place making. In other words, places are sometimes better strengthened by making constructive shifts in environmental ensembles rather than emphasizing self-conscious behavioral or attitudinal shifts in the human beings associated with those places.[7]

This possibility points toward one of the most important questions that our hypermodern world faces today: Can supportive places be made to thrive intentionally through thoughtful design, equitable policy, and the manner of civilized politics-in-place as pointed to by Daniel Kemmis? In the past, these supportive kinds of places mostly happened unself-consciously because construction, transportation, and communication technologies were mostly limited geographically, entrepreneurship was largely local, and most human beings were very much bodily-bound to place. Today, all places on the earth are more or less equally accessible and a crucial question arises: In spite of our human abilities to do almost anything, can we find practical ways to energize place and lived emplacement? In this book, I have argued that we must begin by understanding what places are in human life, why they are important, and how they work. I have suggested that a phenomenological approach offers much toward this understanding and points, particularly through the six place processes, to practical means and methods whereby the places of the world might be made stronger and more durable.

I end with a claim made in Chapter 2: that human beings are always already inescapably immersed, enmeshed, and entwined in their worlds, which most of the time, "just happen" without the intervention of anything or anyone. An integral part of this lived immersion is place and lived emplacement. In turn, I have argued that an integral constituent of place is its physical, spatial, and material elements – the environmental ensemble as I have identified it. Perhaps the most important conclusion I offer is that human wellbeing depends on circumstances, of which one of the most malleable and makeable is the environmental ensemble. Environmental aspects of place do not determine a person or group's lives, but they do elicit specific possibilities, actions, and situations that contribute to life's being one way rather than another. For good or bad, whether we realize it or not, we are all always emplaced, and some emplacements facilitate wellbeing while others fester unkindness, distress, or outright despair. Who we are contributes hugely to what we become, but how we are emplaced also matters. Working to understand lived emplacement and locating ways whereby it can be nurtured rather than enfeebled is the crucial directive I offer in this book. Even in today's hypermodern world, life *always* takes place. We must understand, act, envision, and create accordingly.

Notes

1 My discussion of Kemmis is partially based on Seamon, 2004, pp. 124–127.
2 Much of this discussion is drawn from Seamon, 2013b, pp. 160–166. The geographer John Tomaney (2010, 2012) provides perceptive critique of these two ways of understanding place.
3 E.g., Amin, 2004; Cresswell, 2013, 2014; Dainotto, 2000; Massey, 1997, 2005, 2009; Morley, 2000; Naficy, 1999; Paasi, 2011; Paasi and Metzger, 2016; Rose, 1993, 1995.

4 These early phenomenological studies of place include Bollnow, 1967; Buttimer, 1976; Norberg-Schulz, 1971, 1980; Relph, 1976; Tuan, 1974a, 1974b, 1977, 1980.
5 E.g., Allen and Cochrane, 2007; Connolly, 1995; Cresswell, 2006; Deleuze and Guattari, 1987; Hardt and Negri, 2000.
6 The exact estimate of the world's displaced people is 65.6 million, including 2.8 million refugees and asylum seekers who fled their home country and seek international protection. Significantly, about 40 million people were displaced *within their home country*, a particularly troubling situation in that people who would more than likely stay in place otherwise are forced to be elsewhere (*NYT*, June 19, 2017, p. A5).
7 Discussions of architecture, planning, and environmental design as place making include Bermudez, 2015; Carmona et al., 2010; Frumkin et al., 2004; Kopec, 2012; Montgomery, 2014; Sadik-Khan and Solomonow, 2016; Schwartz, 2015; Seamon, 2014b; Speck, 2012; Steinfeld and White, 2010; Williams Goldhagen, 2017.

POSTSCRIPT

Experience versus Knowledge and the Lived versus the Conceptual

One reader of the first draft of this book suggested that my approach was conceptual rather than phenomenological. He made the claim that Bennett's systems impose a predetermined structure to place and place experience. If one assumes that phenomenology is "a return to the things themselves," how phenomenologically can I justify Bennett's progressive approximation? This reviewer brought forward the related question of whether phenomenology is experiential description or cerebral interpretation. Does phenomenology remain close to the phenomenon and involve mostly narrative explication arising from lived expressions of the phenomenon? Or does phenomenology move away from pure experiential description and toward an interpretive structure grounded in the phenomenon but understanding the phenomenon more broadly? Where, phenomenologically, are the ontological, epistemological, and methodological lines between experience and knowledge and between lived description and intellectual understanding?

These concerns are important, and I address them in this postscript. On one hand, I agree that Bennett's systematics claims broad qualitative structures that may seem arbitrary, intellectually derived, and not directly accessible experientially. On the other hand, as someone who has worked with Bennett's systematics for over three decades, I suggest that, with practice and firsthand investigation, one can discover Bennett's systems experientially and find perceptive insights not otherwise accessible. In this sense, I am proposing that his systems *arise out of lived experience* and offer one productive, originative means to consider the actions, situations, and processes that constitute human life and the worlds in which we find ourselves as enmeshed human beings.

Phenomenology founder Edmund Husserl claimed that phenomenologists are perpetual beginners and must continually begin from and return to lived experience for descriptive and interpretive evidence (Moran, 2000, p. 62). At the same time, however, most phenomenologists emphasize that accurate experiential engagement and description are only first steps in phenomenological efforts (e.g., Finlay, 2011, pp. 109–112; Giorgi, 2009; Spiegelberg, 1982, pp. 682–715). Eventually, one works to place specific descriptive discoveries in relation to broader lived structures and patterns – "phenomenological concepts" as I call them here. One obvious example is Merleau-Ponty's explication of the lived body and related phenomenological concepts like perception and body–subject. His exceptional contribution is locating these phenomena directly in human experience and, through his written explications, making them visible and available for other phenomenologists to probe and develop further (as I have attempted to do through place-grounded concepts like body routines, time–space routines, and place ballet).

Experiencing versus Knowing

In relation to the question of lived experience versus intellectual conception, the key point is that the direct lived discoveries of one phenomenologist become secondhand, cerebral formulations for other phenomenologists. The concepts that Merleau-Ponty discovered directly via lived experience, I first recognized intellectually via his written articulations. For sure, I eventually verified the lived validity of his conceptual accounts in my own lifeworld, but my original understanding of these accounts was grounded in cognitive knowledge rather than in direct experience. In this sense, phenomenological research is a collective undertaking whereby the lived discoveries of one phenomenologist become part of an intellectual body of knowledge that guides and sparks further lived discoveries of other phenomenologists. For example, Casey and Malpas' phenomenologies of place would be impossible without the conceptual groundwork laid by Husserl, Heidegger, and Merleau-Ponty (Casey, 2009; Malpas, 1999, 2006).

Another significant point in discussing experiential versus intellectual understanding is the obvious fact that the lifeworld and natural attitude are the starting point for all phenomenological investigation. As I emphasized throughout this book, the most remarkable existential quality of the lifeworld and natural attitude is their *taken-for-grantedness*. They are normally outside the awareness of conscious attention and therefore hidden from cerebral understanding until exposed phenomenologically. As Husserl (1970, p. 142) wrote,

> [T]he lifeworld for us who wakingly live in it, is always already there, existing in advance for us, the "ground" of all praxis, whether theoretical or extra-theoretical. The world is pregiven to us, the waking, always somehow practically interested subjects, not occasionally but always and necessarily as the universal field of all and possible praxis, as horizon. To live is always to live-in-certainty-of-the-world.

As Moran (2000, p. xiii) explains, Husserl's signal accomplishment was to bring Western thinking back "from abstract metaphysical speculation wrapped up in pseudo-problems, in order to come into contact with the matters themselves, with concrete living experience." Perhaps Husserl's most fruitful contribution was his "discovery" of the lifeworld and natural attitude – concepts never before fully recognized in Western philosophy and psychology. In turn, other phenomenologists like Heidegger and Merleau-Ponty identified additional lived structures – again, I think it fair to call them concepts – that emerged from the lifeworld's concealment in the natural attitude. Obviously, I never directly discovered the concepts of body–subject and perception myself, but once Merleau-Ponty's writings made them known to me, I realized intellectually their workings in my own life and eventually saw, *via my own lifeworld experiences*, that they accurately described an integral dimension of who and how we are as human beings (Seamon, 1979, 2018b). In time, I came to recognize how central these concepts are for understanding the human experience of place and for affording better place making.

As I illustrated in Chapter 13 on place intensification, there are aspects of the lifeworld that, *even through phenomenological efforts*, are not immediately visible or identifiable as contributors to the lifeworld's constitution. Perhaps the most convincing example is Hillier's theory of space syntax, which demonstrates empirically and quantitatively that the spatial configuration of pathways plays a significant role as to whether people come together physically in place or remain apart. Though it might be possible to devise a phenomenological study whereby one experiences and observes how pathway configurations enhance or stymy intersubjective corporeality, one more comprehensively understands this phenomenon via secondhand indicators like Hillier's measures of integration and their cartographic portrayals. It may be impossible phenomenologically to see fully the lived relationship between human movement and pathway configuration, but one can, for example, study lively and lifeless stretches of a city's sidewalks and use space–syntax theory as an intellectual adjunct to gain one set of behavioral and experiential clues as to the contrasting degree of sidewalk activity.

In a similar way, one might argue that the systems of Bennett's progressive approximation are not directly accessible via lifeworld experiences and are therefore questionable in terms of validity and trustworthiness, even though Bennett himself claims that the monad, dyad, triad, and so forth are primary elements of experience and "not something that is added by the mind" (Bennett, 1966a, p. 9). I would expect that, for most readers, the monad of lived emplacement and the several place dyads described in Chapters 5 and 6 are reasonable phenomenological depictions and are in fact already identified in the phenomenological work of Merleau-Ponty (environmental embodiment), Husserl (homeworld/alienworld), Jager (dwelling/journey and workaday/festive worlds), and Casey and Malpas (lived emplacement). An understanding of the lived significance of place dyads is probably the easiest of Bennett's systems for a newcomer to accept, since movement and rest, insideness and outsideness, and so forth, are relatively simple to locate in one's own experiences (though homeworld and alienworld are perhaps less so because they closely relate to the hiddenness of lifeworld and natural attitude).

Triads as Lifeworld Structures

The much more problematic system argued for in this book is the triad: first, the claim that all relationships and actions are grounded in three impulses; second, the claim that the six combinations of the three impulses delineate six triads that mark all relationships and actions. Does the triadic structure underlie all processual phenomena in human life? Can one, with practice, *really find* the six triads in human experience and in the workings of the world? These questions bring my discussion back to the reviewer's concern with the first draft of this book: Are Bennett's six triads imposed cerebral conjectures, or are they existential structures that he discovered in his own experience, through painstaking trial and error?

I cannot answer this question directly, other than to say that, in auto-biographical asides, Bennett mentions the importance of systematics research at his Institute and suggests that his understanding and mastery of the six triads arose slowly, at least partly through collaborative efforts.[1] To me, the more important concern is whether others can locate the six triads in their own experience and thereby contribute to an "intersubjective corroboration" whereby the triads are demonstrated or disproved in a wide range of lifeworld situations. Since this book has focused on the phenomenon of place, I have sought to explicate Bennett's six triads as they point to a range of lifeworld dimensions in relation to place experiences, place meanings, and lived emplacement. I hope my interpretations and real-world examples offer one kind of qualitative evidence for the reality of these triads in human life.

On one hand, I understand the reviewer's skepticism of Bennett's triads but, on the other hand, point out that central phenomenological concepts like lifeworld, lived body, and body–subject were unavailable until Husserl "invented" the phenomenological attitude and brought it to bear on human consciousness, life, and experience. Though Bennett never claimed to be a phenomenologist, his work is phenomenological in the sense that he attempts to clarify key dimensions of human experience. To the newcomer, the six triads may seem an intellectual imposition, but I would argue that, with prolonged, engaged study, one realizes that they are integral lived structures both of human experience and of the worlds in which that experience unfolds. Significantly, in an early draft of *The Dramatic Universe*, Bennett described three stages in understanding the three impulses and the six triads. He wrote:

> There are three moments of understanding. The first can be called "knowl-edge about understanding" and is expressed in the assertion that reality is

triadic and grows through the accumulation of examples that serve to confirm the truth of this assertion. Nevertheless, in this moment, understanding remains an object of knowledge and not a manifestation of [direct lived experience]. At the second moment of understanding, one's consciousness begins to penetrate into the triad. The effort to understand is made by a special division of attention in which the three impulses of the triad are separately contemplated and seen in their coming together. This discipline leads to a third stage of "active pondering" that involves the consciously directed effort to grasp the triadic character of any situation. Such pondering calls first of all for a direct perception of the character of each of the three impulses. This is attained only through experience of life and a sustained effort of attention. It starts with recognizing the meaning of the abstract principles of affirmation, denial, and reconciliation and moves toward the recognition that all reality is pervaded by the three impulses. The movement is from vagueness to clarity, from abstraction toward concreteness, from a rigid formula to a dynamic participation.

(Bennett, 1952, p. 292–293)

A Progressive Understanding

Though Bennett relates this way of progressive understanding to the triad, one can fairly say that this three-stage process applies to the phenomenological method broadly, since, as a newcomer to phenomenology, one typically begins with secondhand intellectual insights that become progressively more real and grounded as one looks for their lived presence via the specific phenomenon in which the phenomenologist is interested. For example, newcomers to the concept of "lifeworld" often encounter considerable intellectual difficulty in understanding what it is because, in ordinary life, it is hidden from view and only "catchable" in glimpses that readily "disappear." Over time, if one perseveres, one realizes how the lifeworld, through its automatic being-what-it-is, allows human life to unfold regularly, normally, and mostly without disruption. In short, one experiences a process of progressive understanding that moves from the ill-defined to the distinct, from secondhand, pre-established description to firsthand, experiential validation, from an arbitrary concept claimed by others to a firsthand recognition of an essential constituent of human life.

Eventually, via practicing the phenomenological attitude, one recognizes the reality of phenomenological concepts in one's lived experience. In this way, those concepts become concrete and unquestionable. Once one recognizes the always–already presence of lifeworld or body–subject, one sees without doubt that they are concepts arising from concrete experience and deftly assisting in understanding the constitution of human experience more broadly. Via the three-stage process he delineates above, Bennett suggests that such concrete understanding can also be had with the six triads.

Let me illustrate via my experience of writing this book. In the sabbatical year I had available, I set myself each weekday to write for three hours each afternoon.

Almost always, as I set myself to work, there arose the dyad of "I must work" but "I don't really feel like working." Through the repeated effort of writing many articles and chapters, I have learned that, to transform this recalcitrant dyad into a working triad, I must "get on with things," a difficult but necessary demand that shifts my situation from dyad to triad. Most days, I make this shift by performing repetitive tasks: locating materials I might need for the day; looking for a specific reference; or rereading and editing what I wrote the day before. All these actions are ordinary, humdrum interaction triads, but their value is that, collectively, they shift my writing efforts into a more engaged triadic state in which I actually begin to write. From a situation of "making myself start to write" by doing easy-to-conduct actions, I sooner or later find myself actively engaged with my work. Words and ideas begin to flow, and the writing takes on "a life of its own." The "trying to write" of interaction triads becomes the "actually writing and often writing quite well" of creation and freedom triads.

Once I am writing rather than trying to write, I might suddenly remember that I should bring another thinker's ideas into the discussion or I might realize that the idea I just expressed would be better discussed earlier. The most invigorating moments are when I suddenly understand something that I had not understood a moment before and can incorporate that understanding into my writing. All these actions relate to the freedom triad, whereby a connection, placement, or inspiration arises "out of the blue" and strengthens my writing by intensifying the creation triad. When I began this book, I had only a general sense of its order and format: I envisioned a single chapter that would integrate the place monad and dyad; I pictured three chapters, each of which would cover two triads each. As I became clearer about what I could say (concentration triads), I realized that the place monad, dyad, and six triads all demanded their own chapters (a series of insights marked by freedom triads). Processually, I worked to place myself receptively before the book's potential outline and open myself to the "best organizational fit." This active receptivity illustrates a series of concentration triads that eventually helped shape the final organizational structure of the book as published.

Throughout this process, I have strengthened my phenomenological sensibilities, my understanding of Bennett's systematics, and my respect for the significance of lived emplacement in human life. In this sense, writing this book has involved me in progressive triads of concentration and identity whereby my sense of self has been invigorated and strengthened. I know I understand more than when I started, and this sense of accomplishment is reassuring and ennobling. Though my focus on place, lived emplacement, and place making is only a part of what human life is about, my discoveries point to the rich field of theoretical and applied possibilities that phenomenology offers broadly and Bennett's work offers as one innovative means to focus phenomenological inquiry through the multivalent perspective of his interpretive systems.

Place as Unpredictable and Marvelous

Just as I was pondering how to end this postscript, an inspiring story of place serendipity appeared in the *New York Times*' "Metropolitan Diary." As a man left the New York Sports Club on West 73rd Street, he waved to the adjacent building's doorman, who came running after him. The man had been saying hello to this doorman for the past two years. "Wait," shouted the doorman, "What's your name?" "Andrew," said the man, to which the doorman replied: "I ask because there is a woman in my building who saw you the other day and wondered who you were. Her name is Rachel and she's beautiful. Can I give her your name?" "Sure," said Andrew, who provided the doorman with his cell-phone number. Three days later Rachel texted Andrew, and three days after that, they met for drinks. A year later they married, and their first son was born in May. "Thank you, Juan," was how Andrew ended his account. Juan, of course, was the doorman (*NYT*, September 25, 2017, p. A21).

I end my postscript with this story because it points to the unpredictable and marvelous dynamics of place. For sure, this serendipitous event relates to the triad of place release, but it also illustrates how Andrew and Rachel would probably never have met if Andrew were not a member of the New York Sports Club, if both Rachel and Juan had not had ties to the building next door, if Rachel had not spotted Andrew leaving the club, or if Andrew had not waved regularly to Juan, who therefore felt comfortable enough to approach Andrew with Rachel's query. Place and lived emplacement are miraculous but taken-for-granted aspects of *all human being*. I hope this book demonstrates how phenomenology provides a road map into the extraordinariness of place and lived emplacement, further concretized via the trailblazing perspective of Bennett's systematics.

Geographer Edward Relph (2001, p. 159) asserts that "The world continually outruns theories and descriptions of it," and this contention is as true for phenomenology as it is for all other past and current ways of knowing – poststructuralism, social constructionism, critical theory, analytical science, and all the rest. Though no conceptual approach can ever afford a complete, perfect fit between experiencing and thinking, I do insist that conceptual structures arising from the lifeworld are more real and useful than conceptual structures generated by thinking alone. Whether the phenomenology of place I offer here arises accurately from lived experience is up to readers to decide. Bennett's systematics may seem to contradict my claim, but I say with confidence that, if readers work with Bennett's systematic method and give it a fair chance, they will be surprised and gratified by experiential discoveries not readily discernible otherwise.

In the preface to *Phenomenology of Perception*, Merleau-Ponty (1962, p. xiii) writes that phenomenology "slackens the intentional threads that attach us to the world and thus brings them to our notice." One such intentional thread is the pivotal presence of place in human life. Here, I have sought to probe this pivotal presence and, particularly, to clarify its processual unfolding. For sure, life does take place.

Note

1   For discussion of the role of collaboration in the development of systematics, see Bennett, 1966a, pp. v–ix; Bennett, 1966b, pp. ix–x. In comparing the earlier 1952 *Dramatic Universe* draft with the six triads' final rendition in volume two of the published *Dramatic Universe*, one notes several shifts in Bennett's understanding, particularly with the triads of order and freedom. In the 1952 draft, Bennett used different labels for some of the triads; he called the triad of interaction, "exchange"; the triad of expansion, "involution"; the triad of concentration, "evolution"; and the triad of order, "determination."

Throughout the development of systematics, one notes that Bennett and his colleagues were continuously questioning, rephrasing, and honing its perspective, method, and conceptual discoveries. I take this intellectual flexibility to indicate a sincere, robust effort to *really understand* human life and world existence. In the third volume of *The Dramatic Universe*, Bennett (1966a, p. viii, p. ix) summarized his aim as follows:

> I have set myself to show that a unified world picture can be constructed that embraces all human experience and all human knowledge as it presents itself to us in the second half of the twentieth century. The picture must, of necessity, be *defective*; but this is not so important as the demonstration that some sort of total picture is *possible* . . . . If some of the notions developed prove fruitful and contribute to the great reconstruction of human thinking that is bound to come during the next century, I shall have accomplished all that I could hope.

REFERENCES

Abramson, D.M. (2016). *Obsolescence: An architectural history*. Chicago, IL: University of Chicago Press.

Alexander, B. (2017). *Glass house: The 1% economy and the shattering of the all-American town*. New York: St. Martin's Press.

Alexander, C. (2002a). *The nature of order, vol. 1: The phenomenon of life*. Berkeley, CA: Center for Environmental Structure.

Alexander, C. (2002b). *The nature of order, vol. 2: The process of creating life*. Berkeley, CA: Center for Environmental Structure.

Alexander, C. (2004). *The nature of order, vol. 4: The luminous ground*. Berkeley, CA: Center for Environmental Structure.

Alexander, C. (2005). *The nature of order, vol. 3: A vision of a living world*. Berkeley, CA: Center for Environmental Structure.

Alexander, C. (2007). Empirical findings from the nature of order. *Environmental and Architectural Phenomenology*, 18(1), 11–19.

Alexander, C. (2012). *Battle for the life and beauty of the earth*. New York: Oxford University Press.

Alexander, C., Anninou, A., King, I., and Neis, H. (1987). *A new theory of urban design*. New York: Oxford University Press.

Alexander, C., Ishikawa, S., and Silverstein, M. (1977). *A pattern language*. New York: Oxford University Press.

Alexander, R. (1997). *Metropolitan diary: The best selections from the New York Times column*. New York: William Morrow and Company.

Allen, C. (2004). Merleau-Ponty's phenomenology and the body-in-space: Encounters of visually impaired children. *Environment and Planning D: Society and Space*, 22(5), 719–735.

Allen, J. and Cochrane, A. (2007). Beyond the territorial fix: Regional assemblages, politics and power. *Regional Studies* 41(9), 1161–1171.

Amin, A. (2004). Regions unbound: Towards a new politics of place. *Geografiska Annaler*, 86B(1), 33–44.

Arnade, C. (2016). McDonald's: You can sneer but it's the glue that hold communities together. *The Guardian*, Wednesday, June 8, 2016; https://www.theguardian.com/business/2016/jun/08/mcdonalds-community-centers-us-physical-social-networks (accessed May 8, 2017).

Bachelard, G. (1964). *The poetics of space*. Boston, MA: Beacon Press.

Bandura, A. (1982). The psychology of chance encounters and life paths. *American Psychologist*, 37(7), 747–755.

Barry, J. (2012). My dad's story: The house he lived in for sixty-five years. *Environmental and Architectural Phenomenology*, 23(2), 4–10.

Behnke, E. (1997). Body. In L. Embree, ed. *Encyclopedia of phenomenology* (pp. 66–71). Dordrecht, the Netherlands: Kluwer.

Bennett, J.G. (1950). The triad [unpublished early chapter of *The dramatic universe*, photocopy].

Bennett, J.G. (1952). *The dramatic universe: An examination of the significance of human existence* [unpublished early draft of *The dramatic universe*, photocopy].

Bennett, J.G. (1956). *The dramatic universe, vol. 1: The foundations of natural philosophy*. London: Hodder & Stoughton.

Bennett, J.G. (1961). *The dramatic universe, vol. 2: The foundations of moral philosophy*. London: Hodder & Stoughton.

Bennett, J.G. (1963). Systematics and general systems theory. *Systematics*, 1(2), 105–110.

Bennett, J.G. (1966a). *The dramatic universe, vol. 3: Man and his nature*. London: Hodder & Stoughton.

Bennett, J.G. (1966b). *The dramatic universe, vol. 4: History*. London: Hodder & Stoughton.

Bennett, J.G. (1970). Systematics and system theories. *Systematics*, 7(4), 273–278.

Bennett, J.G. (1974). *Witness: The autobiography of John Bennett*. London: Turnstone Books.

Bennett, J.G. (1993). *Elementary systematics*. D. Seamon, ed. Santa Fe, NM: Bennett Books.

Bentley, I., Alcock, A., Murrain, P., McGlynn, S., and Smith, G. (1985). *Responsive environments: A manual for designers*. London: The Architectural Press.

Bermudez, J., ed. (2015). *Transcending architecture*. Washington, DC: Catholic University of America Press.

Bertalanffy, L. von (1965). *Perspectives on general system theory*. New York: George Braziller.

Blake, A. (2003). *The meaning of the triad*. Charles Town, WV: DuVersity Publications.

Bohm, D. (1980). *Wholeness and the implicate order*. London: Routledge.

Bollnow, O. (1967). Lived-space. In N. Lawrence and D. O'Connor, eds. *Readings in existential phenomenology* (pp. 178–186). Englewood Cliffs, NJ: Prentice-Hall.

Bollnow, O. (2011). *Human space*. London: Hyphen Press [originally 1963].

Borch, C., ed. (2014). *Architectural atmospheres*. Basel, Switzerland: Birkhäuser.

Borgmann, A. (1992). *Crossing the postmodern divide*. Chicago, IL: University of Chicago Press.

Borgmann, A. (1999). *Holding on to reality*. Chicago, IL: University of Chicago Press.

Bortoft, H. (1971). The whole: Counterfeit and authentic. *Systematics*, 9(2), 43–73.

Bortoft, H. (1985). Counterfeit and authentic wholes: Finding a means for dwelling in nature. In D. Seamon and R. Mugerauer, eds. *Dwelling, place and environment* (pp. 289–302). Dordrecht, the Netherlands: Martinus-Nijhoff.

Bortoft, H. (1996). *The wholeness of nature*. Edinburgh, UK: Floris Books.

Bortoft, H. (2012). *Taking appearance seriously*. Edinburgh, UK: Floris Books.

Böhme, G. (2014). Urban atmospheres. In C. Borch (ed.) *Architectural atmospheres* (pp. 42–59). Basel, Switzerland: Birkhäuser.

Böhme, G., Griffero, T., and Thibald, J., eds. (2014). *Architecture and atmosphere*. Espoo, Finland: Tapio Wirkkala Rut Bryk Foundation.

Brittan, G.G., Jr. (2001). Wind, energy, landscape: Reconciling nature and technology. *Philosophy and Geography*, 4(2), 169–184.

Brittan, G.G., Jr. (2002a). The wind of one's sails: A philosophy. In M.J. Pasqualetti, P. Gibe, and R.W. Righter, eds. *Wind power in view* (pp. 59–79). San Diego, CA: Academic Press.

Brittan, G.G., Jr. (2002b). Fitting wind power to landscape: A place-based wind turbine. *Environmental and Architectural Phenomenology*, 13(2), 10–15.

Burch, R. (1989). On phenomenology and its practices. *Phenomenology + Pedagogy*, 7, 187–217.

Burch, R. (1990). Phenomenology and lived experience: Taking a measure of the topic. *Phenomenology + Pedagogy*, 8, 130–160.

Burch, R. (1991). Phenomenology and the human sciences reconsidered. *Phenomenology + Pedagogy*, 9, 27–69.

Buttimer, A. (1972). Social space and the planning of residential areas. *Environment and Behavior*, 4(3), 279–318.

Buttimer, A. (1976). Grasping the dynamism of lifeworld. *Annals of the Association of American Geographers*, 66(2), 277–292.

Cameron, J. (2005). Place, Goethe and phenomenology: A theoretical journey. *Janus Head*, 8(1), 174–198.

Carman, T. (2008). *Merleau-Ponty*. London: Routledge.

Carmona, M., Tiesdell, S., Heath, T., and Oc, T. (2010). *Public places, urban spaces: The dimensions of urban design*. London: Architectural Press/Elsevier.

Casey, E.S. (1997). *The fate of place: A philosophical history*. Berkeley: University of California Press.

Casey, E.S. (2001a). Between geography and philosophy. *Annals, Association of American Geographers*, 91(4), 683–693.

Casey, E.S. (2001b). J.E. Malpas's Place and experience. *Philosophy and Geography*, 4(2), 225–231.

Casey, E.S. (2009). *Getting back into place*, 2nd edn. Bloomington, IN: Indiana University Press.

Cerbone, D.R. (2006). *Understanding phenomenology*. Durham, UK: Acumen.

Cerbone, D.R. (2008). Perception. In R. Diprose and J. Reynolds, eds. *Merleau-Ponty: Key concepts* (pp. 121–131). Stockfield, UK: Acumen Publishing.

Compton, J. (1997). Existential phenomenology. In L. Embree, ed. *Encyclopedia of phenomenology* (pp. 205–209). Dordrecht, the Netherlands: Kluwer.

Cohn, D. and Morin, R. (2008). *Who moves? Who stays put? Where's home? Pew Demographic Trends*. Washington, DC: Pew Research Center. http://pewsocialtrends.org/assets/pdf/Movers-and-Stayers.pdf (accessed July 5, 2017).

Connolly, W. (1995). *The ethos of pluralization*. Minneapolis, MN: University of Minnesota Press.

Creswell, J.W. (2007). *Qualitative inquiry and research design*. Thousand Oaks, CA: SAGE.

Cresswell, T. (2006). *On the move: Mobility in the modern world*. New York: Taylor & Francis.

Cresswell, T. (2013). *Geographic thought: A critical introduction*. Oxford, UK: Wiley-Blackwell.

Cresswell, T. (2014). *Place: A history*. Oxford: Blackwell.

Dahlberg, K. (2006). The essence of essences – The search for meaning structures in phenomenological analysis of lifeworld phenomena. *International Journal of Qualitative Studies in Health and Well-Being*, 1(1), 11–19.

Dainotto, R. (2000). *Place in literature: Regions, culture and communities.* Ithaca, NY: Cornell University Press.

Davis, H. (2012). *Living over the store.* London: Routledge.

Dardel, E. (1952). *L'homme et la terre: Nature de la réalité géographique.* Paris: Presses Universitaries de France.

Deleuze, G. and Guattari, F. (1987). *A thousand plateaus.* Minneapolis, MN: University of Minnesota Press.

Diprose, R. and Reynolds, J., eds. (2008). *Merleau-Ponty: Key concepts.* Stockfield, UK: Acumen Publishing.

Doczi, G. (2005). *The power of limits: Philosophy and practice.* Boston, MA: Shambhala.

Donohoe, J. (2011). The place of home. *Environmental Philosophy*, 8(1), 25–40.

Donohoe, J. (2014). *Remembering places.* New York: Lexington Books.

Donohoe, J. (2017a). Hermeneutics, place, and the environment. In Bruce Janz, ed. *Place, space and hermeneutics* (pp. 427–436). Cham, Switzerland: Springer.

Donohoe, J., ed. (2017b). *Place and phenomenology.* New York: Roman & Littlefield.

Dorfman, E. (2009). History of the lifeworld from Husserl to Merleau-Ponty. *Philosophy Today*, 53(3), 294–303.

Dovey, K. (1985). The quest for authenticity and the replication of environmental meaning. In D. Seamon and R. Mugerauer, eds. *Dwelling, place and environment* (pp. 33–49). Dordrecht, the Netherlands: Martinus Nijhoff.

Dovey, K. (2010). *Becoming places.* London: Routledge.

Durrell, L. (1971). Landscape and character. In A.G. Thomas, ed. *Spirit of place* (pp. 159–163). New York: Dutton.

Erickson, K.T. (1976). *Everything in its path: Destruction of community in the Buffalo Creek flood.* New York: Simon and Schuster.

Evans, F. (2008). Chiasm and flesh. In R. Diprose and J. Reynolds, eds. *Merleau-Ponty: Key concepts* (pp. 184–193). Stockfield, UK: Acumen Publishing.

Fathy, H. (1973). *Architecture for the poor.* Chicago, IL: University of Chicago Press.

Fine, G.A. and Deegan, J. (1996). Three principles of serendipity: Insight, chance, and discovery in qualitative research. *Qualitative Studies in Education*, 9(4), 434–447.

Finlay, L. (2006). The body's disclosure in phenomenological research. *Qualitative Research in Psychology*, 3(1), 19–30.

Finlay, L. (2011). *Phenomenology for therapists: Researching the lived world.* Oxford: Wiley/ Blackwell.

Fisher, C. (1982). *To dwell among friends.* Chicago, IL: University of Chicago Press.

Fried, M. (1972). Grieving for a lost home. In R. Gutman, ed. *People and buildings* (pp. 229–248). New York: Basic Books.

Frumkin, H., Frank, L., and Jackson, R.J. (2004) *Urban sprawl and public health: Designing, planning, and building for healthy communities*, Washington, DC: Island Press.

Fullilove, M.T. (2004). *Root shock.* New York: Ballantine Books.

Fullilove, M.T. (2011). *Urban alchemy.* New York: New Village Press.

Gallagher, S. (1986). Lived body and environment. *Research in Phenomenology*, 16(1), 139–170.

Gans, H. (1962). *The urban villagers.* New York: Free Press.

Gardner, W.H., ed. (1953). Introduction. In G.M. Hopkins, *Poems and prose* (pp. xiii–xxxvi). London: Penguin.

Gearty, C. (2010) Do human rights help or hinder environmental protection? *Journal of Human Rights and the Environment*, 1(1), 7–22.

Gehl, J. (1987). *Life between buildings*. New York: Van Nostrand Reinhold.

Gieryn, T.F. (2000). A space for place in sociology. *Annual Review of Sociology*, 26(1), 463–496.

Gieryn, T.F. (2002). Give place a chance: Reply to Gans. *City & Community*, 1(4), 341–343.

Giorgi, A. (2009). *Descriptive phenomenological method in psychology*. Pittsburgh, PA: Duquesne University Press.

Gladwell, M. (2008). *Outliers*. New York: Back Bay Books.

Goffman, E. (1963). *Behavior in public places*. New York: Free Press.

Goffman, E. (1983). The interaction order. *American Sociological Review*, 48(1), 1–17.

Goldstein, A. (2017). *Janesville: An American story*. New York: Simon & Schuster.

Grabow, S. (1983). *Christopher Alexander and the search for a new paradigm in architecture*. London: Oriel Press.

Greenfield, A. (2017). *Radical technologies: The design of everyday life*. London: Verso.

Griffero, T. (2014). *Atmospheres: Aesthetics of emotional spaces*. Burlington, VT: Ashgate.

Griffero, T. (2017). *Quasi-Things: The paradigm of atmospheres*. Albany: State University of New York Press.

Gruenewald, D.A. (2003). Foundations of place: A multidisciplinary framework for place-conscious education. *American Educational Research Review*, 40(3), 619–654.

Hammond, D. (2003). *The science of synthesis*. Boulder: University Press of Colorado.

Hanson, J. (1998). *Decoding homes and houses*. Cambridge, UK: Cambridge University Press.

Hanson, J. (2000). Urban transformations. *Urban Design International*, 5(2), 97–122.

Hardt, M. and Negri, A. (2000). *Empire*. Cambridge, MA: Harvard University Press.

Harries, K. (1997). *The ethical function of architecture*. Cambridge, MA: MIT Press.

Harte, B. (1961). *Selected stories of Bret Harte*. New York: Pyramid Books.

Hay, P. (2002). *Major currents in Western environmental thought*. Bloomington: University of Indiana Press.

Heidegger, M. (1962). *Being and time*. New York: Harper and Row.

Heidegger, M. (1969). *Identity and difference*. New York: Harper and Row.

Heidegger, M. (1971a). Building dwelling thinking. In *Poetry, language, thought*. New York: Harper and Row.

Heidegger, M. (1971b) *Poetry, language, thought*. New York: Harper and Row.

Heinämaa, S. (2012). The body. In S. Luft and S. Overgaard, eds. *The Routledge companion to phenomenology* (pp. 222–232). London: Routledge.

Hillier, B. (1989). The architecture of the urban object. *Ekistics*, 56(334/33), 5–21.

Hillier, B. (1996). *Space is the machine*. Cambridge, UK: Cambridge University Press.

Hillier, B. (2005). Between social physics and phenomenology: Explorations towards an urban synthesis? In A. van Nes, ed. *Proceedings of the 5th international space syntax symposium* (pp. 3–23). Delft, the Netherlands: Delft Techne Press.

Hillier, B. (2008). The new science and the art of place. In T. Haas, ed. *New urbanism and beyond* (pp. 30–39). New York: Rizzoli.

Hillier, B. and Hanson, J. (1984). *The social logic of space*. Cambridge, UK: Cambridge University Press.

Hopkins, G.M. (1953). *Gerard Manley Hopkins: Poems and prose*. London: Penguin.

Horan, D. (2000) *Digital places*. Washington, DC: Urban Land Institute.

Husserl, E. (1970) *The crisis of European sciences and transcendental phenomenology*. Evanston, IL: Northwestern University Press.

IOM (2010). International Organization on Migration, World migration report 2010; http://www.publications.iom.int (accessed July 17, 2017).

Jacobs, J. (1958). Downtown is for people. In W. Whyte, ed. *The exploding metropolis* (pp. 157–184). Garden City, NY: Doubleday & Company.

Jacobs, J. (1961). *The death and life of great American cities.* New York: Vintage.

Jacobson, K. (2010). The experience of home and the space of citizenship. *The Southern Journal of Philosophy*, 48(3), 219–245.

Jager, B. (1975). Theorizing, journeying, dwelling. In A. Giorgi, C. Fischer and E. Murray, eds. *Duquesne studies in phenomenological psychology, vol. 2* (pp. 235–260). Pittsburgh, PA: Duquesne University Press.

Jager, B. (1983). Theorizing the elaboration of place: Inquiry into Galileo and Freud. In A. Giorgi, A. Barton, and C. Maes, eds. *Duquesne studies in phenomenological psychology, vol. 4* (pp. 153–180). Pittsburgh, PA: Duquesne University Press.

Jager, B. (1985). Body, house and city: The intertwinings of embodiment, inhabitation and civilization. In D. Seamon and R. Mugerauer, eds. *Dwelling, place and environment* (pp. 215–225). Dordrecht, the Netherlands: Martinus Nijhoff.

Jager, B. (1997). Concerning the festive and the mundane. *Journal of Phenomenological Psychology*, 28(2), 196–235.

Jager, B. (2001a). Introduction. *Journal of Phenomenological Psychology*, 32(2), 103–117.

Jager, B. (2001b). The birth of poetry and the creation of the human world. *Journal of Phenomenological Psychology*, 32(2), 131–154.

Jager, B. (2007). Memories and myths of evil: A reflection on the fall from paradise. In C. Thiboutot, ed. *Essais de psychologie phénoménoguique-existentielle: Réunis en homage au professeur Bernd Jager* (pp. 394–421). Montreal, Canada: Cercle interdisciplinaire de recherches phénoméologiques.

Jager, B. (2009). Thresholds and inhabitation. *Environmental and Architectural Phenomenology*, 20(3), 8–10.

Jager, B. (2010). Towards a psychology of homo habitans: A reflection on cosmos and universe. In T.F. Cloonan and C. Thiboutot, eds. *The redirection of psychology: Essays in honor of Amedeo P. Giorgi* (pp. 229–249). Montreal, Canada: Cercle interdisciplinaire de recherches phénoméologiques.

Jager, B. (2013). Psychology as an art and as a science: A reflection on the myth of Prometheus. *The Human Psychologist*, 41(3), 261–284.

Janz, B.B. (2005). Walls and borders: The range of place. *City & Community*, 4(1), 87–94.

Janz, B.B., ed. (2017). *Place, space and hermeneutics.* Cham, Switzerland: Springer.

Jargon, J. (2017). McDonald's offers franchises help to regain business. *Wall Street Journal*, Friday, May 12, p. B5.

Johnson, S. (2010). *Where good ideas come from.* New York: Riverhead Books.

Jonas, A. (2012). Region and place: regionalism in question. *Progress in Human Geography*, 36(2), 263–272.

Jones, L. (2000). *The hermeneutics of sacred architecture*, 2 vols. Cambridge, MA: Harvard University Press.

Jung, C.G. (1973). *Synchronicity: An acausal connecting principle.* Princeton, NJ: Princeton University Press.

Kelly, K. (2016). *The inevitable: Understanding the 12 technological forces that will shape our future.* New York: Viking.

Kemmis, D. (1990). *Community and the politics of place.* Norman: University of Oklahoma Press.

Kemmis, D. (1995). *The good city and the good life.* New York: Houghton Mifflin.

Klemek, C. (2011). Dead or alive at fifty? Reading Jane Jacobs on her golden anniversary. *Dissent*, Spring, 73–77.

Klinenberg, E. (2002). *Heat wave*. Chicago, IL: University of Chicago Press.

Koestler, A. (1972). *The roots of coincidence*. New York: Vintage.

Kogl, A. (2008). *Strange places: The political potentials and perils of everyday spaces*. New York: Rowman & Littlefield.

Kopec, D. (2012). *Environmental psychology for design*, 2nd edn. New York: Fairchild.

Krafel, P. (1989). *Shifting*. Cottonwood, CA: P. Krafel.

Krafel, P. (1998). *Seeing nature*. White River Junction, VT: Chelsea Green [a revised edition of Krafel, *Shifting*].

Lane, B. (2000). *Landscapes of the sacred*. Baltimore, MA: Johns Hopkins Press.

Larsen, S.C. and Johnson, J.T. (2017). *Being together in place: Indigenous coexistence in a more than human world*. Minneapolis: University of Minnesota Press.

Laurence, P.L. (2011). The unknown Jane Jacobs: Geographer, propagandist, city planning idealist. In M. Page and T. Mennel, eds. *Reconsidering Jane Jacobs* (pp. 15–36). Washington, DC: APA Planners Press.

Laurence, P.L. (2016). *Becoming Jane Jacobs*. Philadelphia: University of Pennsylvania Press.

Lawlor, R. (1982). *Sacred geometry: Philosophy and practice*. London: Thames and Hudson.

Leder, D. (1990). *The absent body*. Chicago, IL: University of Chicago Press.

Leidner, R. (1993). *Fast food, fast talk: Service work and the routinization of everyday life*. Berkeley: University of California Press.

Lessing, D. (1969). *The four-gated city*. New York: Bantam.

Lessing, D. (1984). *The diaries of Jane Somers*. New York: Vintage.

Lewicka, M. (2011). Place attachment: How far have we come in the last 40 years? *Journal of Environmental Psychology*, 31(3), 207–230.

Lewis, P. (1979). Defining a sense of place. In W.P. Prenshaw and J.O. McKee, eds. *Sense of place: Mississippi* (pp. 24–46). Jackson: University of Mississippi Press.

Lively, P. (1998). *Spiderweb*. London: Penguin.

Lively, P. (2007). *Consequences*. London: Penguin.

Lively, P. (2011). *How it all began*. London: Penguin.

Lively, P. (2013). *Dancing fish and ammonites: A memoir*. London: Penguin.

Lofland, L.H. (1985). *A world of strangers: Order and action in urban public space*. Prospect Heights, IL: Waveland.

Lofland, L.H. (1998). *The public realm*. New York: Aldine de Gruyter.

Low, S. (2003a). *Behind the gates: The new American dream*. New York: Routledge.

Low, S. (2003b). Embodied space(s). *Space and Culture*, 6(1), 9–18.

Madison, G.B. (1988). *The hermeneutic of postmodernity*. Bloomington: Indiana University Press.

Main, R. (1997). *Jung on synchronicity and the paranormal*. Princeton, NJ: Princeton University Press.

Main, R. (2007) *Revelations of chance*. Albany: State University of New York Press.

Malpas, J.E. (1999). *Place and experience*. Cambridge, UK: Cambridge University Press.

Malpas, J.E. (2001). Comparing topographies: Across paths/around place: A reply to Casey. *Philosophy and Geography*, 4(2), 231–238.

Malpas, J.E. (2006) *Heidegger's topology*. Cambridge, MA: MIT Press.

Malpas, J.E. (2009). Place and human being. *Environmental and Architectural Phenomenology*, 20(3), 19–23.

Malpas, J.E. (2012a). *Heidegger and the thinking of place*. Cambridge, MA: MIT Press.

Malpas, J.E. (2012b). Putting space in place: Philosophical topography and relational geography. *Environment and Planning D: Society and Space*, 30(2), 226–242.

Malpas, J.E. (2014). Human being as placed being. *Environmental and Architectural Phenomenology*, 25(3), 8–9.

Malpas, J.E., ed. (2015). *The intelligence of place: Topographies and poetics*. London: Bloomsbury.

Manzo, L.C. (2003). Beyond house and haven. *Journal of Environmental Psychology*, 23(1), 47–61.

Manzo, L.C. (2005). For better or worse: Exploring multiple dimensions of place meaning. *Journal of Environmental Psychology*, 25(1), 67–86.

Manzo, L.C. and Devine-Wright, P., eds. (2014). *Place attachment: Advances in theory, methods and research*. New York: Routledge.

Marshall, S. (2012). Science, pseudo-science and urban design. *Urban Design International*, 17(4): 257–271.

Martin, D. (2006). Jane Jacobs, urban activist, is dead at 89 [obituary]. *New York Times*, April 26, 2006.

Massey, D. (1997). A global sense of place. In T. Barnes and D. Gregory, eds. *Reading human geography* (pp. 315–323). London: Arnold.

Massey, D. (2005). *For space*. London: SAGE.

Massey, D. (2009). The possibilities of a politics of place beyond place? *Scottish Geographical Journal*, 125(3/4), 401–420.

Mbembe, A. (2001). *On the postcolony*. Berkeley: University of California Press.

McFarlane, C. (2011). The city as assemblage. *Environment and Planning D: Society and Space*, 29(4), 649–671.

McGilchrist, I. (2009). *The master and the emissary: The divided brain and the making of the Western world*. New Haven, CT: Yale University Press.

Mehta, V. (2013). *The street*. London: Routledge.

Merleau-Ponty, M. (1962). *Phenomenology of perception*. New York: Humanities Press.

Merleau-Ponty, M. (1968). *The visible and the invisible*. Evanston, IL: Northwestern University Press.

Merton, R. and Barber, E. (2004). *The travels and adventures of serendipity*. Princeton, NJ: Princeton University Press.

Meyrowitz, J. (2015). Place and its mediated re-placements. In J. Malpas, ed. *The intelligence of place* (pp. 93–128). London: Bloomsbury.

Michael, S. (2018). *Expanded understandings of place making through genre painting: A heuristic study in the Mid North of South Australia*. Doctoral thesis, Department of Visual Art, University of South Australia, Adelaide.

Miller, V. (2016). *The crisis of presence in contemporary culture*. London: Sage.

Miles, M. (2006). Utopias of mud? Hassan Fathy and alternative modernisms. *Space and Culture*, 9(2), 116–139.

Minton, A. (2009). *Ground control: Fear and happiness in the twenty-first-century city*. London: Penguin.

Montgomery, C. (2014). *Happy city: Transforming our lives through urban design*. New York: Farrar, Straus and Giroux.

Moores, S. (2012). *Media, place and mobility*. Basingstoke, UK: Palgrave Macmillan.

Moran, D. (2000). *Introduction to phenomenology*. London: Routledge.

Moran, D. (2001). Phenomenology. In C. Meister and J. Beilby, eds. *The Routledge companion to modern Christian thought* (pp. 349–363). London: Routledge.

Moran, D. (2005) *Edmund Husserl: Founder of phenomenology*. Cambridge, UK: Polity.

Moran, D. (2008). The phenomenological approach: An introduction. In L. Introna, F. Ilharco, and E. Fay, eds. *Phenomenology, organization and technology* (pp. 21–41). Lisbon, Portugal: Universidade Católica Editora.

Moran, D. (2011). Edmund Husserl's phenomenology of habituality and habitus. *Journal of the British Society for Phenomenology*, 42(1), 53–76.

Moran, D. (2014). The ego as substrate of habitualities: Edmund Husserl's phenomenology of the habitual self. *Phenomenology and Mind*, 6, 26–47.

Moran, D. (2015a). Between vision and touch: From Husserl to Merleau-Ponty. In R. Kearny and B. Treanor, eds. *Carnal hermeneutics* (pp. 214–234). New York: Fordham University Press.

Moran, D. (2015b). Everydayness, historicity and the world of science: Husserl's life-world reconsidered. In L. 'Učník, I. Chvatík, and A. William, eds. *The phenomenological critique of mathematisation and the question of responsibility* (107–132).

Morgan, P. (2009). Towards a developmental theory of place attachment. *Journal of Environmental Psychology*, 30(1), 1–12.

Morley, D. (2000). *Home territories: Media, mobility and identity*. London: Routledge.

Morley, J. (2010) It's always about epoché. In T. Cloonan and C. Thiboutot, eds. *The redirection of psychology* (pp. 293–305). Quebec, Canada: Interdisciplinary Circle of Phenomenological Research, University of Quebec.

Morris, D. (2004). *The sense of space*. Albany: State University of New York Press.

Morris, D. (2008). Body. In R. Diprose and J. Reynolds, eds. *Merleau-Ponty: Key concepts* (pp. 111–120). Stockfield, UK: Acumen Publishing.

Mugerauer, R. (1988). *Heidegger's language and thinking*. Atlantic Highlands, NJ: Humanities Press.

Mugerauer, R. (1994). *Interpretations on behalf of place*. Albany: State University of New York Press.

Mugerauer, R. (2008). *Heidegger and homecoming*. Toronto, Canada: University of Toronto Press.

Naficy, H., ed. (1999). *Home, homeland, exile*. New York: Routledge.

Norberg-Schulz, C. (1971) *Existence, space and architecture*. New York: Rizzoli.

Norberg-Schulz, C. (1980). *Genius loci: Towards a phenomenology of architecture*. New York: Rizzoli.

Norberg-Schulz, C. (1985). *The concept of dwelling*. New York: Rizzoli.

Oldenburg, R. (1999). *The great good place*, 2nd edn. New York: Marlowe & Company.

Paasi, A. (2011). The region, identity, and power. *Procedia: Social and Behavioral Sciences*, 14, 9–16.

Paasi, A. and Metzger, J. (2016). Foregrounding the region. *Regional Studies*, 51(1)1–12.

Pallasmaa, J. (2005). *The eyes of the skin: Architecture and the senses*. London: Wiley.

Pallasmaa, J. (2009). *The thinking hand*. London: Wiley.

Pallasmaa, J. (2014). Space, place, and atmospheres. In C. Borch, ed. *Architectural atmospheres* (pp. 18–41). Basel, Switzerland: Birkhäuser.

Pallasmaa, J. (2015). Place and atmosphere. In J. Malpas, ed. *The intelligence of place* (pp. 129–155). London: Bloomsbury.

Palmer, R. (1969). *Hermeneutics: Interpretation theory in Schleiermacher, Dilthey, Heidegger, and Gadamer*. Evanston, IL: Northwestern University Press.

Pasqualetti, M.J., Gipe, P., and Righter, R.W. (2002). *Wind power in view*. San Diego, CA: Academic Press.

Patterson, M. and Williams, D. (2005). Maintaining research traditions on place: Diversity of thought and scientific progress. *Journal of Environmental Psychology*, 25(4), 361–380.

Pearson, T.R. (1985). *A short history of a small place*. New York: Penguin.

Pendergast, M. (2017). *City on the verge: Atlanta and the fight for America's urban future*. New York: Basic Books.

Pietersma, H. (1997). Maurice Merleau-Ponty. In L. Embree, ed. *Encyclopedia of phenomenology* (pp. 457–461). Dordrecht: Kluwer.

Quillien, J. (2012). *Clever digs: How workspaces can enable thought*. Ames, IA: Culicidae Press.

Pyla, P. (2007). Hassan Fathy revisited. *Journal of Architectural Education*, 60(3), 26–39.

Rae, D.W. (2003). *City: Urbanism and its end*. New Haven, CT: Yale University Press.

Relph, E. (1976). *Place and placelessness*. London: Pion.

Relph, E. (1981). *Rational landscapes and humanistic geography*. London: Croom Helm.

Relph, E. (1985). Geographical experiences and being-in-the-world. In D. Seamon and R. Mugerauer, eds. *Dwelling, place and environment* (pp. 15–31). New York: Columbia University Press.

Relph, E. (1993). Modernity and the reclamation of place. In D. Seamon, ed. *Dwelling, seeing, and designing: Toward a phenomenological ecology* (pp. 25–40). Albany: State University of New York Press.

Relph, E. (2001). The critical description of confused geographies. In P.C. Adams, S. Hoelscher, and K.E. Till, eds. *Texture of place: Exploring humanist geographies* (pp. 150–166). Minneapolis: University of Minnesota Press.

Relph, E. (2007). Spirit of place and sense of place in virtual realities. *Techné*, 10(3), 1–8.

Relph, E. (2008). Sense of place and emerging social and environmental challenges. In J. Eyles and A. Williams, eds. *Sense of place, health and quality of life* (pp. 65–78). Burlington, VT: Ashgate.

Relph, E. (2009). A pragmatic sense of place. *Environmental and Architectural Phenomenology*, 20(3), 24–31.

Relph, E. (2015). Place and connection. In J. Malpas, ed. *The intelligence of place* (pp. 177–204). London: Bloomsbury.

Richards, S. (2012). *Architect knows best: Environmental determinism in architecture from 1956 to the present*. Burlington, VT: Ashgate.

Righter, R. (2002). *Wind energy in America*. Norman: University of Oklahoma Press.

Robbins, P. and Marks, B. (2010). Assemblage geographies. In S.J. Smith, R. Pain, S.A. Marston, and J.P. Jones, eds. *The SAGE handbook of social geographies* (pp. 176–194). London: SAGE.

Robinson, S. and Pallasmaa, J., eds. (2015). *Mind in architecture: Neuroscience, embodiment, and the future of design*. Cambridge, MA: MIT Press.

Romdenh-Romluc, K. (2012). Maurice Merleau-Ponty. In S. Luft and S. Overgaard, eds. *The Routledge companion to phenomenology* (pp. 103–112). New York: Routledge.

Rose, G. (1993). *Feminism and geography*. Cambridge, UK: Polity.

Rose, G. (1995). Place and identity. In D. Massey and P. Jess, eds. *A place in the world?* (pp. 87–132). Oxford: Oxford University Press.

Sadik-Khan, J. and Solomonow, S. (2016). *Street fight: Handbook for an urban revolution*. New York: Viking.

Scannell, L. and Gifford, R. (2010). Defining place attachment: A tripartite organizing framework. *Journal of Environmental Psychology*, 30(1), pp. 1–10.

Schuh, R.T. and Brower, A.V. (2009). *Biological systematics*, 2nd edn. Ithaca, NY: Cornell University Press.

Schwartz, S.I. (2015). *Street smart: The rise of cities and the fall of cars*. New York: Public Affairs.

Sciolino, E. (2016). *The only street in Paris*. New York: Norton.

Seamon, D. (1979). *A geography of the lifeworld*. New York; London: St. Martin's Press; Routledge Revivals.

Seamon, D. (1985). Reconciling old and new worlds: The dwelling-journey relationship as portrayed in Vilhelm Moberg's "Emigrant" novels. In D. Seamon and R. Mugerauer, eds. *Dwelling, place and environment* (pp. 227–245). Dordrecht, the Netherlands: Martinus-Nijhoff.

Seamon, D. (1993). Different worlds coming together: A phenomenology of relationships as portrayed in Doris Lessing's Diaries of Jane Somers. D. Seamon, ed., *Dwelling, seeing and designing: Toward a phenomenological ecology* (pp. 219–246). Albany: State University of New York Press.

Seamon, D. (2004). Grasping the dynamism of urban place: Contributions from the work of Christopher Alexander, Bill Hillier, and Daniel Kemmis. In T. Mels, ed. *Reanimating places* (pp. 123–145). Burlington, VT: Ashgate.

Seamon, D. (2007). A lived hermetic of people and place: Phenomenology and space syntax. In A. S. Kubat, O. Ertekin, Y. I. Guney, and E. Eyuboglu, eds. *6th international space syntax symposium: Proceedings*, 2 vols. (pp. 1–16). Istanbul: Istanbul Technological University [ITU], Faculty of Architecture.

Seamon, D. (2008). Place, placelessness, insideness, and outsideness in John Sayles' Sunshine State. *Aether: The Journal of Media Geography*, 3, June, 1–19.

Seamon, D. (2010). Gaston Bachelard's topoanalysis in the 21st century: The lived reciprocity between houses and inhabitants as portrayed by American writer Louis Bromfield. In L. Embree, ed. *Phenomenology 2010* (pp. 225–243). Bucharest, Romania: Zeta Books.

Seamon, D. (2012a). "A jumping, joyous urban jumble": Jane Jacobs' death and life of great American cities as a phenomenology of urban place. *Journal of Space Syntax*, 3(1), 139–149.

Seamon, D. (2012b). Place, place identity, and phenomenology. In H. Casakin and F. Bernardo, eds. *The role of place identity in the perception, understanding, and design of the built environment* (pp. 1–25). London: Bentham Science Publishers.

Seamon, D. (2013a). Encountering the whole: Remembering Henri Bortoft (1938–2012). *Phenomenology & Practice*, 7(2), 100–107.

Seamon, D. (2013b). Lived bodies, place, and phenomenology: Implications for human rights and environmental justice. *Journal of Human Rights and the Environment*, 4(2), 143–166.

Seamon, D. (2013c). Phenomenology and uncanny homecomings: Homeworld, alienworld, and being-at-home in Alan Ball's HBO television series, Six Feet Under. In D. Boscaljon, ed. *Resisting the place of belonging* (pp. 155–170). Burlington, VT: Ashgate.

Seamon, D. (2014a). Lived-immersion-in-world. *Environmental and Architectural Phenomenology*, 25(3), 5–8.

Seamon, D. (2014b). Physical and virtual environments: Meaning of place and space. In B.A. Boyt Schell, G. Gillen, and M.E. Scaffa, eds. *Willard & Spackman's occupational therapy*, 12th edn. (pp. 202–214). Philadelphia, PA: Lippincott, Williams & Wilkens.

Seamon, D. (2014c). Place attachment and phenomenology. In L. Manzo and P. Devine-Wright, eds. *Place attachment: Advances in theory, methods and research* (pp. 11–22). New York: Routledge.

Seamon, D. (2015a). Lived emplacement and the locality of being: A return to humanistic geography? In S. Aitken and G. Valentine, eds. *Approaches to human geography*, 2nd edn. (pp. 35–48). London: SAGE.

Seamon, D. (2015b). Situated cognition and the phenomenology of place: Lifeworld, environmental embodiment, and immersion-in-world. *Cognitive Processes*, 16(1), 389–392.

Seamon, D. (2015c) Understanding place holistically: Cities, synergistic relationality, and space syntax. *Journal of Space Syntax*, 6(1), 32–43.

Seamon (2016). Christopher Alexander and a phenomenology of wholeness. In K. Pontikis and Y. Rofé, eds. *In pursuit of a living architecture: Continuing Christopher Alexander's quest for a humane and sustainable building culture* (pp. 50–66). Champaign, IL: Common Ground.

Seamon, D. (2017a). Architecture, place, and phenomenology: Buildings as lifeworlds, atmospheres, and environmental wholes. In J. Donohoe, ed. *Phenomenology and place* (pp. 247–263). New York: Roman and Littlefield.

Seamon, D. (2017b). A phenomenological and hermeneutic reading of Rem Koolhaas's Seattle Central Library. In R.C. Dalton and C. Hölscher, eds. *Take one building: Interdisciplinary research perspectives of the Seattle Central Library* (pp. 67–94). London: Routledge.

Seamon, D. (2017c). Hermeneutics and architecture: Buildings-in-themselves and interpretive trustworthiness. In B. Janz, ed. *Hermeneutics, space, and place* (pp. 347–360). Cham, Switzerland: Springer.

Seamon, D. (2018a). Architecture and phenomenology. In D. Lu, ed. *The Routledge companion to contemporary architectural history*. London: Routledge, in press.

Seamon, D. (2018b). Lifeworld, place, and phenomenology: Holistic and dialectical perspectives. In T. Collins and N. Cronin, eds. *Lifeworlds: Space, place and Irish culture*. Cork, Ireland: Cork University Press, in press.

Seamon, D. (2018c). Merleau-Ponty, lived body, and place: Toward a phenomenology of human situatedness. In T. Hünefeldt and A. Schlitte, eds. *Situatedness and place*. Cham, Switzerland: Springer, in press.

Seamon, D. (2018d). Well-being and phenomenology: Lifeworld, natural attitude, homeworld and place. In K. Galvin, ed. *A handbook of well-being*. London: Routledge, in press.

Seamon, D. and Gill, N. (2016). Qualitative approaches to environment-behavior research: Understanding environmental and place experiences, meanings, and actions. In R. Gifford, ed. *Research methods for environmental psychology* (pp. 115–135). New York: Wiley-Blackwell.

Seamon, D. and Mugerauer, R., eds. (1985). *Dwelling, place and environment*. Dordrecht, the Netherlands: Nijhoff,

Seamon, D. and Nordin, C. (1980). Marketplace as place ballet: A Swedish example. *Landscape*, 24, October, 35–41.

Shamai, S. (1991). Sense of place: An empirical measurement. *Geoforum*, 22(3), 347–358.

Simms, E. (2008). Children's lived spaces in the inner city. *The Humanistic Psychologist*, 36(1), 72–89.

Slife, B.D. (2004). Taking practice seriously: Toward a relational ontology. *Journal of Theoretical and Philosophical Psychology*, 24(2),157–178.

Sokolowski, R. (2000). *Introduction to phenomenology*. Cambridge, UK: Cambridge University Press.

Solnit, R. (2009). *A paradise built in hell: The extraordinary communities that arise in disaster*. New York: Penguin.

Speck, J. (2012). *Walkable city*. New York: Farrar, Staus and Giroux.

Spiegelberg, H. (1982). *The phenomenological movement*. The Hague, the Netherlands: Martinus Nijhoff.

Sprout, H. and Sprout, M. (1965). *The ecological perspective on human affairs*. Princeton, NJ: Princeton University Press.

Stambaugh, J. (1969). Introduction. In M. Heidegger, *Identity and difference* (pp. 7–18). New York: Harper & Row.

Stefanovic, I.L. (1991). Evolving sustainability: A re-thinking ontological foundations. *Trumpeter*, 8(4), 194–200.

Stefanovic, I.L. (1998). Phenomenological encounters with place: Cavtat to square one. *Journal of Environmental Psychology*, 18(1), 31–44.

Stefanovic, I.L. (2000). *Safeguarding our common future*. Albany: State University of New York Press.

Steinbock, A. (1994). Homelessness and the homeless movement: A clue to the problem of intersubjectivity. *Human Studies*, 17(2), 203–223.

Steinbock, A. (1995). *Home and beyond: Generative phenomenology after Husserl*. Evanston, IL: Northwestern University Press.

Steinfeld, E. and White, J. (2010.) *Inclusive housing*. New York: Norton.

Storper, M. and Scott, A.J. (2016). Current debates in urban theory. *Urban Studies*, 53(6), 1114–1136.

Tilley, C. (1994). *A phenomenology of landscape*. Oxford: Berg.

Tilley, C. (2010). *Interpreting landscapes: Explorations in landscape phenomenology 3*. Walnut Creek, CA: Left Coast Press.

Tilley, C. and Cameron-Daum, K. (2017). *An anthropology of landscape*. London: University College London Press.

Timberg, S. (2015). *Culture crash: The killing of the creative class*. New Haven, CT: Yale University Press.

Tomaney, J. (2010). Parish and universe: Patrick Kavanagh's poetics of the local. *Environment and Planning D: Society and Space*, 28(2), 311–325.

Tomaney, J. (2012). Parochialism: A defense. *Progress in Human Geography*, 37(5), 658–672.

Toombs, S.K. (1995). The lived experience of disability. *Human Studies*, 18(1), 9–23.

Toombs, S.K. (2000). *Handbook of phenomenology and medicine*. Dordrecht, the Netherlands: Kluwer.

Trentelman, C.K. (2009). Place attachment and community attachment: A primer grounded in the lived experience of a community sociologist. *Society and Natural Resources*, 22 (3), 191–210.

Tuan, Y. (1974a). Space and place: Humanistic perspective. In C. Board, R.J. Chorley, P. Haggett, and D.R. Stoddard, eds. *Progress in human geography, vol. 6* (pp. 111–152). London: Edward Arnold.

Tuan, Y. (1974b). *Topophilia*. Englewood Cliffs, NJ: Prentice-Hall.

Tuan, Y. (1977). *Space and place*. Minneapolis: University of Minnesota Press.

Tuan, Y. (1980). Rootedness and a sense of place. *Landscape*, 24, January, 3–8.

UN DESA (2010). Trends in international migrant stock. United Nations Department of Economic and Social Affairs. http://esa.un.org/migration/index.asp?panel=1 (July 17, 2017).

van Eck, D. and Pijpers, R. (2017). Encounters in place ballet: A phenomenological perspective on older people's walking routines in an urban park. *Area*, 49(2), 166–173.

van Manen, M. (2014). *Phenomenology of practice*. Walnut Creek, CA: Left Coast Press.

Vesely, D. (2003). The humanity of architecture. In N. Leach, ed. *Architecture and revolution* (pp. 139–145). London: Routledge.

Wachterhauser, B.R. (1996). Must we be what we say? Gadamer on truth in the human sciences. In B.R. Wachterhauser, ed. *Hermeneutics and modern philosophy* (pp. 219–240). Albany: State University of New York Press.

Weiss, G. (2008). *Intertwinings: Interdisciplinary encounters with Merleau-Ponty*. Albany: State University of New York Press.

Weiss, G. and Haber, H.F., eds. (1999). *Perspectives on embodiment*. New York: Routledge.

Whyte, W. (1980). *The social life of small urban spaces*. New York: Project for Public Spaces.

Whyte, W. (1988). *City: Rediscovering the center*. New York: Doubleday.

Wiggins, B.J., Ostenson, J.A., and Wendt, D.C. (2012). The relational foundations of conservation psychology. *Ecopsychology*, 4(3), 209–215.

Williams Goldhagen, S. (2017). *Welcome to your world: How the built environment shapes our lives*. New York: HarperCollins.

Willig, C. (2001). *Introducing qualitative research in psychology*. Philadelphia, PA: Open University Press.

Wood, S. (2014). Favorite places: Spatial and temporal dimensions of place attachment, *Environmental and Architectural Phenomenology*, 25(2), 10–16.

Wood, S. (2016a). Moving: Remaking a lifeworld. *Environmental and Architectural Phenomenology*, 27(1), 14–17.

Wood, S. (2016b). Moving and ongoing place processes. *Environmental and Architectural Phenomenology*, 27(2), 13–15.

Wylie, L. (1957). *Village in the Vaucluse*. Cambridge, MA: Harvard University Press.

Yardley, L. (2008). Demonstrating validity in qualitative psychology. In J.A. Smith, ed. *Qualitative psychology*, 2nd edn. (pp. 235–251). Thousand Oaks, CA: SAGE.

Zukin, S. (2010). *Naked city: The death and life of authentic urban places*. New York: Oxford University Press.

INDEX

Bolded page numbers indicate tables; *italicized* page numbers indicate figures